Class and Conflict

Class and Conflict

Revisiting Pranab Bardhan's Political Economy of India

Edited by
Elizabeth Chatterjee
and
Matthew McCartney

OXFORD
UNIVERSITY PRESS

OXFORD
UNIVERSITY PRESS

Oxford University Press is a department of the University of Oxford.
It furthers the University's objective of excellence in research, scholarship,
and education by publishing worldwide. Oxford is a registered trademark of
Oxford University Press in the UK and in certain other countries.

Published in India by
Oxford University Press
22 Workspace, 2nd Floor, 1/22 Asaf Ali Road, New Delhi 110 002

© Oxford University Press 2020

The moral rights of the authors have been asserted.

First Edition published in 2020

ISBN-13 (print edition): 978-0-19-949968-7
ISBN-10 (print edition): 0-19-949968-3

ISBN-13 (eBook): 978-0-19-909880-4
ISBN-10 (eBook): 0-19-909880-8

Typeset in Bembo Std 10.5/13
by The Graphics Solution, New Delhi 110 092
Printed in India by Replika Press Pvt. Ltd

To the pleasures of being a scholar of India, made so much easier by standing on the shoulders of so many inspiring teachers and academics

Table of Contents

Figures and Tables

FIGURES

TABLES

Acknowledgements

This book is the result of a collective effort, stretching across many months and several countries. We are grateful for the generosity of All Souls College, Oxford, for supporting and hosting both Pranab Bardhan's original 1983 Radhakrishnan Lectures and the symposium that gave rise to this book. The latter event was also generously supported by the Radhakrishnan Memorial Fund and the South Asia Research Cluster at Wolfson College, Oxford. We would especially like to thank the eleven contributors who provided the wonderful chapters you are about to read, as well as those who presented but for various reasons could not contribute to the volume—including Nandini Gooptu, Vijay Joshi, Bhaskar Vira, and Kanta Murali. We received warm encouragement from Oxford University Press, Oxford, when Matthew McCartney originally approached them to discuss the idea of revisiting Pranab Bardhan's classic work. Elizabeth Chatterjee in particular engaged with the helpful and endlessly patient editors from Oxford University Press, New Delhi. Finally, we would like to thank the anonymous reviewers for their thoughtful comments on the manuscript.

—Elizabeth Chatterjee and Matthew McCartney
London and Oxford
22 September 2019

I

Overview

1 Revisiting *The Political Economy of Development in India*

Elizabeth Chatterjee and
Matthew McCartney

If we suppose influential books must be large and forbidding, we would be surprised by *The Political Economy of Development in India* (hereafter *PEDI*) by Pranab Bardhan. Published in 1984, the original contains only 83 pages of text and 22 pages of tables. Bardhan describes the book as 'taking on the vast panorama of the political economy of development in contemporary India with a few quick, impetuous brush-strokes' (Bardhan, 1998: vii).[1]

Despite—or because of—this concision, *PEDI* has had enduring influence. For students of Indian political economy, it quickly became a scholarly touchstone. The revised 1998 edition, which contained a short epilogue on the political economy of reform in India after the 1980s, is regarded as a minor classic in its own right. By the turn of the twenty-first century, Bardhan's slim volume was hailed as 'the

---

[1] For a sense of this striking terseness, compare its rivals: writing at the close of the twentieth century, John Harriss depicted *PEDI* as one of only two 'standard works on the political economy of India' (1999: 3371); the other, Francine Frankel's magisterial *India's Political Economy, 1947–1977: The Gradual Revolution* (1978, updated 2005), came in at over six times *PEDI*'s length.

prevailing consensus' on state–society relations in India (Fuller and Harriss, 2001: 7).

In the years after *PEDI*'s publication, however, political economy and especially class-based analysis fell out of favour in South Asian studies. By the later 1980s, academic interest in class and capitalism was declining. The fall of the Soviet Union confirmed the replacement of class analysis by a resurgent free-market ideology, carried throughout the Global South by international financial institutions, alongside the embrace of identity politics on both sides of the political spectrum. In India, class-based organizations and political parties increasingly fell by the wayside or abandoned long-standing ideological commitments as state and national governments converged on the necessity of economic liberalization. Instead, mobilizations increasingly tended to be identity-driven and often conservative, such as the Hindu-nationalist agitations of the early 1990s around Ayodhya's Babri Masjid and upper-caste protests against the Mandal Commission's recommendations on reservations. In the academy too, class analysis was replaced by social–scientific formalism on the right and postcolonial theory on the left (Chibber, 2006; Herring and Agarwala, 2006). South Asian studies proved especially vulnerable: in the United States of America it already had a well-consolidated internal culture—classical Orientalism rooted in the teaching of religion, language, and literature (Chibber, 2006). This culturalist emphasis only accelerated with the rise of Indian postcolonial theorists in elite North American universities, who increasingly shaped the agenda of South Asian research and the training of young Indian academics. Together these dynamics led to the marginalization of *PEDI*-style class analysis, leaving *PEDI* ever more isolated as an intellectual totem.

Scholarship on the political economy of South Asia did not cease, and more recently the socio-economic changes that have attended India's economic growth have helped to rejuvenate an interest in class. Many have posited that India's political economy has undergone 'a great transformation' since the 1980s, to quote the title of one recent collection (Ruparelia et al., 2011). Such scholarship often points to the 'three Ms'—market, *mandir* (temple), and Mandal—to summarize the key changes: economic liberalization, the rise of identity politics, and democratic mobilizations from below. The state has revised its economic development strategy to favour the private sector, especially big business (Corbridge and Harriss, 2000; Kohli, 2012). Together, market competition and the power of regional business groups have helped to shift the centre of political gravity from the federal government to the states (Basu, 2000; Sáez, 2002). Contrasting sharply with widespread perceptions of agrarian crisis, newly visible are both a consumerist middle class and assertive, upwardly mobile lower-class groups. However, both have often been associated less with a reinvented politics of class-for-themselves than a turn to identity politics, whether through caste-based parties or Hindu nationalism (Fernandes, 2006; Jaffrelot, 2003). The dimensions of this great transformation—each of which is interrogated by the contributors to this volume—might appear to cast doubt on *PEDI*'s analytical relevance in the economic reform era, even as its method has crept back into the academic mainstream.

Yet a competing strand of literature stresses continuities that echo much of the discussion in *PEDI*. In retrospect, the hallmark of the 2000s was arguably a new path of ultimately unsustainable growth based on the extraction of raw materials, burgeoning infrastructure, dispossessing and amalgamating land for big construction, and jostling over telecommunication spectrum allocations (Sen and Kar, 2014). All these sectors push the supposedly liberated private sector back towards the state bureaucracy to acquire the necessary land, licences, and permits (Chandra, 2015). Despite promises to roll back state intervention, the bureaucracy continues to exercise regulatory discretion over many aspects of the economy. The state's new pro-business tilt has met resistance from popular protest movements, regulatory agencies, and the judiciary. To counter its worst effects, national politicians have felt compelled to offer social protection schemes, often characterized as populist subsidies. The last decade saw the launch of a wide range of new welfare programmes for guaranteed rural employment, the right to education, and a rejuvenated food subsidy scheme. The growth of registration schemes and the discretionary authority passed to state officials in allocating these welfare benefits were clear examples of rolling the state *forward* rather than backward. Most recently, and ranging far beyond India's own borders, *PEDI*'s provocative suggestion that inequality is not necessarily caused by economic growth but that the line of causation might run the other way—that inequality could *retard* growth—has found echoes in the work of Joseph Stiglitz and others in the aftermath of the 2008 global financial crisis (Chapter 3).

Thus, more than 30 years after Bardhan delivered the short lectures that became *PEDI*, the time is ripe for a re-evaluation of his seminal arguments and their relevance in the twenty-first century.

BARDHAN'S 'HERETICAL' EXPERIMENT

Internationally celebrated for his contributions as a development economist on topics as wide-ranging as corruption and agricultural institutions, Bardhan (Chapter 2) notes that *PEDI* has received 'nothing but benign neglect' from mainstream economists in the three decades since its original publication. This indifference is likely the flipside of the book's deep appeal for non-economists: it eschewed the dense formal exposition of much economics literature in favour of freewheeling interdisciplinary engagement. *The Political Economy of Development in India* sought to synthesize several competing and influential political–economic paradigms with what Bardhan elsewhere wryly called his 'heretical eclecticism' (1988a: 67). From Marxism, the book took its overarching emphasis on class analysis and the structure of state–society relations. Yet, it also incorporated rational-choice microfoundations and a focus on collective action and rent-seeking associated with the 'New Political Economy', alongside a quite different reading of the state that drew on neo-Weberian institutionalist scholarship (Toye, 1988: 113–4; Sridharan, 1993).

In this masterful synthesis, *PEDI* was not simply opportunistic, but was rather an experiment in a much more ambitious and collaborative intellectual project. In 1982, Bardhan had joined an informal international collective of 'democratic, egalitarian scholars', including philosophers, historians, and sociologists as well as other economists.[2] As he explained in a short autobiographical essay,[3] they were drawn

---

[2] Alongside Bardhan, its fairly stable membership was a veritable who's who of leftist scholars on both sides of the Atlantic: Samuel Bowles, Robert Brenner, G.A. Cohen, Joshua Cohen, Jon Elster, Erik Olin Wright, Adam Przeworski, John Roemer, Hillel Steiner, Philippe van Parijs, and Robert van der Veen. For a sense of the group's range of interests, see the collection edited by Roemer (1986).

[3] Bardhan has also published a Bengali-language memoir, *Smriti-Kanduyan* ('Memory-Scratching', Ananda Publishers, 2013).

together by their conviction that 'Marx asked important questions (even though his answers were often wrong) but one needs analytical methods to properly study them' (Bardhan, n.d.). The plausibility of each theoretical argument had to be treated as a matter for empirical scrutiny. Their influential movement was, therefore, often known by outsiders as analytical Marxism, though Bardhan and his colleagues preferred a saltier term that emphasized its commitment to analytical rigour: 'non-bullshit Marxism'.[4]

Although the movement was spearheaded by the philosopher G.A. Cohen under the influence of his classic work *Karl Marx's Theory of History: A Defence* (1978),[5] several members quickly moved away from Cohen's overt functionalism and methodological collectivism, notably the political scientist Jon Elster and the economist John Roemer. Their methodologically individualist variant of the analytical approach— often called rational-choice Marxism—and especially Elster's game-theoretic tendencies would particularly influence Bardhan in the 1980s.

These rational-choice microfoundations brought structuralist class analysis into conversation with a quite different, neoclassical body of theory emerging from Bardhan's fellow economists. Drawing on public choice theory first developed in the Global North, neoclassical economists provided a cynical picture of a state systematically mined by a parasitic bureaucracy, albeit one in which the state played a much more dominant role than in Northern analyses. A.O. Krueger (1974) accordingly analysed India as a 'rent-seeking society' in which interest groups competed for windfall gains from state-endorsed monopoly licences, an interpretation later influentially extended by Jagdish Bhagwati (1982). *The Political Economy of Development in India* nodded towards their emphasis on the rent-seeking bureaucracy within an overweening state,[6] although it pushed beyond the static equilibria

---

[4] By 'bullshit' the group meant pretentiously obscure and intellectually sloppy academic writing, singling out French, and especially Althusserian, Marxism in particular; see Cohen (2002).

[5] It was at G.A. Cohen's home institution, All Souls College, Oxford, that Bardhan delivered the 1983 Radhakrishnan Lectures that were published as *PEDI* the following year.

[6] *The Political Economy of Development in India*'s depiction of a distinct class of rent-seeking bureaucrats (see Chapter 8) also resembles Krueger

of these neoclassical models to incorporate a diachronic analysis of interest-group change over time more akin to the new institutional economics.

In particular, the institutional economist Mancur Olson, and especially his *The Rise and Decline of Nations* (1982), provided the immediate inspiration (Bardhan, 1998: 69).[7] Olson's seminal work, *The Logic of Collective Action* (1965), had provided a powerful critique of the assumption that actors with congruent interests—such as the working class—were able to act collectively, a mainstay of orthodox Marxism and an insight whose importance was recognized by rational-choice Marxists. He pointed out that free-rider problems often weakened the ability of large collectives to cooperate, while narrow, homogeneous groups could better coordinate to advance their interests. *Rise and Decline* extended this argument to suggest that countries' divergent economic trajectories could be explained through the accumulation of such narrow—and therefore well-organized—interest groups over time. Such special interests were able to extract excludable benefits, and thereby gradually reduced overall economic efficiency in stable societies ('institutional sclerosis'). A related collective action dilemma provided *PEDI*'s overarching theme. Bardhan would later describe the book as deploying 'an implicit analytical framework of a noncooperative Nash equilibrium': it read the fiscal crisis of the Indian state as the result of 'an infinitely repeated game between a number of powerful interest groups that compete over a common pool of public saving' (2005b: 202–3).

Nonetheless, *PEDI*'s political economy of institutions was not purely cynical. Both neoclassical and Marxist scholars took too passive a view of the state, Bardhan charged: it was not simply the arena for competition between the three dominant classes, but in certain times and places could act in the national interest in its own right. The book, therefore, included short but suggestive remarks on potential state

---

(1974), though Bardhan himself preferred to credit Marx's critique of Hegel's *Philosophy of Right* for the emphasis on bureaucrats as a class which held 'the essence of the State' as its private property (Bardhan, 1989a: 156).

[7] Olson's influence was felt in broad theoretical terms; Bardhan ignored his ahistoric claim that India's economic stagnation was caused by the caste system (Olson, 1982: 152–61).

autonomy. Accordingly, *PEDI* did not simply prescribe state retreat but instead drew on the contrast between India and South Korea to outline criteria for success that resembled the then newly emergent notion of the 'developmental state' (discussed below in the section 'State versus society-centred political economy').

Rational-choice Marxism is now often treated as a mere historiographical footnote, and Bardhan himself subsequently declared *PEDI* an 'oversimplified exercise' (1986: 76n18). Nonetheless, the synthesis offered in its 83 pages was strikingly bold and catholic, ranging far beyond the narrow confines of area studies and disciplinary or ideological boundaries. Despite Bardhan's modesty, it continues to be regarded as 'the most elaborate and influential approach to the political economy of India's arrested development', at once elegant, terse, and sweepingly ambitious (Jenkins, 1999: 31).

MAIN THEMES OF *THE POLITICAL ECONOMY OF DEVELOPMENT IN INDIA*

The Political Economy of Development in India marked a late intervention in an ongoing debate amongst Indian economists and political scientists on this 'arrested development', especially on slow industrial growth (see Chapter 3; Varshney, 1984; Ahluwalia, 1985). While others had attributed its causes to everything from planning errors to the misguided nature of import substitution industrialization, Bardhan provided an interpretation focused on the relationship between India's society and state. The deceleration in industrial growth *PEDI* attributed to a decline in public investment.

Yet this was only the proximate cause. The economist's explanation—rooted in a regression analysis finding a significant link between public investment and economic growth—was embedded in a rich political economy framework. As the following section explains, *PEDI* argued that the fundamental basis for India's economic stagnation lay in a collective action dilemma, created by the heterogeneous and competitive nature of India's governing class coalition. At the risk of providing a summary almost as long as the original volume, we also outline two of the book's key sub-theses. One has proven perhaps even more famous among political scientists of India than the central collective action thesis: the idea that Indian political economy is best understood

by reference to *three dominant proprietary classes* of industrial capitalists, wealthy farmers, and urban professionals. The second remains less
well known: *PEDI*'s attempt to balance out the society-centric bent
of this tripartite class competition with the theoretical potential for
autonomous state action.

India's Collective Action Problem

India is a famously diverse country in both social and ethno-linguistic
terms, and *PEDI*'s starting premise is that the country's dominant elites
are also heterogeneous. The paradox, Bardhan argued, is that India's
greatest success and failure both stemmed from the way it accommo-
dated this heterogeneity: through a complex 'machine' model of politics
in which spoils were distributed in return for support (Bardhan, 1998:
77–8). Formal democracy provided mechanisms to manage conflict,
absorb dissent, and articulate, negotiate, and balance demands from different interest groups. Rather than risk domination or extremism from
their rivals, India's disparate elites, therefore, continued to invest in the
democratic system (75–8). Other scholars have seen the workings of
political parties, particularly the rise and fall of the 'Congress system', as
being crucial to the functioning of political machines (Kothari, 1964).
This was an institutional debate that *PEDI*, for all of its richness, side-
stepped.

Nonetheless, the same machine politics also undermined the state's
ability to implement meaningful policy change in the face of conflict
between these heterogeneous elites and rising pressure from newly
vociferous 'lower classes' (Bardhan, 1998: 78). The fragmentation of
India's elites, with 'none of them … individually strong enough to
dominate the process of resource allocation', made it increasingly difficult to organize cooperation towards long-term problem solving or
investment. Instead, these plural elites 'pull in different directions', pre-
dictably leading to 'the proliferation of subsidies and grants to placate
all of them' (61).

The result of proliferating subsidies was reduced public investment
and, therefore, industrial stagnation and fiscal crisis. As *PEDI* put it, 'a
patron-client regime fostered by a flabby and heterogeneous dominant coalition preoccupied in a spree of anarchical grabbing of public
resources tends to choke off efficient management and utilization of

capital in the public sector', such as long-term investments in infra-structure (70–1). Meanwhile, the increasing intensity and visibility of this 'unseemly' bargaining process—and the 'brokers' and 'political middlemen' on whom it relied—risked weakening the legitimacy of the state (66).

The Political Economy of Development in India thus marks a sustained exploration of the thesis that underlying social or ethnic heterogeneity can help to explain institutional underperformance. While India had already begun to shift from economic stagnation into a period of more rapid growth from around 1980, Bardhan would later contend that this central thesis remained relevant into the liberalization era. His epilogue to the updated 1998 edition of *PEDI*, on the first decade of eco-nomic reforms, acknowledged that there had been an increase in the 'diversity, fluidity and some fragmentation of the dominant coalition'. Nonetheless, it re-emphasized that 'the system' continued to 'settle … for short-run particularist compromises in the form of sharing the spoils through an elaborate network of subsidies and patronage distri-bution' (131). The epilogue concluded that '[t]he prospects for more reforms are not bleak, but one should not underestimate the scale and nature of opposition' (137). Bardhan's more recent monograph-length comparison of India and China concluded similarly on the persistence of India's collective action problems (Bardhan, 2010).

The purchase of the thesis was not confined to India. Matthew McCartney (Chapter 3) notes that *PEDI* pre-empted a set of later scholarly debates with implications well beyond the subcontinent. It anticipated much later and more rigorous statistical work by scholars such as William Easterly and Paul Collier, who have painstakingly measured social heterogeneity and found it causally related to a failure to provide public goods, and so to lower economic growth (Easterly and Levine, 1997) or to political conflict (Collier, Honohan, and Moene, 2001). Bardhan himself has continued to build on this central thesis, synthesizing recent research on the role of distribu-tive conflicts in the persistence of dysfunctional institutions with a wider theoretical argument about scarcity, conflict, and cooperation across the Global South (Bardhan, 2005b). Bardhan's contribution on this theoretical front deserves its own volume. Nonetheless, it is on *PEDI*'s Indian case study, and the influential—and controver-sial—framework that the book offered to decipher the subcontinent's political and socio-economic complexity, that the present collection modestly concentrates.

The Three Dominant Proprietary Classes

At the core of *PEDI*'s collective action dilemma were India's plural and heterogeneous elites, and the competition between these elites that undermined the possibility of long-term collective action. Today, the book is especially remembered for its depiction of India's political economy as a complex 'ménage à trois', as Bardhan jokingly called it, between three 'dominant proprietary classes' (Bardhan, 1998: 66). The selection of these three classes was a triumph of *PEDI*'s eclectic borrowings from a range of scholarly traditions, as mentioned earlier, united by the innovative suggestion that each class was proprietary— that it could be defined by the 'property' that entitled it 'to acquire part of the surplus generated in society' (Bardhan, 1989a: 155).

The first dominant class was a conventional Marxist category: industrial capitalists. While this class was already 'reasonably strong at the time of Independence', it had also succeeded in wresting financial advantages from the interventionist Indian state (Bardhan, 1998: 40). Since the 1950s, the state had created lending institutions that became the predominant source of finance for large private industrial capital. Despite this financial interest, the state refrained from interference even in cases of indifferent private firm governance, while still 'act[ing] as a risk-absorber of the last resort and a charitable hospital where the private sector can dump its sick units' (42). Richer and better-connected industrialists also successfully subverted the 'licence raj' to their own advantage, appropriating the bulk of licences and freely violating regulations without fear of prosecution. Nonetheless, Bardhan noted some flux in the class's composition: new regional family capitalists were emerging to contest the dominance of old business conglomerates; policy changes presaged greater foreign involvement (although this was yet to materialize); and the informal economy appeared increasingly important, even if this trend often masked actual control by large corporate houses disguised for tax purposes (42–3). Unlike the powerful bourgeoisies of the 'industrially advanced countries' (40), however, *PEDI* was emphatic that India's industrial capitalists were far from triumphant.

The second dominant class was comprised of wealthy farmers who often explicitly positioned themselves in opposition to 'the city' (54–5), echoing scholarship on urban–rural conflict that developed in reaction to Lipton's (1977) controversial 'urban bias' thesis (see, for example, Byres, 1979).This group, '*numerically* the most important proprietary class' if empirically difficult to define, had benefited from post-Independence land reforms that accelerated the ongoing process of land transfer from non-cultivating absentee landlords to profit-minded farmers (Bardhan, 1998: 45–8). Such rich farmers benefited from high government procurement prices for their marketable surpluses, as well as from subsidies on farming inputs, cheap credit, and the minimal taxation of agricultural incomes. They were particularly influential within provincial state legislatures, especially in the northwest plains and parts of the agrarian south. Even there, though, they remained more diffuse, factional, and reliant on pure numerical weight than their wealthier urban rivals, if still far better organized than the landless labourers who might otherwise resist them (55–7). In particular, caste at once divided wealthy agriculturalists and opened possible avenues for wider mobilizations in their class interests (47–51). *The Political Economy of Development in India*'s delightful brevity can be seen in his succinct definition and analysis of the wealthy farmers when compared with the then concurrent 'mode of production debate' in India; the latter ran from the late 1960s to the early 1980s and was eventually lost amidst confusing technical terms, rival definitions, and Marxist obscurantism (reviewed in Nadkarni, 1991).

Finally, *PEDI* argued that if physical capital could be the basis of class stratification, so too could human capital. This was the primary 'property' of the third dominant class: urban professionals who enjoyed scarcity rents from their education, skills, and technical expertise, none of which was widespread in the population. Their secondary property, however, was based on their access to the state: a segment of this 'rentier' class acquired 'license-giving powers at various levels of bureaucracy' and thereby 'increased their capacity to multiply their rental income' (Bardhan, 1998: 52).While in many other societies this group was treated as a mere subset or instrument of other classes, Bardhan claimed that in India it was a class in its own right. The country had a long tradition of powerful bureaucratic functionaries, who unlike their equivalents in Europe habitually had little personal link to or stake in trade or industry.

They were instead recruited from traditional 'literati groups', insulated by caste barriers, at least into the 1970s. Yet, this group should not simply be equated with the state, *PEDI* cautioned: alongside the three canonical dominant classes appeared a fourth distinct actor—the 'state elite'.

State versus Society-Centred Political Economy

'Our theories of economic policy need a good theory of the state,' declared Bardhan shortly after *PEDI*'s publication (1988a: 64). Accordingly, *PEDI* contained an evocative but sometimes unsettling analysis of the Indian state, which in practice appears more like a *dual* theory. Its famous society-centric paradigm of the three dominant proprietary classes coexisted with a somewhat underspecified state-centric alternative, which preserved an ambiguous role for autonomous action by policymaking elites. The relationship between the two—and how countries such as India could move from one to the other—was only loosely sketched.

In a tantalizingly brief chapter titled 'The State as an Autonomous Actor' (Bardhan, 1998: 32–9), Bardhan asserted that the state enjoyed not merely the relative autonomy posited by Poulantzas (1973) in which it simply acted '*on behalf of* the dominant proprietary classes', nor could it be simply equated with the bureaucracy (emphasis added). Instead, he drew on now-classic works by Weberian historical institutionalists to argue that under some circumstances the state was able to actively make policy in its own right, including the famous paper by Skocpol that would be published the following year (citing Stepan, 1978; Trimberger, 1978; Skocpol, 1985; see Bardhan, 1998: 33–4, and Chapter 6). The state's structural role enabled it to play the dominant classes off against each other, so securing the latitude to pursue its own goals (Bardhan, 1998: 75–6). On occasion, the direction of influence was even reversed, so that the state could actually shape 'class realignments in civil society' (33–5)—a strikingly state-centric claim.

This presented empirical difficulties, however; it ran dangerously close to reifying the state as an abstract and monolithic actor against the rigorously individualistic rational-choice tenets of analytical Marxism—after all, what *is* the state, if not its bureaucrats?[8] In response,

---

[8] Rudra (1985) thus complained that Bardhan's state had a dual existence, as both an abstract actor enacting policy in the interstices of societal forces and a concrete agglomeration of interest groups.

PEDI distinguished between the 'political leadership representing the state', responsible for agenda setting and policy formulation, and 'the white-collar workers in the public bureaucracy', who are 'supposed to implement' those decisions (51n8). While the source of the state elite's autonomy and the bureaucracy's dominance both flowed from the state's control over the economy's 'commanding heights' and the distribution of licences and credit, their interests were often diametrically opposed as principles and agents. In this fashion, as Bardhan clarified elsewhere, the state elite strategically operated 'in a game of mixed conflict and cooperation' with the dominant classes (1988a: 65). *The Political Economy of Development in India*'s *ménage à trois* thus might be reconsidered as containing *four* crucial actors, although the state elite was not just another class: at times it could and did act in the name of a genuine (and ideological) 'conception of the national interest' (Bardhan, 1998: 34).

Yet, by 1984, societal constraints on the state elite 'became binding' (38–9). Why was the state elite not able to exploit its structural role, when it might have been expected that a deadlock between the three dominant classes would increase its manoeuvrability? State autonomy is notoriously difficult to define or measure, and *PEDI* only loosely sketched its enabling conditions. The public sector's economic weight was not sufficient for the exercise of state autonomy, it argued. Turning the collective action dilemma on its head, we might expect that when the state takes the initiative, the society and its dominant proprietary classes would be too heterogeneous to coordinate resistance against reform efforts, as Jenkins (1999) contended of the state's successful liberalization agenda after 1991. This threatened the very premise of *PEDI*'s collective action thesis, however, and it remained largely silent on this 'class-balance theory of the state' (to borrow a term from a slightly later analytical Marxist classic [Elster, 1985: 422–8]).

Instead, Bardhan's diagnosis focused on institutions. The book unfavourably contrasted India with South Korea's similarly interventionist state to suggest that it was not the extent but the *quality* of state intervention that was determinant.[9] The two countries' divergent economic performances could be explained by their state elites' varying abilities: first, 'to insulate economic management from political processes of

---

[9] This is made explicit in Bardhan (1990: 4). Nor was the problem regime type (Korea was then an autocracy): democratic Japan and Sweden also possessed comparatively insulated bureaucracies (Bardhan, 1988a: 66).

distributive demands, rent-seeking and patronage disbursement' (72); and second, to exert control over 'the white-collar workers in public bureaucracy' (74). India's state elite had once enjoyed greater autonomy thanks to its prestige and ideological coherence around Independence (38). The enabling conditions for state autonomy could presumably re-emerge, although it was not quite clear how—except that this would depend on *institutional* factors, such as bureaucratic structure and cohesion, as well as the changing balance of power among the three dominant classes. It was left to the later authors such as Adrian Leftwich, Robert Wade, and Alice Amsden to deepen the analysis of case studies such as South Korea and to clarify the concept and political economy of 'the developmental state'. The political prerequisites they discussed—such as a determined developmental elite, relative state autonomy, a powerful, insulated and competent economic bureaucracy, a weak and subordinated civil society, the effective management of non-state economic interests, and a judicious mixture of repression and legitimacy (Leftwich, 1995)—were mostly rigorous formulations of *PEDI*'s loose sketch.

The ambiguities surrounding the conditions which would nominally enable a transition from the society-driven state capture to state autonomy meant that, for all the book's great influence, 'the state itself remains rather shadowy' in its analysis (Fuller and Harriss, 2001: 7). Many subsequent readers largely chose to disregard its state-centric arguments in favour of a simplified, static vision of interest-group gridlock. Herring thus classified Bardhan's theory as a 'version of Indian pluralism' in which '[p]olicy is the vector sum of bargaining among the three proprietary classes' (1999: 314), while Fuller and Harriss argued that in practice *PEDI*'s state was 'virtually subsumed by the relationships of power among the dominant classes' (2001: 7). But this characterization came at a heavy cost: it erased the dynamic potential of *PEDI*'s state theory—with its resemblance to the emergent idea of the developmental state—just as a number of major transformations were beginning to reshape the country's political economy.

THE BOOK'S CHAPTERS

Looking back with three decades of hindsight, how much analytical traction do *PEDI*'s main theses still have? The contributors to this volume explore this question from different angles. After the following chapter, in which Pranab Bardhan revisits his slender book three decades on, Part II assesses *PEDI*'s arguments about the Indian economy. McCartney interrogates its treatment of economic stagnation, while Maitreesh Ghatak and Ritwika Sen test the hypothesis that subsidies retard economic growth.

Part III turns to examine the class configurations that underlie *PEDI*'s political economy framework: how have Bardhan's three dominant proprietary classes fared in the years since *PEDI*'s publication in 1984? Chapters by Rob Jenkins, John Harriss, and Elizabeth Chatterjee consider the fates of industrial capitalists, wealthy farmers, and the urban professionals respectively.

Part IV then offers some significant alternative interpretations of India's political economy and how they might analytically supplement or contradict *PEDI*. Leela Fernandes uses *PEDI* as a lens on the newly fashionable concept of 'the middle class'. Barbara Harriss-White, Muhammad Ali Jan, and Asha Amirali take the very different vantage point of the 'rest of India', the mass of the economy and population which lie largely outside the reach of formal state control. Finally, Part V concludes with Michael Walton's bold re-examination of *PEDI*'s collective action thesis.

Together the chapters aim to provide a nuanced picture of the continuities and changes that have characterized India's political economy since 1984, indicating both the ongoing relevance of *PEDI*'s analysis and the modifications it requires to capture new economic and political realities. The contributions testify, first, to the value of *PEDI*-style class analysis in explaining India's pattern of growth and the persistence of structural inequalities, even if its contours must be updated with the times; second, to *PEDI*'s emphasis on the state's centrality to Indian political economy and the high cost of seeking access to state subsidies and other rents in the long term; and third, to the appeal of *PEDI*'s stylish combination of concise analysis and judiciously deployed empirical examples. Yet they also highlight areas of contestation that challenge or push beyond *PEDI*'s original analysis.

Explaining Economic Stagnation

As noted above, the book sought to explain India's economic stagnation after 1965. The most dramatic change that it thus appeared to miss was the near-doubling of the growth rate from around 1980, even as the original lectures were being delivered. The hitherto closed economy began to become progressively more open to foreign capital, while some sectors of the economy were deregulated, albeit slowly and partially. Accordingly, the first part of this collection interrogates *PEDI*'s economic theses in the light of India's subsequent economic reforms and higher growth trajectory.

Extending *PEDI*'s analysis beyond the stagnation of the mid-1960s, there now exists a substantial economics debate on both how to detect and explain episodes of growth and stagnation. McCartney's chapter probes episodes of relative acceleration and slowdown in India, both before and after *PEDI*'s publication, including analysis of the 1980 upturn that Bardhan (and most other scholars working in the 1980s) overlooked. *The Political Economy of Development in India*'s examination of the stagnation episode from around 1965—an innovative example of the case-study method for researching the causes and sustainability of economic growth—has subsequently been complemented by a veritable subfield of development economics on the measurement and explanation of growth episodes. Drawing on this recent literature, McCartney engages with the apparent paradox that the ostensible arrival of 'big bang' liberalization in 1991 did not bring a break in growth, which instead arrived later, around 2003. This paradox disappears once we return to *PEDI* and consider instead its eclectic list of drivers of growth. Placing *PEDI* back in conversation with competing explanations from the 1980s of India's industrial stagnation, McCartney suggests that some of the book's arguments remain relevant for the 1980 and 2003 growth episodes. However, McCartney contests *PEDI*'s claim that after the mid-1960s the Indian state was largely confined to 'regulatory functions', arguing that its successful developmentalism continued into the era of stagnation—both through Green Revolution agricultural policies and support for sectors such as information technology (IT).

Ghatak and Sen interrogate the 'Bardhan subsidy hypothesis' of a negative and one-way relationship between 'the subsidy Raj' and economic growth. *The Political Economy of Development in India* suggested that interest-group gridlock leads to escalating populist subsidies, draining resources for long-term public investment in infrastructure and other developmental goods. It thereby argued that subsidies were the most important binding constraint on economic growth in the 1980s. Ghatak and Sen use data on central budgetary subsidies to challenge this thesis. They show that the subsidy hypothesis is not supported beyond the 1980s. Except for the cutbacks of the early to mid-1990s, subsidies have grown *alongside* economic growth, suggesting that other factors may be better explanations for stagnation. Instead, they suggest that the relationship between subsidies and growth is two-way: while subsidies may hamper growth, growth also provides additional resources for subsidies until it is choked off or undermined by some other factor. They, therefore, posit a modification of *PEDI's* subsidy hypothesis that might incorporate some of its findings for the 1980s: growth and government spending on subsidies may be cyclically related, although they leave the nature of these cycles to be analysed by other political economists.

The importance of thinking carefully about the underlying political economy determinants of subsidies has enduring value. Pritchett (2009) used the failure of public service delivery in contemporary India as evidence for state weakness—what he called a 'flailing state'. Mooij (1999) deployed similar evidence, more in the spirit of *PEDI*, to depict a state embedded in social relationships but utilizing subsidies to secure in part its own interests. The apparent failure of the public distribution system of subsidized foodgrains is more than a matter of incompetence, she argues. Politicians are utilizing the scheme to support their own interests, in this case by allocating licenses to run fair-price shops—with concomitant opportunities for profit by diverting subsidized foodgrains onto the open market—to supporters. Such positions are often traded in return for known fees, the revenue from which is re-allocated upwards through the bureaucracy and political hierarchy. The importance of 'political middlemen', who feature in *PEDI's* analysis only in passing, opens up a rich seam of analysis that contemporary anthropologists and others have only just begun to explore (Piliavsky, 2014; Vaishnav, 2017). Walton's closing chapter suggests that updated conceptualizations of rent-sharing in contemporary India must accord a substantial role for politicians as more than mere intermediaries, graphically illustrated for the case of Andhra Pradesh.

The peripheral role that *PEDI* accorded to political middlemen was mirrored by a comparative silence on party politics. Focusing on a specific aspect of the contemporary subsidy regime, James Manor's chapter exposes this lacuna, pushing against Bardhan's implicit suggestion that political regimes do not matter. Instead, he provocatively argues that there was a major difference between the Congress-led United Progressive Alliance (UPA) administration and the Bharatiya Janata Party (BJP)-led administration that took power under Narendra Modi in May 2014. The leadership of the former was ideologically committed to a social–democratic programme and so introduced substantive welfare projects, some of the largest the world has ever seen. Their beneficiaries largely lay well outside the original dominant classes, a point to which several chapters return as they interrogate the resilience of the older elites' dominance.

The Pro-business Tilt

The acceleration of India's economic growth from the time of *PEDI*'s publication coincided with a widely perceived shift in state attitudes and policies to become more favourable to the private sector. This shift, alongside the even more rapid rise in billionaire wealth and a series of high-profile corruption scandals, have led many commentators to speculate on the belated victory of industrial capitalists in India. Accordingly, perhaps the most dominant reinterpretation of India's political economy—and one which Bardhan himself has tentatively endorsed—is that the Indian state has undergone a 'pro-business tilt'. As Atul Kohli put it, in an interpretation gripping in its parsimony and whiff of conspiracy: 'India's economy has grown briskly because the Indian state has prioritised growth since about 1980, and slowly but surely embraced Indian capital as its main ruling ally' (2006a: 1251).[10] This close alliance between big business (mainly domestic, much less so foreign) and the state both unleashed economic dynamism in India and has been responsible for limiting the gains of that growth (Kohli, 2012).

The pro-business interpretation is hotly contested across this collection. Several authors endorse it, albeit with important caveats. Michael Walton agrees that the private sector in India has become

---

[10] For similar arguments, which give a sense of this thesis's popularity, see Corbridge and Harriss (2000); Chatterjee (2008); Evans and Heller (2015); Gupta and Sivaramakrishnan (2011); and Jaffrelot, Kohli, and Murali (2019).

increasingly dominant, both politically and economically, in a fashion that appears to render irrelevant *PEDI's* theory of interest-group gridlock. However, he emphasizes that the business class is not unitary but has 'two faces': one entrepreneurial, the other more like Bardhan's old rentier capitalists with their heavy reliance on close links with the state (see also Gandhi and Walton, 2012; Sen and Kar, 2014). More than this, he concludes that India's collective action problems have not ended so much as altered. Business, the first dominant class, has consolidated its position—but the state's relationship with interest groups still remains one of *PEDI*-style 'particularist compromises', even as the old classes of farmers and bureaucrats have been joined by other formations such as caste alliances.

In contrast, Rob Jenkins contests the emergent pro-business orthodoxy. Instead, he argues that the state elite retains greater autonomy than is typically appreciated, in terms of its overall control over economic levers, the space opened up by continued competition between the three dominant classes, and the persistence of the 'anti-market streak' in Indian public life that Bardhan documented 15 years earlier (Bardhan, 1998: 136). Following Bardhan's analysis of the potentially autonomous state, he thus attributes the initiation of economic liberalization not to business capture of the state but to the state elite's revised conception of the 'national interest'. Like Manor, then, Jenkins disputes the notion that dominant classes can shape a policy agenda that consistently favours their own interests, instead arguing that economic liberalization has *increased* state autonomy.

Where Walton and Jenkins agree, though, is on the importance of federalism in conditioning liberalization. Both note that the rise of business coincided with the increasing regionalization of Indian politics, as in the 1990s ascendant new regional business classes, originating in the agrarian economy and other low-technology sectors, were quick to promote and embrace liberalization through the funding of regional political parties (Basu, 2000). State–business relations, the influence of wealthy farmers, and preferred policy strategies vary considerably from state to state (Sinha, 2005). If *PEDI* acknowledged India's federal system largely in passing, many of the contributions here highlight the importance of recognizing regional variation, both in institutional and socio-economic terms.

The Resilience of the Original Dominant Classes

In terms of Bardhan's original *ménage à trois*, we might expect the ascendancy of industrial capitalists to have seen a parallel diminution of the influence of Bardhan's other two classes: wealthy farmers and urban professionals. The reality is not quite so clear-cut.

The Political Economy of Development in India had suggested that India's large farmers were relatively weak in comparison with the 'urban lobbies', because of the money power of the latter. Yet John Harriss shows that, even as Bardhan's book was published, rich farmers had begun exercising the power of their numbers in striking public demonstrations through disruption and massive political rallies. Nonetheless, this movement dissipated; by the 1990s big farmers were clearly no longer playing such a prominent role in Indian politics, and discussion of an agrarian crisis has subsequently become widespread. Providing a synoptic overview of recent scholarship, Harriss treads a careful line through this debate. Noting the simultaneous fragmentation of small landholdings and the rise in inequality, he concludes that a small minority of rich farmers, especially in certain western and southern states, continue to capture a disproportionate share of state subsidies—but at the cost of a crisis of public investment in agriculture as a whole. While endorsing Kohli's claim that a narrower state–business alliance now 'determines the pattern of Indian development', Harriss points out that 'the dominant partners have still had to make compromises with rural interests for electoral reasons', for all the current administration's pro-business promises.

Surveying the fate of the bureaucrats who form the rentier core of Bardhan's white-collar professional class, Elizabeth Chatterjee suggests that their fate in the liberalization era has been a similarly ambivalent one. Given their ability to extract rents from their privileged location within the state apparatus, superficially they were the class with most to lose from the rollback of the state that economic reformers repeatedly promised. Chatterjee shows that in practice state rollback has been exaggerated: although their relative size has diminished, senior bureaucrats still receive healthy emoluments and are able to extract both old and new forms of rents. This does not mean that the third dominant class is intact. As part of the broader class of urban professionals, bureaucrats also had a second source of rent derived from the scarcity value of their human capital (education and networks). This has helped to fragment the class between specialist technocrats best able to leverage their scarce skills, who have welcomed at least some elements of reform, and generalists more inclined to provide the resistance predicted by conventional political economy. In this resistance, the latter have been joined, especially at the state level, by junior bureaucrats who stymy policy *implementation*—but who do not form a competing class, being both internally heterogeneous and owing their position to political patronage.

Class Homogenization or Fragmentation?

Even as it was published, *PEDI* predicted a number of socio-economic and political changes that threatened to undermine the cohesion or influence of the original three dominant classes. Bardhan (1989a) noted that the boundaries between the three classes appeared increasingly blurred thanks to economic diversification and social interpenetration. This threatened to undercut the antagonism between the classes, and to weaken their internal coherence. Across this volume, scholars differ on whether these changes to India's class structure are more accurately characterized as a process of *homogenization* or *fragmentation*.

Echoing Bardhan's earlier predictions, both Harriss and Chatterjee provide some evidence that dominant class boundaries are weakening: rich farmers are diversifying into trading, agro-industry, moneylending, education, and real-estate speculation, while educated professionals seek to exploit a host of new opportunities in the private sector, blunting older conflicts with the business class. Reflecting this homogenization, over recent years both popular and scholarly interest in the nebulous idea of an Indian 'middle class' has grown. Fernandes's chapter interrogates this concept through the lens of *PEDI*'s framework. She contests the popular view that frames the middle class in terms of support for economic liberalization, consumer goods imports, and private sector employment and shows that a reliance on the state—upon which *PEDI*'s analysis centred—is a pillar both of these classes' economic standing and their political demands, even though it stands at odds with market ideology. Like McCartney, Manor, Jenkins, and Chatterjee, then, she challenges the conventional drawing of 'easy dichotomies between state-led development and the age of neoliberal economics'.

Nonetheless, Fernandes argues that the notion of a homogenous 'middle class' is more ideological claim than social reality. The middle classes are structurally stratified by caste, language, religion, and more. Building on *PEDI*'s class analysis, Fernandes singles out socio-economic heterogeneity in particular. To conflate the prosperous upper middle classes, who resemble Bardhan's third dominant proprietary class, with the growing, aspirational, yet economically precarious 'neo-middle class' is to obscure structural inequalities. At the same time, the ubiquity of the 'middle classes' as a concept and an ideal emphasizes the importance of ideational as well as structural understandings of class. Like Fernandes, several other contributors nod to the fraught link between identity politics and socio-economic hierarchy, in contrast to *PEDI*'s comparative silence, while in the final analysis resisting the unproductive temptation to collapse class into just another category of identity.

If Fernandes challenges the notion that India's political economy today is best understood with reference to a homogenous middle class, other chapters present a picture of the dominant classes themselves as increasingly fragmented, undermining their ability to act collectively. Wealthy farmers may be split between those export-oriented farmers for whom some aspects of liberalization appeal and more protectionist elements. Chatterjee depicts a fragmentation of the bureaucracy into more generalist and specialist elements, and into the upper and lower bureaucracy, in ways that undermine the group's sense of itself as a class. Big business, already fractured by competition, emerges from these analyses with a host of fissures. While Walton emphasizes the need to distinguish between innovative and rent-seeking capitalists, Harriss-White, Jan, and Amirali go beyond this to critique the notion of class cohesion not just today, but even in 1984. Surveying petty capitalism outside the formally regulated arena of corporate capital's operations, they cast doubt upon the solidity of Bardhan's original categories, even while calling for greater attention to bottom-up field studies and the vast informal economy. How can we draw conclusions from data mainly drawn from the formal sector when perhaps 60 per cent of the economy lies in the informal sector? Political economists and policymakers alike, they contend, must grapple more seriously with the characteristics and demands of the 'rest of India' outside the dominant classes.

While the authors here broadly agree that class fragmentation and not homogenization is the dominant trend, they differ on its implications. If for Jenkins inter- and intra-class competition opens up room for state autonomy in directing apex-level policy change, for Harriss-White and her co-authors class fragmentation frequently sabotages the state's operations at the street level. In his contribution, Bardhan endorses this more pessimistic interpretation: thanks to demographic growth, regionalization, democratic assertion, and rising economic (if not social) inequality, '[t]he polity is more fragmented'. Notwithstanding the present administration's attempts to centralize power, then, 'by and large the consequent problems for collective action may have become more severe'.

Democratic Deepening and the Anti-business Backlash

As this ferment suggests, over the last three decades the state elite's tilt to favour big business has gone far from unchallenged. There is little hint in *PEDI* that the sharing of the spoils by the three dominant proprietary classes, though leading to economic stagnation, was anything other than *politically* sustainable. The book depicted non-elite groups as, at most, an occasional irritant to the dominant proprietary classes: 'from time to time a significant number of crumbs have to be thrown at these clamouring groups banging at the gates just outside the periphery of the dominant coalition', and 'equally expensive is the process of manning and securing those gates' (Bardhan 1998: 67). Was this a reasonable conclusion, given the highly politicized nature of Indian society?

Even as state policy shifted in several sectors to become more supportive to private capital, it has faced counter-mobilizations. On the one hand, the dominance of the three narrow proprietary elites has been challenged by 'the intermediate groups banging at the gates', as *PEDI* predicted (67). Scholars have documented a shift away from the concentration of political power in the hands of Bardhan's narrow set of dominant classes in the face of a 'second democratic upsurge' (Yadav, 1999; Jaffrelot, 2003). Insurgent lower groups have entered the fray, demanding their own share of the public sector's spoils. Such groups began to compete increasingly vociferously for state favours such as the extension of reservations for government jobs and public education, especially in the face of persistent 'jobless growth'. These groups do not necessarily recognize themselves as sharing class interests, however: there has instead been a political shift away from overt class politics to foreground identity, whether in the form of caste or religious nationalism.

On the other hand, the exclusionary growth path of the 2000s and the highly visible rents earned by political and economic elites have prompted a surge of popular discontent and a backlash from state agencies themselves (Sen and Kar, 2014). Marginalized groups have emerged to contest land and resource dispossession, mobilizing against the extra-legal coercion used to acquire land for big business. As Jenkins argues, this has sometimes forced central and state governments into compromises that attempt to mitigate the most egregious excesses of the pro-business tilt.

A reaction has also emerged from increasingly powerful regulatory institutions such as the Comptroller and Auditor General (CAG) and the Supreme Court, and from middle-class citizens irritated by persistent corruption (most famously, the electoral victories of the Aam Admi Party in Delhi). These 'accountability institutions' both identified and investigated corruption and in some cases deprived the corrupt of their gains; the Supreme Court cancelled coal block licenses, for example. Observing these developments, Walton's concluding chapter points out that this might suggest that 'Polanyi's sequential double movement is happening simultaneously in India': the new dominance of the market in the liberalization era has prompted a parallel counter-movement for social protection. Opening this volume, Bardhan warned of 'a brewing "legitimization crisis" of capitalism in India', and raised doubts about the institutional capacity of regulatory bodies, political parties, or social movements to negotiate constructive political solutions to head this off. In closing, Walton provides instead a source of cautious hope. He develops not just an increasingly common comparison between India's contemporary billionaires and the Rockefellers and Carnegies of the so-called 'Gilded Age' of the United States of America, but draws more optimistic lessons that might be gleaned from the regulatory and welfare developments of the Progressive Era. '[I]n a democracy as competitive and vigorous as India's there is always hope' that a similarly transformative political coalition might eventually coalesce, Walton concludes, even if 'the paths to such a transition remain unclear'.

When Bardhan delivered his original lectures in the spring of 1983, independent India was 35 years old. As we write today, it is about to celebrate its 72nd anniversary. Half of India's history as an independent nation thus lies outside the book's purview. Yet *PEDI* is far more than a historical curiosity, a mere snapshot of a country in the midst of a midlife crisis. Innumerable weighty tomes have been composed in the past seven decades on the improbable if imperfect survival of Indian democracy, but very few continue to provoke as many questions and fruitful new lines of inquiry. As the Indian polity becomes perhaps more heterogeneous, fractious, and noisy than ever, Bardhan's nimble little book feels as relevant as it did three decades ago.

2 Reflections on Indian Political Economy

Pranab Bardhan

On the 1984 book around which this volume is organized, I have noticed over the years a remarkable asymmetry in its reception among mainstream economists as opposed to others.[1] It has received nothing but benign neglect from the former group. I am pretty sure most of my colleagues in the major economics departments in the United States of America have never heard of this book, even though many of them may be aware of my more technical articles in journals. Looking back, I have sometimes thought that maybe it would have attracted more attention from economists if I published in the book the background theoretical notes I had for a couple of its main messages. One such message was about the difficulty of organizing collective action towards long-term common economic goals such as encouraging public investment in infrastructure, a key ingredient of economic growth, in a country where even the elite is fragmented and finds it difficult

---

[1] This is a revised version of the text of the opening keynote lecture I gave at a conference at All Souls College, Oxford, United Kingdom, to mark the 30th anniversary of the publication of my book *The Political Economy of Development in India*, which was originally presented as the Radhakrishnan Lectures at that college in 1983. The text was originally published in the *Economic and Political Weekly* on 2 May 2015.

to get its act together in doing something that would have benefited most of its members. With this failure of collective action, the public surplus is often frittered away in short-term subsidies and handouts. Since writing this book, I have elsewhere[2] elaborated on my theoretical ideas on the adverse effect of social heterogeneity and inequality on collective action, not just on matters of macroeconomic growth but also in the microeconomic issues of management of local commons. The other message (which even non-economists have not paid much attention to) enunciated in the last chapter of the book, for which I had some unpublished theoretical notes, was how the same elite fragmentation that acts as a constraint on economic growth can work as a safeguard for the resilience of democracy in India, where the divided groups may agree on the procedures of democracy as a means of keeping one another within some bounds of moderation in their transactional negotiations.[3]

In this short chapter, I shall first reflect on how the collective action issue for long-term growth that I had identified more than three decades ago remains acute even today in India. Then I move onto a few of the structural issues, not considered in the 1984 book, that have become prominent in recent years.

I think it is relatively easy to see that the economic growth fundamentals for India are potentially quite strong (stronger than it seemed in 1984):

- Domestic saving and investment rates are relatively high for a poor country.
- After the opening of the Indian economy, the alacrity with which part of hitherto protected Indian business adapted to the demands of global competition and thrived suggests a remarkable adaptability.
- Vigorous entrepreneurial spirit in all corners of the economy has been rejuvenated by the infusion of business entries from hitherto subordinate castes and regional capitalists.

---

[2] See, for example, Bardhan (2005b).
[3] For a recent game-theoretic model of intra-elite conflicts and democracy on broadly related lines, see Ghosal and Eugenio (2009).

- The majority of the population is quite young, thus creating the potential of a large and productive young work force.
- With better transport and communication (particularly with the remarkably fast spread of mobile phones), connectivity is increasing in a way that is likely to speed up enhancement of productivity.

But there are major structural and institutional problems blocking the full realization of these strong growth fundamentals.

(1) While the business dynamism in the private corporate sector (and the part of the informal economy linked with it in supplier relationships) has been impressive since the reform process started, the physical infrastructure (roads, electricity, ports, railways, and so on) to sustain it remains weak. Particularly in the last few years of stagnant exports and domestic private investment, public investment in infrastructure has again become crucial. But public budgets laden with heavy subsidies, salaries, and debt servicing have very little left for infrastructure investment, leading to increasing frequency of public–private partnerships on infrastructure. But these have often been saddled with problems of mismanagement, too high debt–equity ratios, opportunistic renegotiation, non-transparent regulations, corruption, and now a mountain of bad loans on the books of public banks. In addition, caught in the crossfire between corporate lobbies on the one hand and social activists and the judiciary on the other, official land and environmental clearances for infrastructure projects have become extremely slow, non-transparent, or erratic (lurching from one side to the other in different regimes) in recent years.

(2) Secondary education is a minimum qualification for many good non-farm jobs, and yet the children from poor families overwhelmingly drop out before entering or completing secondary schools on account of economic and, particularly in the case of girls, also social compulsions.

(3) The average quality of school and college education is not sufficient for employable skills for many, even for some manual, jobs. The provisions for vocational training and skill formation along with connections with potential employers, particularly for rural youths, are extremely deficient. In a so-called 'labour-surplus'

country, there is now a serious shortage of employable labour in many factories and other enterprises.

(4) Despite the robust economic growth of recent years, a major social and organizational failure, almost at a disastrous level, over many decades has been in matters of public health and sanitation, where India lags behind even some African countries.[4] Building more toilets has not yet resolved the problem of why they remain underutilized. Poor public health and sanitation continue to keep the Indian disease burden high and productivity of workers low.

(5) Environmental degradation has been a major drag on net economic growth. It has been reported in the 2014 United Nations Development Programme (UNDP) *Human Development Report* that the annual depletion in natural resources (depreciation of 'natural' capital) in India as a proportion of national income (conventionally measured) is nearing 5 per cent per year (not very different from the growth rate in national income in recent years), compared to 3.6 per cent for Brazil and 0.1 per cent for Costa Rica.[5] It has been assessed by the World Health Organization that of the 20 most air-polluted cities in the world, 13 are in India. (Indoor and outdoor) air pollution kills an estimated 1.6 million people every year.

All of the above—infrastructure, education, public health and sanitation, and the environment—involve the governance effectiveness issue with respect to delivery of key public goods and services, which is rather low in India, and, of course, varies a great deal between different states. A recent ranking by Mundle et al. (2012) of 17 major Indian states in terms of a composite score for quality of governance (taking into account delivery of infrastructure, social and judicial services, fiscal performance, law and order, and quality of legislators) suggests,

[4] According to the *Human Development Report* of the UNDP, the deaths of children under age 5 due to unsafe water, unimproved sanitation, or poor hygiene per hundred thousand children numbered 316 in India in 2004, whereas the number was 255 in Sudan, 256 in Zimbabwe, and 286 in Gambia.

[5] A recent book edited by Mani (2014) estimates that in 2009 the cost of environmental degradation in India came to 5.7 per cent of gross domestic product (GDP).

unsurprisingly, that the six states that occupy the top ranks, across alternative rules of weighting the different indices, are Andhra Pradesh, Gujarat, Haryana, Kerala, Punjab, and Tamil Nadu; the bottom ranks are largely occupied by seven states: Assam, Bihar, Jharkhand, Madhya Pradesh, Uttar Pradesh, and West Bengal.

Governance ineffectiveness is often regarded as a lack of state capacity, which many point to as India's major failing. While it is true that the bureaucracy is often inept or corrupt or simply truant (apart from the large numbers of continuing vacancies in police, judiciary, and bureaucracy), it is equally important to keep in mind that state capacity is sometimes weak not necessarily because of a dearth of capable people but because of a systemic impasse.

Extraordinary state capacity may be observed in some episodic matters, for example, in organizing the complex logistics of the world's largest election, the world's second-largest census, and some of the world's largest religious festivals. But extraordinarily poor state capacity is displayed in, for example, some regular essential activities such as cost-effective pricing and distribution of electricity—the key input for the economy. There exist regular under-recovery of costs, erratic supply, and anaemic investment in electricity caused not so much by an inherent lack of administrative capacity but more by factors relating to complicity in a sinister political nexus of populist pressures and outright theft. Min and Golden (2014) provide evidence that in Uttar Pradesh, the largest state, transmission losses in electricity from public distribution utilities go up sharply before the state assembly elections. Similarly, much of the police and bureaucracy are highly politicized and often deliberately incapacitated to be subservient to the ruling political party. Corruption in India is often more dysfunctional than in, say, the more politically centralized countries of East Asia, primarily because it is fragmented with no encompassing centralizing entity internalizing the distortions ('negative externalities') of each act of corruption.[6]

The apparent lack of state capacity may be more a symptom of the underlying difficulty of organizing collective action (or collectively working out a political or 'social pact') in India, a problem exacerbated by its large heterogeneous population, fragmented polity, and extreme social and economic inequality. In such a context, commitments on the

---

[6] For an analytical discussion of this issue, see Bardhan (2005b: Chapter 8).

part of the state are often not credible and, anticipating that, different interest and identity groups agitate and settle for short-run patronage and subsidies.

This brings me back to the main theme of the difficulty of collective action emphasized in the 1984 book.

Since 1984, the population has increased considerably both in size and the diversity of now-assertive groups. The polity is more fragmented.[7] While social inequality may be on a slow decline, economic inequality has almost certainly increased.[8] Thus, by and large, the consequent problems for collective action may have become more severe, and the rare absolute majority of the ruling party and the apparent centralization of power in the Prime Minister's Office under the new regime has not made much of a difference in the policy implementation stage, despite all the hype. With the current disarray of policy implementation at the local level, collective action will remain problematic for the Indian polity.

STRUCTURAL ISSUES

Let me now move to the second part of this chapter by pointing briefly to at least four types of structural issues, not considered in the 1984 book, where there are significant unresolved tensions that the Indian political economy will have to grapple with in the coming years.

Changing Pattern of the Regulatory State

In the 1984 volume, I discussed the nature and impact of the dominant public sector and pervasive state regulations over the private sector in the form of fields of operation and various licences and permits. Since economic liberalization the dominance of the public sector has

---

[7] The recent unusually aggregative and presidential national elections do not negate high political fragmentation at the regional and local levels where most important policies are implemented. The 'Modi wave' does not apply to many of the economic policy complexities at those levels.

[8] Evidence for income inequality rising between 2004–05 and 2011–12 is available from the India Human Development Survey data; evidence for wealth inequality rising between 1991 and 2012 is available from National Sample Survey (NSS) data.

diminished, but unlike in China the commercialization of the public sector enterprises has been rather shallow, and by and large they remain under the thumb of the relevant ministries. As for the private sector, the earlier regime of permits and licences has declined in importance (though this applies more to the central regulations for trade and industry than at the state level), but with the expansion of private domestic and foreign investment in many fields, a whole range of regulatory bodies to oversee them has come up.

The proliferation of these bodies, instead of adding transparency and coherence to the system, has, with few exceptions, made it murkier and more fragmented. Quite often, they have just added another layer to the bureaucracy, with similar hidebound procedures and with post-retirement officers brought in from the ministry at whose behest they work. In the case of some regulatory bodies, such as that for telecommunications, they operate only in an advisory capacity and often overruled by the ministry. A landmark Electricity Act of 2003 has been neutered by the state regulatory commissions who obediently follow the state governments in preventing open access to the inter-state grids. Nor do they fail to connive at the state politicians' distribution of electricity to select groups at throwaway prices. In general, the control by politicians is often exerted in the form of selective implementation of the regulations.

In any case, most regulatory bodies have no penal power for non-compliance of their regulations. It looks like the regulatory bodies have mainly expanded the scope for sinecure jobs for professionals (identified as a dominant class in my 1984 book) and cemented state–business relationships between the regulator and the regulated. Prime minister after prime minister has promised at the beginning of their tenure a thorough administrative reform and yet ended up doing very little on that front. This has less to do with lapse of memory and more with the grip of strong vested interests in the class of professionals (including the powerful Indian Administrative Service officers' association), in spite of the various divisions in this class and the frequent need for compromises with their politician bosses. In this sense, there is a remarkable 'resilience' in this class, as noted in Chapter 8 of this volume.

As I have already indicated, the new mode of public–private partnerships has been saddled with problems, and sustainable regulatory protocols governing them are yet to be institutionalized. In this respect, the private sector has to give up on its tendency in such partnerships to privatize the profits and 'socialize' the losses, if the state–business relationship is to keep some semblance of democratic legitimacy. On the other hand, the state has to work out reasonable modes of long-term risk management and renegotiation as initial conditions unpredictably change, with decisions preferably delegated to an independent body that can avoid the suspicion of indulging in crony capitalism. The history of maintaining the independence of non-elected bodies has been rather poor, and recent years have seen assault on and erosion of even semi-independent institutions.

Accumulation versus Legitimization

For the last few decades, there has been a brewing 'legitimization crisis' of capitalism in India for many sections of the people on account of,

- the rising inequality of wealth;
- the flourishing of 'crony' capitalism, with regulatory favours to select business groups;
- the displacements and dispossession of common people from their land and degradation of their environment; and
- deterioration in the supply of basic public services (water, safety, and so on) in the burgeoning cities and towns, while the rich arrange for private access to these services.

In reaction, quite often politicians try to placate with short-run populist measures.

But the legitimization issue has also induced vigorous social movements and pressures for the recognition of various kinds of citizen rights and accountability institutions over the last couple of decades. These movements, however, have occasionally ended up stalling industrial progress—in collaboration with judicial activism they have made mining, infrastructural, and environmental clearances sometimes very difficult to obtain, slowing industrial growth.

The debates all around have become polarized on this matter, and political decisions seem to lurch from one end to the other: under the United Progressive Alliance (UPA) regime (2004–14) in the early years the rights movement flourished, but in the last few years or so the pendulum has swung again in favour of corporate lobbies and governments that harass and repress activists (compare Chapter 6). Since the social movements have not yet taken the form of mass political organizations, it has been relatively easy for business-friendly governments to bypass or dilute earlier welfarist legislative actions in actual implementation. To negotiate some kind of political balance in this tug of war between competing interests will be complex and time-consuming and the Indian polity will go on vacillating on these issues. And following usual political practice, parties in opposition will agitate against policies they themselves supported while in power.

The mainly elite-led non-governmental organizations and other voluntary organizations often act as strident single-interest lobbies, making compromise difficult. In this respect, they are poor substitutes for large multifarious political parties. But with the decay of inner-party democracy in all the parties, political parties no longer act as a forum for deliberation and transactional negotiations between contending interest groups within the party on controversial policy issues, where there are always trade-offs which could be negotiated.

On the other side, in the arena of organized politics, with the institutional decay of political parties the politics of legitimization has sometimes been usurped by forms of plebiscitary democracy, which depend more on the antics of blustering popular leaders and of the media often driven by crony capital interests, than on liberal procedures of accountability or structured social movements.

Jobs and Reservations

More than citizen rights and welfare, the young people who are the majority of 'aspirational' India seem to be demanding jobs. Over the next decade or so, this may be a major source of political turmoil, particularly because over many decades job growth in India has been very sluggish. It has been estimated on the basis of NSS data—see Ghose (2016)—that nearly 8 million workers are added to the labour force every year, on top of the backlog of over 60 million surplus workers (both openly unemployed and underemployed) in 2015–16 (this does not include those, mostly women, who have dropped out of the labour force but are potentially available with appropriate jobs). Outside the construction sector, growth elasticity of job creation so far has been extremely low. Most recent economic success stories in India have been in relatively skill-intensive or capital-intensive industries (software, pharmaceuticals, vehicles, auto parts, and so on).

There are several constraints on large-scale labour-intensive industrialization in India—infrastructure, skill formation, credit, regulatory environment, contract enforcement problems, red tape and the 'inspector raj', and so on. We do not yet have good statistical decomposition exercises on the net impact of these various factors on job creation or lack of it.

The business press and some liberal economists habitually put much of the blame on trade unions supporting stringent labour laws. But they overlook the fact that, while many of the labour laws do require modification and upgrading, trade unions (particularly of unskilled workers) are now substantially weaker than before, partly on account of technological change and increased capital mobility both across countries and across states in India. Even in the organized sector, more than one-third of workers are now 'contract labourers' without security or benefits, sometimes working side by side with regular workers.

Even when jobs are created, there is a major regional discrepancy between job demand and supply, which may turn the so-called demographic dividend from large numbers of young people into a ticking time bomb in parts of the country.[9] For demographic reasons, these young people are more in the large populous states of North India (where poor governance and infrastructural deficiencies limit job growth as well as delivery of welfare services). But jobs, when created, emerge more in states in western and southern India. Inter-state migration can be a partial relief but, given the staggering numbers, cannot be a solution if one wants to avoid large costs of dislocation and nativist unrest.

The last Finance Commission has encouraged more devolution of finance and responsibility to the states. With large initial differences in state capacity and infrastructural deficit, this is likely to accentuate regional inequality and discontent. With capital being much more

[9] It is estimated that even if one takes only the males in the 15–29 age group (likely to be socially the most restless young people), currently there are about 14 million unemployed or underemployed among such people, with about 6 million new entrants each year.

mobile across states than unskilled labour, many states are likely to compete in giving concessions to capital while indulging in populist measures for the poor. It also means that states where the dominant caste-coalition is generally pro-business will have advantage in attracting capital. At the same time, there are now some signs that even dominant castes (such as Patidars, Jats, or Marathas) are showing some cracks, as those sections in the same aggregative caste that are not doing well in terms of jobs and general economic conditions (while being pushed out of their traditional occupations by agrarian distress) are getting restive.

General reservations (in public sector jobs, higher education, and political representation), which have long constituted the default redistributive option in much of the public realm in India, are increasingly seen less as a way of fighting the historical legacy of discrimination against marginalized groups, and more as a way of staking a share in the spoils of the system, with even dominant castes demanding more for their share. As the job situation in India's non-agricultural sector becomes more acute, such demands are going to cause a great deal of tension in the political economy of the socio-economic arrangements.

Tension between Rentier and Entrepreneurial Capitalism

While there is vigorous productive capitalism in some sectors of the Indian economy, given the nature of the Indian political–business relationships there are few sectors that are untouched by factors that involve some form of rent (see Chapter 11). Apart from the usual temporary monopoly rent enjoyed by innovating companies in most countries, India has at least three major sources of quite unproductive (and thus socially wasteful) rent:

- Traded natural-resource-intensive goods (for example, minerals): in the first decade of this century, the mining mafia had its way, but with global recession and slowing down of the Chinese economy this source of rental income is a bit weaker now.
- Non-traded natural-resource-intensive goods and services (for example, land and real estate).
- Political rent in other activities (following from collusion between politicians or bureaucrats and connected sets of favoured

businessmen).[10] Even after economic liberalization, capital crucially depends on various kinds of regulatory discretion of officials as well as loans from public banks (which have seen many large 'wilful defaulters').

- There is hardly any major state or political party in India which has not been corrupted by land and real-estate interests. As the economy grows and land prices in a densely populated country gallop, this is unlikely to diminish in importance. (There is some evidence that land price rise in India in recent years has been one of the highest in the world [Chakraborty, 2013]). While auctions of public resources have now become somewhat cleaner than before and land acquisition and eviction of poor people has been made somewhat more difficult under the new laws, crony capitalism and rent-sharing between business and politicians continue relentlessly in different forms. In fact, politics and business are increasingly intertwined.

On the creation and maintenance of political rent, which is promoted by lack of competition, there are, of course, some built-in checks in economic competition (if scale economies are not large barriers to entry), particularly from abroad, and the political competition of democracy. Though the domestic non-traded sector is large, the Indian economy is now sufficiently globally integrated for the economic check to be quite significant in many sectors. There is, however, not much evidence that the dominance of incumbent firms has declined in the Indian industrial sector even after economic liberalization (Alfaro and Chari, 2012). On political competition, the barriers to political entry are getting stiffer, as elections become inordinately expensive and all campaigning politicians are increasingly dependent on scarce, often illicit, financial and organizational resources. A large part of undocumented election funds from the corporate sector for major political parties is a form of quid pro quo for the political rents enjoyed by business referred to above (although it has been pointed out that the uncertainty in the flow of kickbacks sometimes keeps the businessmen on tenterhooks).

[10] In some sectors (for example, liquor, real estate, construction, transport, private colleges, and so on), politicians themselves are now major business investors.

The impact of rentier capitalism on politics is to encourage oligarchic forces. As Walton argues in Chapter 11 of this volume, in US history the 'robber barons' of the nineteenth century were partially checked by the institutions created by the politics of the 'Progressive Era'. Much will depend on if or how a sufficient number of accountability institutions develop in India. Our elections are vigorous but our democracy is enormously flawed in terms of various kinds of accountability failures. It is this uphill democratic struggle that will shape the future of Indian political economy.

II

The Indian Economy Three Decades On

3 The Stagnation Debate

An Enduring Legacy

Matthew McCartney

Economics has not in recent decades been noted for its accessibility, diversity, and eclecticism. As an academic discipline, it frequently relies on a formal exposition revolving around the use of mathematics, which can be forbidding to those without graduate-level training. Economics has a rich legacy of schools of thought (Keynesian, Austrian, post-Keynesian, Marxist, Institutional, among others) but many students and practitioners utilize only one: the neoclassical school. Economics in its own past has seen itself as an embedded social science—its early exponents such as Adam Smith were known as political economists—and as an academic discipline, it drew freely on and contributed to discussion in history, politics, sociology, and demography. More recently, economics has been perceived to have disappeared into splendid isolation, structuring itself around forbidding mathematics and its own recent-vintage theoretical perspectives, offering contributions to but not drawing from other disciplines—'economics imperialism', as some have called this process. Reading academic writings about economic liberalization in India after 1991, one could be forgiven for criticizing the debate in all these terms. Studies looking at the impact of trade liberalization on productivity can often be densely mathematical and technical. Other schools of thought have been neglected in the rush to evaluate economic liberalization through the key pillars of the neoclassical paradigm—efficiency, resource allocation, and markets. The debate has been dominated by economists, often those resident in North American university departments not noted for drawing on other disciplines. The disappearance of class or political economy has been a widely noted feature of economics post-1991 (Keen, 2001).

This chapter is structured around one book, *The Political Economy of Development in India* (*PEDI*), written by Pranab Bardhan in 1984, and one debate: to explain industrial stagnation in India after 1965. It expands outwards from this focus and argues the book and debate to be forerunners of a then new research paradigm in economics, to explain episodes of economic growth and stagnation. Over the last decade an outpouring of cross-country statistical work has shown that the key feature of growth in developing countries is short to medium episodes of growth and stagnation. The division of the world into long-term growth success stories (South Korea and Taiwan) and long-term growth failures (Philippines, Egypt, and South Africa) is less tenable. Most countries in the world experience short periods of rapid growth followed by periods of economic slowdown.

This chapter begins by outlining the facts of industrial stagnation in India after 1965 and introduces the wider debate regarding episodes of growth and stagnation. The section titled 'The Facts to be Explained: Stagnation' goes on to show how thinking about economic growth in India since 1950 can be structured around this debate. The section, 'The Debate and Its Afterlives' introduces the key themes of the original industrial stagnation debate in India (including heterodox ideas such as income distribution, public investment, and the role of the state) and shows how this eclectic mix can be extended to provide a framework to think about all episodes of growth and stagnation in the Indian economy after 1947. The last section concludes. Among the pleasures of *PEDI* are its accessibility (less than a hundred pages of discussion with enough accompanying data), and its diversity and eclecticism (drawing on formal economics, the writing of Marx, digressions about the Mughal Empire, econometrics, and the impact of Nehru's leadership). Returning to *PEDI* and combining it with more recent work on the empirics of economic growth can help return economics to its roots as a social science and by doing so offer us deep insights into big contemporary problems—industrialization, employment and poverty, inequality, the global financial crisis, and sustainable economic growth in the twenty-first century.

THE FACTS TO BE EXPLAINED: STAGNATION

The central empirical fact that *PEDI* sought to explain was industrial stagnation in India after 1965, specifically in heavy industry. Industrial production had been expanding by 9 per cent per annum between 1961 and 1965 (Rangarajan, 1982: 292), which represented one of the best interludes of industrial growth in India over the entire twentieth century. Comparing the years 1956–57 to 1965–66 with the period from 1966–67 to 1979–80, *PEDI* found that growth had slowed across the (heavy) industrial sector, including basic metals, metal products, machinery (electrical and non-electrical), and transport equipment. In more labour-intensive sectors such as food processing and textiles, growth was slow (1984: 94–5). This stagnation was striking relative to the industrial bias of state planning efforts and the continuing aspirations of the political leadership to build an industrial base in India. From the 1960s onwards, planning documents targeted annual industrial growth of 12 per cent per annum and kept doing so. The stagnation was not just a failure to add new capacity to production but increasingly a failure to use the capacity created in the 15 years after Independence (Raj, 1976). In the capital goods industry, for example, capacity utilization fell from 85.9 per cent between 1960 and 1965 to 66.4 per cent between 1966 and 1970 (Ahluwalia, 1985: 109).

Episodes: A New Way of Thinking About Economic Growth

The stagnation debate in India was an early pioneer in thinking about economic growth in terms of episodes of growth and stagnation. This central analytical prop of *PEDI* has had enduring relevance. A wave of statistical work over the last decade or so has shown that the dominant feature of developing country growth is not rapid or slow growth clubs or perennial failures or take-offs into long-term growth success, but instead short to medium episodes of growth and stagnation. Hausmann, Pritchett, and Rodrik (2005) define an 'episode of growth' as an increase in per capita growth of 2 per cent or more sustained for at least eight years and post-acceleration growth of at least 3.5 per cent. They identify 80 such episodes between 1957 and 1992: Asia had 21, Africa 18, Latin America 17, and the Middle East and North Africa 10. While refining the definition (to include episodes of stagnation, for example) and expanding the sample, subsequent scholarship has confirmed the central thesis (Jones and Olken, 2008; Cuberes and Jerzmanowski, 2009; Jong-a-Pin and De Haan, 2011; Berg, Ostry, J. Zettelmeyer, 2011). This is no less true in India, where scholarship on growth after *PEDI* has retained the concept of 'episodes of growth and stagnation' as an organizing framework.

The 1980 Episode of Growth in India

There is widespread agreement that economic growth in India increased from its post-Independence average of around 3.5 per cent per annum to 5 per cent after around 1979. This growth occurred in both the public and private sectors (Nagaraj, 1991) and was driven by growth in mining and quarrying, manufacturing, transport, storage and communications (Bhargava and Joshi, 1990), finance, real estate and business services (Wallack, 2003), and registered manufacturing (Balakrishnan and Parameswaran, 2007). (The statistics related to this later episode of growth advanced beyond the simple averages used in *PEDI* by incorporating ever more sophisticated econometric techniques that served to isolate this new debate about growth from the broad audience of *PEDI* and included selecting the most statistically significant F-test over all possible years [Wallack, 2003], or selecting the largest Chow statistic for all possible years [Hatekar and Dongre, 2005], the growth trend in a Hodrick–Prescott filtered gross domestic product [GDP] series [Virmani, 2004], or a methodology to simultaneously estimate multiple structural breaks in growth [Balakrishnan and Parameswaran, 2007].)

Was There a Break in Growth in 1991?

There is widespread agreement that 1991 marked a significant shift in the policy framework—towards liberalization. Very few scholars have identified 1991 as ushering in a statistically significant increase in growth rates, however. Those familiar with the episodes literature would not find this a surprise. Hausmann, Pritchett, and Rodrik (2005), for example, found that only 14.5 per cent of growth accelerations are associated with liberalization, while 85.5 per cent of growth accelerations are not preceded or accompanied by liberalization. The typical empirical finding is represented by Nagaraj (2000), who used simple pre- and post-1991 averages of GDP growth to show that growth continued at a rate of 5.7 per cent throughout the 1980s and 1990s.

To squeeze out evidence for a break in growth after 1991 some scholars have engaged in statistical gymnastics. A. Panagariya (2004), for example, argues that growth was only high in the 1980s due to the growth average of 7.6 per cent between 1988 and 1991. This interlude should not be considered, he suggests, as it was driven by a demand-side boost provided by an unsustainable fiscal expansion and build-up of external debt. Foreign debt rose from $20.6 billion in 1980–81 to $64.4 billion in 1989–90 (Joshi and Little, 1994: 186). Government current expenditure, boosted mainly by subsidies, rose by 5 per cent of GDP and the government fiscal deficit reached 10 per cent of GDP annually after 1985; the 'eventual outcome of these developments was the June 1991 crisis' (Panagariya, 2004: 22; 2008 : 103). Panagariya (2004) also argues that the year 1991–92 was a crisis year (slow economic growth) and that the liberalizing reforms of 1991 onwards were made in response to the crisis rather than causing it; he, therefore, argues that it is a distortion to include 1991–92 (as is the convention) in the averages for post-reform growth. His data for the 1990s thus only begins with the revival of growth in 1992–93. So if we exclude 1988 to 1991, we find an average growth between 1980–81 and 1987–88 of only 4.6 per cent, close to the 4.1 per cent average between 1951–52 and 1964–65. Starting from the post-reform period, later we find an average growth of 6.3 per cent between 1992–93 and 1999–2000 (Bhagwati and Panagariya, 2013). Hey presto, we have an episode of economic growth in the 1990s. This chapter sticks with the more conventional view and does not include c. 1992 as heralding a new episode of growth.

The 2003 Break in Growth in India

There is an exuberance in the reporting of economic growth statistics after 2003, using impressive averages but not making the rigorous efforts used to demonstrate the statistical break in c. 1980. This breathless enthusiasm is perhaps not surprising as India became for the first time one of the fastest-growing economies in the world. A typical example is Nagaraj (2008), who writes that between 2002–03 and

2006–07 India's GDP grew annually by 8.7 per cent per annum, and manufacturing and service output by 8.8 and 9 per cent per annum respectively. Annual growth in beverages, textile products, basic metals, transport equipment, and electric and non-electric machinery all exceeded 10 per cent per annum (2008: 56). Investment, which as a share of GDP had remained barely above 20 per cent since the early 1990s, now surged to 33 per cent in 2006–07. In a later paper, Nagaraj (2013) was even more enthused about this growth episode, arguing that it was not just more rapid, but also sustainable (unlike the c. 1980 episode). He noted that the nation's finances were much improved; rising profitability boosted corporate savings, while tax reforms and the better financial performance of public sector enterprises turned around public savings. India's exports-to-GDP ratio increased from 14 per cent in 2002 to 25 per cent in 2009, and he argued that social networks of Indian professionals in Wall Street firms, Indian academics in US universities, and Indian entrepreneurs leveraged this integration to create a remarkable success story.

THE DEBATE AND ITS AFTERLIVES

The Political Economy of Development in India was one of the last canonical contributions to the debate about industrial stagnation. Although the debate about and concern with industrial stagnation faded with the acceleration of economic growth around 1980, and even more so with the shift to liberalization in c. 1991, the quality of the contributions continued to be acknowledged. In a collection of many of the seminal articles (published in 1994), Nayyar wrote an introduction that discussed how the India-focused debate had influenced a wider analysis of economic growth in developing countries. The India debate had encompassed neoclassical concerns with relative prices and resource allocation and a consequent emphasis on the 'static' economic efficiency costs of import-substitution industrialization, while also reaching into the dynamics of industrialization to incorporate heterodox ideas in the tradition of Keynes and Kalecki (Nayyar, 1994). This is the important legacy of *PEDI* and the stagnation debate: the idea that the economics of growth is a broad and eclectic debate. During the 1990s, scholarship related to India became ever more narrowly focused on the causes and consequences of economic liberalization. The emphasis in this chapter on the occurrence and timing of episodes of growth in India and corresponding debates reveals a much richer continuing engagement with competing schools of thought from the radical to the orthodox and, though not the focus of this chapter, from orthodox economics to political economy. This section reviews each of the key arguments in the original stagnation debate—income distribution, agriculture–industry linkages, import substitution, state failure, the policy framework constraint, and public investment—then discusses their relevance to the subsequent episodes of growth in India in 1980 and 2003.

Income Distribution

The conventional link between growth and income distribution is whether growth leads to more or less inequality. Famously, Kuznets (1955) suggested the relationship was an inverted U-shape. More recently, Piketty (2014) has suggested that the declining inequality leg of the inverted U is a historical anomaly and much of the world is trending back to historical norms of significant inequality. The novelty of the stagnation debate in India was to reverse this line of causation and to argue that inequality could influence economic growth via its influence on the pattern or level of demand. Increasing inequality in the distribution of income could divert demand from mass consumption goods to luxury production, changing the pattern of demand. The production of mass consumption goods in India is labour-intensive and stimulates linkages with the local economy. Luxury production was import-intensive or produced by technology- and capital-intensive methods of production that generated little employment and wage-based consumption demand in India (Nayyar, 1978). Rising income inequality may stimulate savings by the rich at the expense of consumption by the poor and thus reduce the level of aggregate demand (Chakravarty, 1979).

The Political Economy of Development in India noted that the evidence on income and expenditure inequality is mixed for India after 1965. Also, output growth in the consumer goods industries actually increased in the years after 1965—not something we would expect if rising inequality was choking off the growth of consumption for basic necessities. Other scholars have not found rigorous evidence to suggest a failing of demand amongst the poorest in 1970s India. Between 1977–78 and 1993–94, average consumption grew by 0.9 per cent per annum and by 1.5 per cent per annum amongst the poorest half of the rural population (Nagaraj, 2000). *The Political Economy of Development in India* also noted that inequality did not stop rapid growth in other countries in the 1960s such as Brazil and South Korea.

After the stagnation debate, discussion of this heterodox approach all but disappears. Some lingering influence can be teased out of the literature regarding the episode of growth after c. 1980. Bhattacharya and Mitra (1990; 1991) offered an explanation based on income distribution and inequality between economic sectors. They noted that the rapid growth of the service sector in India was creating income and consequently consumption expenditure. This demand was still directed at the output of the manufacturing sector (services accounted for less than 20 per cent of aggregate consumer expenditure in the 1980s). Incomes, without corresponding commodity production, they suggested would generate excess demand for imports or inflationary pressures and render the service-led growth path unsustainable. There is little evidence that the Indian economy was failing to produce consumption goods in the 1980s. Nagaraj (1990), for example, finds that the growth rate of consumer durables output averaged 16 per cent per annum between 1980–81 and 1988–89, compared to only 7.4 per cent per annum for manufacturing as a whole. The service-led growth path in India, rather than failing, soared into an even more dramatic growth episode in c. 2003.

In regard to the 2003 episode of growth, there has been a surge of studies looking at the more conventional argument: whether economic growth is accompanied by rising inequality (Sarkar and Mehta, 2010), and how that inequality is structured according to discrimination (Banerjee et al, 2009), class (Vakulabharanam, 2010), caste (Thorat and Newman, 2007), between states (Baddeley et al., 2006), among various others. This reflects the growing global discourse about rising inequality (Piketty, 2014). There remain a few exceptions. The slowdown in economic growth after 2011, argue Sen and Kar (2014), was due to the growing popular discontent at the unequal sharing of the material benefits generated by the 2003 episode of growth; they offered a political economy explanation linking income distribution to GDP rather than one working through aggregate demand. There was mass political mobilization against the attempts by the state of Odisha and West Bengal to use extra-legal/coercive means to provide land to big business/ mining. In response to the controversy, an activist Supreme Court banned iron ore exports, and the Comptroller and Auditor General of India (CAG) investigated corruption in allocation of 2G mobile phone licences and coal mining licences. Increasingly, the ruling party at the centre lost the authority to credibly commit to new deals in the face of popular and legal challenges. Investor perception of investment risk started increasing after 2006, and as a consequence, corporate investment and economic growth declined (Sen and Kar, 2014: 22).

While the causal impact of inequality has faded from discussion in India, it has gained more widespread interest elsewhere. Thirty years after *PEDI*, J.E. Stiglitz was writing well-received bestsellers arguing that inequality in the United States of America was an underlying cause of the 2008 global financial crisis. Growing inequality, he argued, redistributed incomes from the poorest (who would be more likely to consume) to the richest (who were more likely to save). To sustain consumption demand and so economic growth required an 'artificial prop, which in the years before the crisis came in the form of a housing bubble fuelled by Fed policies' (Stiglitz, 2013: 106). It is not surprising that this debate has had so little traction in contemporary India. In India, unlike the United States of America, monetary measures of poverty are falling (Datt and Ravallion, 2010) and the debate is almost entirely about the extent of that fall, not the fact of it (Deaton and Kozel, 2005). In India, again unlike the United States of America, real wages among the poorest are rising, not stagnating, over recent decades (Kijima, 2006; Sarkar and Mehta, 2010). Consumption amongst the poorest in India is increasing over time (Deaton and Drèze, 2009), and concerns revolve instead about whether rising prices of privatized education and health are crowding out expenditures on nutrition, health, and other important necessities (Pal, 2013).

Agriculture–Industry Linkages

The key mechanisms by which agriculture can influence industrial growth include agriculture as a supplier of wage goods (food) and labour to the industrial sector, as a provider of raw materials for agro-based industries, to generate final incomes that provide a demand for industrial outputs, and more indirectly as a source of savings and tax revenue to pay for industrial investment. Most traditional industries in mid-1960s India such as cotton and jute textiles, sugar, vegetable oils, and tobacco were agro-based.

Some scholars did connect industrial stagnation to a failure of growth and productivity in Indian agriculture (Vaidyanathan, 1977; Rangarajan 1982). Mitra (1977) argued that the slow growth of agricultural output led to an upward pressure on the prices of foodgrains and a resulting pressure for higher wages that reduced the profitability of, and investment in, the industrial corporate sector. Other scholars have disagreed and argued that agricultural output growth was actually higher after 1967–68 (Balakrishnan and Parameswaran, 2007) and that the patterns in the relative price of agricultural products showed no clear trend over time (Desai, 1981). The inherent instability of monsoon-driven agriculture makes any use of average growth rates notoriously mercurial.

There is wide agreement that agricultural growth showed a trend in improvement after 1980, with a few exceptions (such as Nagaraj, 2000). Agriculture showed a better performance in the 1980s (4.75 per cent) over the 1970s (1.4 per cent) and 1990s (3.08 per cent). The averages for the 1970s are partly contingent on how the negative growth rate in 1979–80 (–13.36 per cent) is dealt with; if dropped from the average for the decade as a one-off aberration, the average growth rate in the 1970s is 3.04 per cent. Even constant growth rates would have had a changing impact on industrial growth as the percentage of purchased inputs to total inputs (taken as a proxy for demand for industrial inputs in agricultural production) doubled from 16.4 per cent in 1970–71 to 35.6 per cent in 1983–84 (Thamarajakshi, 1990). Some argue that the agricultural terms of trade did not decline in the 1980s relative to the 1970s (Rodrik and Subramanian, 2005), whilst others disagree (Kotwal et al, 2011). There is little writing for more recent years on the link between this growth of agriculture and the growth of other economic sectors. The contemporary debate has focused more narrowly on the 'crisis of agriculture' seen in terms of the falling growth rate of agricultural output in the 1990s relative to the 1980s (Mathur, Das, and Sircar, 2006; Chand, Raju, and Pandey, 2007; Bhalla and Singh, 2009; Vakulabharanam and Motiram, 2011), and of the slowing of yield growth (Chand and Pendey, 2007; Bhalla and Singh, 2009; Vakulabharanam and Motiram, 2011). Much of this work has focused on individual state-level stories of crisis such as Punjab (Sidhu, 2002) and Odisha (Pattnaik and Shah, 2010), or success in Gujarat (Dixit, 2009) or West Bengal (Harriss, 1993). Gadgil and Gadgil (2006) is a rare exception, which shows that between 1950 and 2003 the impact of changes in rainfall has continued to have a significant impact on foodgrain production and in turn on the growth of GDP, this despite the share of agriculture in GDP declining from 50 per cent in 1950 to 22 per cent in 2000.

In relation to the 2003 episode of growth, agriculture is again treated as a sectoral issue lacking much wider macroeconomic import. Deokar and Shetty (2014), for example, argue that 2004–05 was a turning point for agriculture. The average growth rate of output increased from 2.4 per cent between 1994–95 and 2004–05 to 4 per cent until 2013–14. This, they argue was due to policy changes that included the launching of the National Horticulture Mission, reforms to the Agricultural extension system, launch of the Bharat Nirman Project in 2005–06 (to upgrade rural infrastructure), and efforts to double credit to agriculture in three years after 2004–05. Balakrishnan (2014) does provide a bigger macroeconomic picture, suggesting but not offering rigorous empirical evidence that the poor harvests after 2008–09 contributed to the slowdown of GDP in India in the late 2000s.

Import Substitution

Import substitution as a (potentially) viable development strategy was a much-discussed topic in India, until at least the publication of *PEDI*. There are two crucial parts to the argument linking import substitution to industrial stagnation. First, import substitution accounted for 23 per cent of total industrial growth between 1950–51 and 1965–66. C.P. Chandrasekhar (1988) argued that by the mid-1960s opportunities for further import substitution were exhausted. By 1965–66 the share of imports in domestic availability exceeded 20 per cent in only four (petroleum products, basic metals, non-electrical machinery, and electrical machinery) from 20 industrial groups. A second argument suggests that the inefficiency of import substitution was acting as a drag to further industrial growth by the mid-1960s. In the 1950s and 1960s, protection was granted to any industry setting up indigenous capacity in India regardless of the relative costs of foreign and domestic production. The size of the domestic Indian market was often not big enough to allow economies of scale. Together these policies are argued to have raised costs and reduced the productivity of Indian industrial production, slowing industrial growth, particularly via exports (Ahluwalia, 1985).

Political Economy of Development in India notes that the growth deceleration after the mid-1960s was not necessarily associated with the end of import substitution. It includes a table (Bardhan, 1984: 96) that shows the volume of imports as a percentage of availability being still high in paper and paper products, petroleum products, basic metals, non-electrical machinery, and non-metallic mineral products even in 1978–79. This implies there was still scope for continued growth based on import substitution. In the 1980s, the discussion in India shifted to the incipient process of trade liberalization and export promotion, and the debate about import substitution disappeared into the realm of discursive history.

The Failure of the State

Bardhan argued that the Indian state had become 'in spite of its pervasive economic presence largely confined to regulatory functions, avoiding the hard choices and politically unpleasant decisions involved in more active developmental functions' (1984: 74). The failure hypothesis receives support from other scholars. There were inefficiencies that covered the entire public sector investment programme from project formulation to implementation. Inefficiencies in the management of the state-owned railway system, for example, included a poor performance on net tonne kilometres moved per wagon per day, net tonne kilometres moved per tonne of wagon capacity, engine utilization, and engine speed. The minimum time overrun for the construction of hydroelectric power was two years and the maximum was nine years. Cost overruns were typically over 100 per cent. Thermal power plants operate at a norm of 80 per cent, but in India actual plant availability reached a high of only 77 per cent in the mid-1970s, then declined to 66 per cent in 1980–81. The plant load factor (PLF) of power plants reached a maximum of 56 per cent against a recommended norm of 58 per cent and then showed a steady decline from the mid-1970s onwards (Ahluwalia, 1985). Shetty focused on 'the impact of the absence of sustained developmental efforts', which he argued by the mid-1960s was evident 'in the generation of apparent surpluses of foodgrains and foreign exchange reserves ... in the midst of rising malnutrition, poverty and unemployment ... and persistent sluggishness in domestic investment' (1978: 132). S.L. Shetty further argues that there was an 'atmosphere of permissiveness in the deployment of industrial control mechanisms' (1978: 141). While the availability of wage goods (such as soap, cotton yarn, and textiles) was increasing slowly, there were 'disproportionate' increases in luxury goods (such as toothpaste and polyester fibre). Shetty argues that the cause of these maladies was a 'downgrading of the planning process' whereby a 'significant proportion of the total public outlays was frittered away in non-developmental expenditure' and 'simultaneously, the rigours of industrial controls—price and distribution controls, industrial licensing, capital issue controls etc—were drastically reduced' (1978: 174). C. Rangarajan (1982) argues that indicators showing the inefficient use of public sector capital were in part due to poor planning, specifically to the lack of complementary investments leading to an inefficient use of available capital. Chandrasekhar (1988) noted that large business houses in India were able to corner a disproportionate share of licences as a strategy to undermine the effort by the government to influence resource allocation and capacity creation.

The Political Economy and Development of India contributed much evidence to the state failure hypothesis. The costs of creating irrigation potential doubled at constant prices, which the book attributes to inefficiency and management failures with public sector capital (1984: 28). Bardhan found that capacity utilization was very low in electricity generation (public sector) and other key sectors such as basic metals, including non-electrical machinery and transport equipment (dominated by the public sector). Where capacity existed in both public and private sectors, *PEDI* suggests that capacity utilization was often lower in the public sector by 15–20 percentage points. Some of these problems arose from the lack of complementary investments and the failure of 'political and administrative mismanagement' (30) and ultimately a consequence of 'the politics of rising capital-output ratios' (31).

The big problem with the state failure hypothesis is that the evidence is not supportive for the first 15 years after Independence. *PEDI* created a rich political economy framework, based around how the nature of the class structure had become a growing constraint on the autonomy of the Indian state. It argues that the state at Independence had enormous prestige and a sufficiently unified sense of ideological purpose that from its control of the commanding heights of the economy it could formulate goals and policy directions neither at the behest of nor on behalf of the dominant proprietary classes. Yet over time, constraints on this autonomy grew stronger as the aura of the Indian leaders waned such that by the mid-1960s 'the plurality of these constraints and the complexity of their mutual interaction in a noisy open polity have generated pressures which have seriously interfered with the accumulation and management functions of the public economy' (39). The clear development successes of the Indian state up to 1965 and abrupt shift to stagnation are difficult to reconcile with an explanation that revolves around the gradual silting up of problems and constraints on the state as documented by *PEDI*.

The pre-1965 development successes are manifold. There was a statistically significant increase in economic growth in c. 1950 that was more marked than any other in India in the entire twentieth century (Nayar, 2006; Hatekar and Dongre, 2005; Balakrishnan and Parameswaran, 2007). The Indian economy grew by over 4 per cent between 1951 and 1964, during which time there were few signs of growth fatigue; if anything industrial growth was accelerating from 1960 to 1965. If there was a productivity failure, it was only after the mid-1960s. Productivity growth (total-factor productivity [TFP]) was relatively rapid (1.78 per cent per annum) between 1950–51 and 1964–65. It was only between 1964–65 and 1980–81 that it slowed sharply (by 0.41 per cent per annum) (Sivasubramonian, 2000: 286; Virmani, 2004: 23).

The state mobilized resources to support a vision of long-term planned economic growth. The state almost doubled the share of national income raised in taxation from 7 per cent at the beginning of the 1950s to nearly 15 per cent by the mid-1960s (Bhagwati and Srinivasan, 1975: 8). Tax mobilization was combined with a strict control of public spending. Government spending as a share of GDP was no more than about 6 per cent until 1960 when it increased to around 8.5 per cent by 1965. Subsidies were controlled: during the 1950s, for example, while the area irrigated by canals increased by 20 per cent, losses from running the government irrigation system were reduced and subsidies per hectare of net sown area or irrigated area declined. By comparison, subsidies and operating losses increased three- or four-fold in the 1960s (Chakravarty, 1987: 127). More tax revenue and controlled public spending led to an increase in public savings from (three-year moving averages) 1.9 per cent of GDP in 1951–52 to 3.5 per cent in 1964–65 (Bardhan, 1984: 99). The management of the public budget facilitated a big increase in public investment from 3.3 per cent of GDP in 1951–52 to 8.3 per cent in 1964–65 (Bardhan, 1984: 97). Over the 1950s, the Indian state made rapid progress in diversifying the structure of industry. By the early-1960s, the industrial structure had shifted from one dominated by textiles and sugar to one with substantial capacity in iron and steel, non-ferrous metals, machine building, coal, and heavy chemicals (Chandra, Mukherjee, and Mukherjee, 2008: 450–1). The aspirations in 1947 to achieve independence encompassed not just a formal end to colonial rule, but also economic independence from the developed economies. This was largely achieved: the 'Indian state has played a decisive role in constructing the most self-reliant and insulated capitalist economy in the third world.... There is no major capitalist country in the third world which has a more powerful state than India's or an indigenous bourgeoisie with more autonomy from foreign capital' (Vanaik, 1990: 8, 11). Increased self-sufficiency was driven by a proactive state. In some sectors, the state entered to produce on its own account (oil, tinplate, electrical equipment, drugs, and shipping) or by encouraging Indian firms to enter/increase market share (matches, soap, industrial gases, rubber tyres, vanaspati: a cheap vegetable oil used as a substitute for ghee or butter) (Kidron, 1965).

Developmental successes continued into the era of stagnation, belying *PEDI's* assertion that the Indian state was largely confined to 'regulatory functions'. From the mid-1960s onwards, the state promoted Green Revolution policies, which sustained agricultural growth. Inflation was kept (brief interludes excepted) at 10 per cent or below and the macroeconomic management of the Indian state differed from the outcome of fiscal and subsidy populism among other developing countries. In 1974, the state tested a nuclear weapon based on indigenous technology. Some scholars have also pointed to the era of stagnation as being crucial for the creation of capabilities in sectors that led economic growth in the 1980s onwards, notably in Information

Technology (IT) (Saraswati, 2013) and pharmaceuticals (Perlitz, 2008; Joseph, 2011).

The output share of the public sector peaked in 1991–92 at 26.1 per cent, which implies that the acceleration of GDP growth after 1980–81 was shared by the public sector. The public investment ratio peaked in 1986–87 at 12.5 per cent of GDP and declined to 6.4 per cent by 2001–02. The public sector delivered a stable share of accelerating domestic output for 20 years even though its investment share halved, an impressive record of productivity growth. This was in stark contrast to the evidence for inefficiency in the public sector in the 1960s and 1970s (Nagaraj, 2006). The 1980s also saw distinct improvements in the functioning of the Indian state. This included greater selectivity in new projects and the concentration of available resources in completing ongoing ones. There was an increase in the output growth of key state-produced industrial inputs such as coal, electricity, nitrogenous fertilizer, phosphatic fertilizers, and cement. The growth in telecommunications (measured by new direct exchange lines added) and railways (recorded by revenue earning traffic) since 1981 was notable (Nagaraj, 1990).

The Policy Framework as Constraint

During the era of industrial stagnation, Bhagwati (1993) argued that there was no problem of resource mobilization as national savings doubled from 10 to 22 per cent of GDP between 1950 and 1984. I.J. Ahluwalia (1985) found that growth in manufacturing output was entirely accounted for by growth in the capital stock, while productivity (TFP) declined. Stagnation was a problem with the productivity of resource utilization, specifically the 'effect of inadequacies in the policy design and framework showed itself in stagnant growth rates' (Bhagwati, 1993: 40).

The Industrial Licensing Act of 1951 mandated that firms acquire a licence to establish a new undertaking for expanding capacity, using new technology, to import, to exit an industry, or to manufacture a new article. From 1967 onwards, some areas of industrial production were reserved for the small-scale sector and by 1977 the list comprised 180 items. The Monopoly and Restrictive Trade Practices Act (MRTP) passed in 1969 added an extra layer of licensing and regulatory oversight to large companies. Policymaking was characterized by administrative delays and overwhelmed ministries were only able to allocate licences using ad hoc rules of thumb such as allocating licences on the basis of already installed capacity. The uncertainties and delays associated with licence allocation discouraged long-term planning by industry. Foreign trade was strictly regulated through the use of tariffs and elaborate quotas and protection was granted to all domestic production regardless of cost on the basis of indigenous availability (Bhagwati and Desai, 1970; Bhagwati and Srinivasan, 1975; Ahluwalia, 1985).

The earliest hint of liberalization, argues Nayar (2006), was in 1974 when the government abandoned its attempts to nationalize the wholesale trade in wheat. This was followed by a creeping devaluation of the rupee, by 20 per cent between 1971 and 1975, and some minor deregulation of the domestic economy. Despite its limited scope, Panagariya (2008) credits this 'first phase of liberalization' with GDP growth of 9 per cent in 1975–76 and an average growth rate of nearly 6 per cent between 1975–76, and 1978–79. Liberalization continued into the next decade, going further than the 1970s under the auspices of the Industrial Policy Statement of Indira Gandhi in 1980. The freedom to import capital goods was increased noticeably and there was some easing of capacity constraints on domestic production and greater freedoms to engage in foreign collaborations. Reforms under Rajiv Gandhi in the 1980s focused on domestic liberalization, easing licenced capacity constraints, reducing the bite of the MRTP, and raising the ceiling on small-scale enterprises. There was a particular push for exports, which included various tax and concessional credit incentives and the opening of more Export Processing Zones (EPZs). The real exchange rate depreciated by about 30 per cent between 1985–86 and 1989–90. The lack of attention to external liberalization can be seen in the effective rates of protection, which reached 149 per cent for intermediate goods, 79 per cent for capital goods, and 112 per cent for consumer goods in the years 1986 to 1990 (Kotwal, Ramaswami, and Wadhwa, 2011: 157). Panagariya (2004) links this liberalization to the 7.6 per cent annual GDP growth experienced between 1988 and 1991. Panagariya (2008) calls the years 1988 to 2006 the 'Triumph of Liberalization'.

The reforms of the 1990s were systemic and deeper. The share of products subject to quantitative restrictions declined from 87 per cent in

1987–88 to 45 per cent in 1994–95. Tariffs were systematically reduced rather than relying on selective exemptions; average tariffs fell from more than 80 per cent in 1990 to 37 per cent in 1996. The Indian rupee was devaluated against the dollar by 20 per cent in July 1991 (Topalova, 2004). Pre-entry scrutiny of investment decisions by MRTP companies was no longer required and instead emphasis was placed on controlling and regulating monopolistic, restrictive, and unfair trade practices. The new policy limited the public sector monopoly to eight sectors on security and strategic grounds. The concept of automatic approval of foreign direct investment (FDI) was introduced and the Reserve Bank of India (RBI) was empowered to approve equity investment up to 51 per cent in 34 priority industries. The public sector dominated the banking sector throughout the 1990s, though private banks were allowed to operate and FDI up to 75 per cent was permitted under the automatic route; by the early 2000s, 50 foreign banks were in operation. Infrastructure was opened up to the FDI under the 100 per cent-under-automatic route for projects in construction and maintenance of roads, highways, bridges, toll roads, ports, and harbours (Panagariya, 2004; 2008).

Many authors have tried to link liberalization and the success of certain economic sectors. By 1996, more than 1,000 products were still reserved for production by small enterprises, but by 2008 all but 20 products had been removed. When products were removed from the reserved list, while the average incumbent stagnated, the average entrant grew in terms of output and employment (Martin et al., 2014). Reductions in import tariffs led to robust and highly significant increases in productivity for private companies but not for government-owned or foreign companies (Topalova, 2004). India's trade liberalization increased firms' access to intermediate inputs from abroad in volume and variety and firms have used these imported inputs to introduce new products into the domestic market (Goldberg et al., 2013). The opening up of services to the FDI led to an increase in the share of services in the FDI from 10.5 per cent in the early 1990s to nearly 30 per cent in the later 1990s. FDI by major software firms enabled the domestic industry to utilize world-class quality processes, tools, and methodologies (Kotwal et al., 2011). The crucial step for the dramatically successful telecommunications revolution was the New Telecom Policy of 1999, implemented from the early 2000s (Bhagwati and Panagariya, 2013). Improved communications (especially cell phones) and diffusion of the internet were not conceivable without the breakup of government monopolies and advent of competition in the telecommunications sector. Under Rajiv Gandhi, while the number of telephone lines rose from 0.4 in 1984–85 per 100 people to only 0.6 in 1989–90, penetration surged to 18 by 2007 (Panagariya, 2008: xxvii). Domestic civil aviation reforms in 1997 freed entry into the airline industry. The rising demand for airline services in the 2000s led to the entry of Spice Jet, GoAir, IndiGo, and Kingfisher among others. These competed against the incumbents: Jet, Sahara, Air Deccan, and Indian (previously Indian Airlines and now Air India). The total number of passengers increased from 8.1 million in 1991 to 22.7 million in 2005 (Panagariya, 2008: 97).

A big problem for those scholars seeking to link liberalization to economic growth is that, as noted below, economic growth and productivity showed no sign of acceleration after 1991. There was no episode of growth to coincide with the shift in policy. This paradox for some has been resolved by considering lags. Any positive impact of economic liberalization working through access to imported capital goods, competitive pressures forcing efficiency improvements, and the re-allocation of factors of production to more efficient uses will take time. In the short term, the transition is likely to be characterized by an initial slowdown in productivity and output growth. This decline is linked to the deterioration in capacity utilization resulting from obsolescence of product lines and loss of demand for capital used to produce it. It also takes time for firms to utilize new capacity and new technology through learning by doing and exploiting scale economies (Virmani and Hashim, 2011).

There is good evidence of such a 'J-curve' in GDP and productivity growth. Capital productivity declined between 1991–92 and 1997–98 but surged by 6 per cent per annum between 2002–03 and 2007–08 (Virmani and Hashim, 2011: 15). There is a clear J-curve pattern of TFP growth in manufacturing. Total-factor productivity grew at 0.6 per cent per annum in the 1980s, slowed to 0.25 per cent per annum in the first years of the 1990s reform, declined by 0.1 per cent during the late 1990s and early 2000s, then accelerated sharply to 1.4 per cent per annum after 2002–03. There is a similar pattern in subsectors such as textile products, chemicals and chemical products, food products and beverages, motor vehicles, electrical machinery, and other transport equipment (Virmani and Hashim, 2011: 22). There is evidence of a substantial contribution of resource reallocation to growth in India after 1991, with a higher gain for deregulated industries. Most of the reallocation gains in the years after deregulation can be attributed to new entrants in deregulated industries. As time elapsed more gains from reallocation were experienced by incumbent firms in those same industries. These findings are consistent with the view that competition effects and other gains from deregulation required time and emerged with a lag (Alfaro and Chari, 2012).

Public Investment

Political Economy of Development in India accepts the well-rehearsed argument that public investment was crucial in creating capacity in sectors such as railways, power, and fuel. By the mid-1960s, public investment provided a near-monopoly source of demand for the output of such sectors. Public investment reached a peak of 9.6 per cent of GDP in 1965–66, then fell with the onset of industrial stagnation to a low of 6.3 per cent of GDP in 1970–71. The slowdown in public investment was borne disproportionately by infrastructure. Infrastructure investment grew by 17 per cent per annum between 1960 and 1965 and by 2 per cent per annum over the next 10 years. Private investment, by contrast, remained stable or even increased slightly between the mid-1960s and early 1970s. After the early 1970s, the level of total investment began to recover, led by increasing public investment and high and rising private investment. This relative stability of aggregate investment between 1965–66 and 1979–80 is the basis of Ahluwalia's (1985) argument that cuts in public investment cannot explain industrial stagnation after 1965. She argues that the demand for the output of capital and basic industries depends on overall investment, public or private. This is wrong. The growth of heavy industries was contingent on public investment. The share of infrastructure investment in total investment rose sharply from 13.2 per cent to 21–3 per cent between 1960–61 and the mid-1960s, then fell to a low of 10.1 per cent in 1973–74 (Ahluwalia, 1985: 78–9). This argument is even more relevant in areas of industry reserved for the state. For example, by the mid-1960s the government was the monopoly purchaser of the output of railway equipment. The share of public investment going to railways fell sharply from 23.1 per cent in 1964 to 6 per cent a decade later (Virmani, 2004). Reduced infrastructure investment after the mid-1960s led directly to a sharp decline in capacity utilization in the capital goods industry from 85.9 per cent between 1960 and 1965 to 66.4 per cent between 1966 and 1970, and to 60.2 per cent between 1971 and 1975 (Ahluwalia 1985: 109). In keeping with *PEDI*'s simple but clear statistics relating to growth rates, Bardhan ran a basic regression using time series data (1951–52 to 1980–81) on investment and showed that public investment has a positive, significant, and lagged impact on private (especially corporate) investment. *Political Economy of Development in India* estimated that the elasticity of private corporate investment with respect to public investment (of the previous year) was as high as 0.73 (23). There is widespread support for this empirical finding (Rangarajan, 1982; Murthy and Soumya, 2007).

The fact that *PEDI* was published in 1984 based on lectures given in 1982 led the study to miss the near doubling of the GDP growth rate that occurred around 1980 (Nayar, 2006). But in important ways, its hypotheses held good. A key explanation for the c. 1980 growth surge was the contemporaneous boost to public investment. The years 1979 and 1980 were, like the mid-1960s, characterized by drought, oil price shocks, and a debt crisis. In contrast with the austerity of the mid-1960s, India responded in the early 1980s with expansionary adjustment. A large International Monetary Fund (IMF) loan was taken out to help fund big increases in public investment, of 14 per cent in both 1981–82 and 1982–83. Private investment showed a strong response. Corporate investment, which had been stagnant in the 1970s, grew by 12 per cent per annum in the 1980s (McCartney, 2009: 151–78). Private equipment investment increased from 2.5 per cent of GDP in 1970–4 to 5.0 per cent in 1985–9 (Sen, 2007: 41). The literature examining cross-country drivers of episodes of growth supports *PEDI*'s earlier argument and finds that growth accelerations worldwide are correlated with increases in investment (Hausman, Pritchett, and Rodrik, 2005a; Jones and Olken, 2008). There is also quite a lot of work on the narrower question of public investment in agriculture. Studies have found that public investment in agriculture was cut in the 1990s relative to the 1980s (Shetty, 1990; Kumar, 1992; Mishra and Chand, 1995) and that such cuts were an important contributory factor behind the slowdown in agricultural growth in the 1990s (Dhawan, 1996; Gulati and Bathla, 2001; Mathur, Das, and Sircar, 2006).

The episode of growth after 2003 was linked to some specific increases in public investment. The National Highways Development Project (NHDP) and Pradhan Mantri Gram Sadak Yojana (PMGSY) after 2000 improved road connectivity between major cities and within rural areas. The centrepiece of the NHDP was the Golden Quadrilateral, which aimed to connect Delhi, Mumbai, Chennai, and Kolkata among other major routes with four-lane highways. The government approved NHDP-I in December 2000, awarding contracts by February 2002. Of the 5,846 km covered by the first phase, 5,521 km had already been converted to four lanes as of January 2007. An estimated $50 billion was to have been invested by 2012 (Panagariya, 2008). Investment in roads increased from 0.4 per cent of GDP in the late 1990s to around 1.2 per cent by the late 2000s (Mohan and Kapur, 2015).

More generally, however, there is evidence that the importance of public investment has been declining in recent years. Sen (2007) finds that the growth in private equipment investment after c. 1980 was explained by the relative price of equipment, financial deepening, and public investment. He notes that, while important in earlier years, by the mid to late 1980s public fixed investment was no longer a crucial influence on private equipment investment. At the beginning of the 1980s, India had one of the highest levels of the relative price of equipment investment among developing countries. The relaxation of import controls that had started with the export–import policy of 1977–78 gained momentum in the 1980s and steadily freed up the import of capital goods and led to sharp falls in the relative price of both domestic and imported capital goods. The liberalization of capital goods imports in the 1990s led to what Desai (2001) called the 'massacre of machine building'. Gross value added of the domestic machine tool manufacturing industry grew by only 1.7 per cent per annum between 1981 and 1997, then declined in each of the next four years, falling by 14 per cent in 2001 alone. Much of the incremental demand was met by imports and the import to consumption ratio nearly doubled from 29 per cent in the 1990s to 56 per cent in 1995 (Nagaraj, 2003). In agriculture as well total gross capital formation as a percentage of agricultural GDP increased from 12.9 per cent in the five-year period ending in 2003–04 to 17 per cent in 2012–13. This was mainly driven by the private sector, with only a modest rise in public investment in agriculture (Deokar and Shetty, 2014). Relatedly, the importance of the public sector, specifically for infrastructure investment, has also been declining. Gross fixed investment as a share of GDP increased from 24 per cent in 1996–97 to 2003–04 to a peak of nearly 34 per cent in 2008 (Mohan and Kapur, 2015). The share of infrastructure spending to GDP increased from 5.0 per cent in 2006–07 to 6.3 per cent in 2008–09. Unlike in earlier years, this increase was driven by the private sector, while public sector infrastructure investment stagnated (Mohan and Kapur, 2015: 16).

While public investment has seemingly become less relevant in driving economic growth in India, Stiglitz has returned to this debate as a policy recommendation for the United States of America to break out of stagnation after the 2008 global financial crisis: 'Government investments—in infrastructure, education, and technology underpinned growth in the last century, and they can form the basis of growth in this century' (Stiglitz, 2013: 354).

★★★

In 83 pages, Pranab Bardhan produced an enduring and influential analysis of the political economy story of a country with (today) 1.2 billion people. In 1984, Bardhan described his book as 'impetuous'; if so, its analysis has proved tenacious and 30 years later regularly appears in the bibliography of publications from across the political spectrum. At one level, *PEDI* was one among many fascinating contributions to a very specific debate—that on industrial stagnation in India after 1965. Compared to the 'lost decade' in Latin American economies of the 1980s, the 1990s collapse of the Soviet Union or the 1997 Asian crisis was not a very dramatic story. Yet the story remains important because it was in these years that India failed to make the breakthrough into sustained industrialization. Study of this period thus helps to explain why India today has failed to generate the factory-based employment that has led poverty reduction elsewhere in the developing world. The stagnation debate was also prescient, if not widely recognized outside India by specialists: it finds striking contemporary echoes in the works of Stiglitz and others discussing the stagnation of the United States of America and other developed countries after the 2008 global financial crisis. The methodology of *PEDI* has also become more common in recent years. The book sought to draw out bigger conclusions about the causes and sustainability of economic growth based on the close analysis of a case study of an episode of stagnation. Twenty years after its publication, it became widely accepted that the dominant pattern of economic growth is not success or failure, but instead that developing countries experience distinct and regular episodes of growth and stagnation.

The most important contribution of *PEDI* was its location in an academic debate about the causes of and constraints on economic growth. This chapter discussed the 1965 episode of stagnation and 1980 and 2003 episodes of growth in India. Since 1965, academic discussion has long-discarded the importance of import substitution as a driver of economic growth and while concern with income distribution and agriculture–industry linkages has declined, they are not quite forgotten. The importance of public investment remained central to discussion into the 1980s and 1990s but empirical work has shown that its real-world influence has been declining after 2003. The widely accepted hypothesis of state failure in relation to stagnation after 1965 gave way to a story of state success in the 1980s and a more nuanced debate in the 2000s. From being first among relative equals in relation to the 1965 stagnation debate, the notion of the policy framework as a constraint on growth has become the most widely debated upon hypotheses in the intervening years.

Just as significantly, the debate recognized the validity of competing schools of thought and of economics as being an embedded social science that should engage with other academic disciplines. This can be contrasted with the lonely isolation of economics, which for much of the last few decades has forgotten this diversity and eclecticism and embraced the neoclassical school to the exclusion of taking any others seriously. Returning to *PEDI* and to the industrial stagnation debate opens up rich possibilities through which we can deepen our understanding of the big contemporary concerns—industrialization, employment and poverty, inequality, the global financial crisis, and sustainable economic growth.

4 Growth and the Subsidy Raj in India

Re-examining the Bardhan Hypothesis[1]

Maitreesh Ghatak and Ritwika Sen

Pranab Bardhan's classic book *The Political Economy of Development in India* (hereafter *PEDI*), first published in 1984, has an air of pessimism about it. Written at a time when the Hindu rate of growth was still a fact of life in India, Bardhan wrote that there simply had not been enough growth for its benefits to trickle down, resulting in high levels of poverty and low levels of human development.[2] In *PEDI*, he goes on to propose what is now a very well-known hypothesis about the reasons for this low-growth regime—interest-group politics in a democracy leads to populism and subsidies, choking off resources for accumulation through public investment in infrastructure.[3] This

[1] We thank Pranab Bardhan, Elizabeth Chatterjee, Matthew McCartney, and Sudipto Mundle for their helpful comments. We also thank the participants of the conference *The Political Economy of Development in India—Redux* at the University of Oxford in March 2015 for their helpful feedback.

[2] The term 'Hindu rate of growth' was coined by Indian economist Raj Krishna in the mid-1970s to describe a period of low and unchanging economic trend growth since the 1950s, of around 3.5 per cent to 4 per cent per annum (Ahluwalia, 1995: 1).

[3] In a subsequent essay, Bardhan (2009) also mentions another channel through which wasteful government expenditure due to interest-group

political economy of constraints, according to Bardhan, seems to have blocked the economy's escape from a low-level equilibrium trap of low growth. Moreover, high levels of social heterogeneity (caste, region, and language) and economic inequality make collective action problems that would help India break out of this trap harder to resolve.

If we fast-forward to 2015, with the benefit of hindsight, we know that Bardhan was writing exactly before massive reforms in the Indian economy in the form of liberalization, privatization, and deregulation that occurred in the early 1990s. High rates of growth have occurred for almost three decades (ignoring the recent deceleration) and so it seems India has broken off from the low-level equilibrium trap of growth that Bardhan was describing. In fact, the trend-break in growth occurred around 1980 and not in the 1990s as is commonly believed, that is, just before he was writing the book (Rodrik and Subramanian, 2005).

Very few would question that growth has helped reduce average poverty and improve human development measures in the last three decades, even though there is controversy over the extent to which poverty has declined.[4] However, it is also impossible to deny that the benefits of growth have not sufficiently trickled down to the poor. In the early 1990s, 45 per cent of the population lived below the poverty line; despite three decades of high growth and a slew of anti-poverty programmes according to the latest numbers, 30 per cent of the population still lives below the poverty line.[5] Cross-country evidence suggests that India's growth elasticity of poverty (to what extent decline in poverty responds to growth) has been lower compared to China and other developing countries (Lengala and Ram, 2010).

---

politics affects growth—the increase in government debt and higher interest rates that raise the cost of capital to private business.

[4] For example, reviewing the state of the debate, Deaton and Kozel (2005) conclude that there is good evidence that poverty fell during the 1990s, but at the same time the official figures for the extent of poverty reduction are too optimistic, especially in rural areas. Sen and Himanshu (2004), who criticize some of the over-optimistic estimates of poverty decline, still conclude that poverty fell by 3 percentage points between 1993–94 and 1999–2000.

[5] These are 2011 figures, reported by the Planning Commission of India (2014). See Kotwal, Ramaswami, and Wadhwa (2011) for comparison of growth rates and poverty rates before and after liberalization.

While there are ongoing debates about the *normative* question of how public investment should be prioritized (for example, whether it is infrastructure or human capital, as in the recent debate between Amartya Sen and Jagdish Bhagwati), *PEDI* remains as relevant as it was before about raising a key *positive* question: what are the factors that drive the composition of public expenditure? Everyone agrees that more public investment in 'general interest' public goods that help the growth process (whether it is infrastructure or human capital) is desirable, as is expenditure on merit-based goods. However, beyond vague allusions to 'political will', with the exception of *PEDI*'s theory of interest-group politics, there is very little discussion of the factors that help to drive government expenditure away from wasteful and to more productive ends.

In this chapter, we look at a specific and somewhat narrow part of *PEDI*'s argument, namely, the relationship between subsidies and growth. We realize that Bardhan was talking about interest-group politics and capture of public resources much more broadly than what subsidies can capture. But because subsidies are a specific and precise category on which data are available over time, despite the limited scope of the exercise, we can study some concrete patterns with precision. Following from the epilogue to *PEDI* (Bardhan, 1998), we interpret 'subsidies' beyond the conventional understanding of the term, as the unrecovered costs that result from public provision of economic and social services.

We should note up front that due to data limitations we focus on explicit budgetary subsidy payments made by the central government over time. There is no consistent time series available either on implicit subsidies (central or state) or on state government subsidies mainly because of the arduous task of preparing such a series. In contrast, a time series on explicit subsidies at the central level is available and that is what we focus on.[6] In particular, we study the patterns of growth in

[6] The few aggregative numbers on the volume and composition (for example, merit-based versus non-merit-based) of subsidies that take into account state-level subsidies that are available and widely quoted are based on *two* years only, namely, 1987–88 and 1998–99. These are from a number of important studies by the NIPFP, namely, Mundle and Rao (1991; 1992) and Srivastava et al. (2003). Very recently, preliminary aggregative estimates based on an as of yet unpublished report has become available for the year 2011–12 (Mundle and Sikdar, 2017).

income per capita and subsidies over the period 1980–81 to 2013–14 and their correlation to examine a part of the Bardhan subsidy hypothesis. We also estimate trends in implicit and explicit budgetary subsidy payments made by the central and state governments using measures of public debt, general government debt, and point estimates from various studies conducted by the National Institute of Public Finance and Policy (NIPFP).[7]

Our main findings are: growth did 'take off' in the decades following liberalization. However, contrary to popular perception, trend growth in the 1990s (post-reform) was not significantly different from that of the 1980s. Evidence for accelerated growth is found only in the 2000–9 decade, from 2003–04 onwards.

However, over the entire period of our analysis, subsidies in per capita terms have grown more than proportionally with income per capita, with the exception of the 1990s (more specifically, from 1990 to 1995) when there was a significant deceleration in the growth of subsidies. It is also worth noting that the elasticity of subsidies with respect to income (in other words, the observed co-movement of the two variables over time) has been similar between the 1980s and the 2000s, but not in the 1990s, when income went up but subsidies went down. We should note that very recent estimates (Mundle and Sikdar, 2017) show that in 2011–12, the share of budget subsidies (explicit and implicit) as a fraction of gross domestic product (GDP) was 10.6 per cent, a more than two percentage point decline from 1987–88 for which comparable numbers exist, when it was 12.9 per cent. However, we do not have sufficient data to estimate whether the current trend will continue to push the fraction of subsidies further down.

From the point of view of *PEDI*'s framework, this analysis suggests that growth has occurred in the post-liberalization period and, except for the early to mid-1990s, subsidies have grown alongside economic growth. We also examine trends in total and public investment since

---

[7] The estimates of budgetary subsidies (both implicit and explicit) by NIPFP (1997), which is cited by Bardhan (1998), were computed from the expenditure items in budget documents. Since public debt (central government liabilities) and general government debt (total liabilities of the central and state governments) correspond to deficit financing of that expenditure, budgetary subsidies are fully reflected in the debt indicators used as proxies.

PEDI and how they have moved with respect to subsidy payments. It is apparent that investment (both private and public) has increased considerably since the 1980s. Moreover, allocations to investment and subsidies have generally moved together, with the exception of the 1990s, which challenges the argument that the divergence of resources to competing special interests have choked off resources for productive investment and growth.

Put together, these trends do not provide evidence in favour of the 'Bardhan subsidy hypothesis' that the subsidy Raj was the most important binding constraint to economic growth in the 1980s. Admittedly, nor do they refute it since both growth rates and subsidies are clearly driven by other factors, and in the absence of an exogenous shock to growth or the composition of subsidies, we cannot make any causal inference about its impact on growth. Also, subsidies may well have been a major constraint on growth. What subsequent trends suggest is that they were not the most important bottleneck, and that there were other, more important, binding constraints at work that were relaxed due to the process of liberalization. It is also possible that subsidies not discussed in this chapter (that is, trends in implicit and explicit subsides provided by the central and state governments) were binding constraints to growth—though our examination of debt indicators, to the extent that they capture the dynamics of total budgetary subsidies, seems to indicate otherwise. We also mention the recent note by Mundle and Sikdar (2017) that throws some additional light on this issue.

Our analysis suggests that *PEDI's* theoretical framework should be extended to allow for a *two-way* relationship between subsidies and growth. Subsidies constrain growth by using up public resources as Bardhan argues, but growth creates resources for more subsidies. This is what our empirical analysis seems to suggest. To the extent changes in other factors lead to growth spurts, this enables governments to continue and even expand the subsidy Raj. This in turn suggests that growth leads to an expansion of the subsidy Raj which eventually chokes off growth, creating pressure for some pro-growth reforms and checks on expansion in subsidies. At the same time, subsidies may be expanded in response to economic problems, for example, more bank lending to mitigate the effects of global financial crisis. Then the statistical relation may be wrongly read as subsidies causing slower growth

(Rodrik, 2012). While this discussion is reminiscent of the literature on electoral cycles and their relationship with government spending, it is beyond the scope of this chapter to develop this theoretical argument carefully in the context of the *PEDI* framework.

EXAMINING THE 'BARDHAN SUBSIDY HYPOTHESIS'

The key hypothesis of *PEDI* was that the competing claims of dominant interest groups in the Indian polity to control public resource allocation resulted in a proliferation of subsidy payments and grants designed to placate these pressure groups. This resulted in the perpetuation of a subsidy network that favoured the rich at the expense of the poor, thus, undermining the social impact of subsidy payments, and also in a reduction of allocations for public investment and consequent economic growth. In an epilogue written in 1998, Bardhan considers the political economy of the post-liberalization era and points to the alarming volume of subsidies as symptomatic of the continued influence of interest groups.

With the advantage of hindsight and recorded macroeconomic performance since 1984, this chapter addresses the following question relating to the Bardhan subsidy hypothesis: were subsidy payments a binding constraint to economic growth in the 1980s, and if so, did they change in a way that contributed to the subsequent increase in average economic growth?

Trends in Subsidies and Economic Growth

The usual rationale for subsidies on certain goods and services is to encourage increased consumption when the net benefit to society at large exceeds the net private benefit to consumers, that is, the presence of positive externalities (for example, healthcare and education). Subsidies are also provided by governments to serve redistributive objectives. It is argued by the NIPFP (1997) that subsidies explicitly stated in budgetary documents in India represent only the 'tip of the iceberg' if one uses the broader definition of budgetary subsidies as unrecovered costs in the public provision of goods and services that are essentially private in nature (for example, losses of unprofitable public sector organizations). The 1997 discussion paper provided a comprehensive estimate of subsidies at the central and all-India level in the year 1994–95. It also classified subsidies as pertaining to merit-based or non-merit-based goods on the basic principle that merit-based goods deserved subsidization (albeit the degree of subsidization would need to be worked out for each instance) and that there was no case for subsidizing non-merit-based goods. This classification was further refined in NIPFP (2001) to 'merit I goods', 'merit II goods', and 'non-merit goods and services' corresponding to high, intermediate, and zero levels of deserved subsidization respectively (this, in turn, follows from the extent of the associated externality).[8]

Estimates by the NIPFP of total non-merit-based subsidies (implicit and explicit, centre and states) whose benefit accrue to the relatively better-off in India is about 11 per cent of GDP (Bardhan, 1998). Just as a benchmark, notice that this is more than 25 times the expenditure on Mahatma Gandhi National Rural Employment Guarantee Act (MGNREGA), the rural employment guarantee programme (less than 0.4 per cent of GDP), a scheme that is often subject to policy debates. In Table 4.1, we summarize the magnitude of total central and state government budgetary subsidies (both explicit and implicit) as estimated by various studies over the years. Bardhan (1998) refers to the subsidy estimates from NIPFP (1997) for the year 1994–95 when budgetary subsidies at the all-India level accounted for about 13.5 per cent of GDP. We update this with a set of relatively comparable estimates from subsequent NIPFP publications, but it should be noted the inter-temporal comparison is not valid in a strict sense due to differences

---

[8] The definitions of these terms are as follows: 'merit I' refers to elementary education, primary health centres, prevention and control of diseases, social welfare and nutrition, soil and water conservation, and ecology and environment; 'merit II' refers to education (other than elementary), sports and youth services, family welfare, urban development, forestry, agricultural research and education, other agricultural programmes, special programmes for rural development, land reforms, other rural development programmes, special programmes for north-eastern areas, flood control and drainage, non-conventional energy, village and small industries, ports and light houses, roads and bridges, inland water transport, atomic energy research, space research, oceanographic research, other scientific research, census surveys and statistics, and meteorology; and 'non-merit' refers to all others.

in the methodology employed by various authors.[9] However, all of these studies aimed to derive comprehensive estimates of budgetary subsidies, and the last four estimates (between 1994 and 1998) are more comparable on grounds of similar estimation methodology.

We can see from this table that total subsidies, both explicit and implicit, provided by the central government increased from 4.25 per cent of GDP in 1994–95 to 4.59 per cent in 1998–99. National Institute of Public Finance and Policy (2003) attributes the rise in central subsidy payments in the year 1998–99 (especially compared to 3.49 per cent estimated by a comparable method for 1996–97) to the following factors: (*i*) salary revisions following from the recommendations of the Fifth Central Pay Commission; (*ii*) declining performance of the railways sector leading to net government subsidization of the sector (as opposed to surplus earnings); (*iii*) substantial increases in central explicit subsidy payments; and (*iv*) increase in input costs without

TABLE 4.1 Summary of Central Government Subsidy Estimates from the Literature

Year	Subsidies as % of GDP		
	Central Government	State Government	All India
1987–88 (M-R)	4.53	7.41	11.94
1992–93 (Tiwari)	4.92	7.82	12.74
1994–95 (NIPFP)	4.25	9.26	13.51
1995–96 (NIPFP)	3.61	–	–
1996–97 (NIPFP)	3.49	–	–
1998–99 (NIPFP)	4.59	8.96	13.55
2011–12 (NIPFP estimate)	–	–	11

Source: (In order) Mundle and Rao (1992), Tiwari (1996), Srivastava et al. (1997), Srivastava and Amar Nath (2001) for both 1995–96 and 1996–97, and Srivastava et al. (2003). The estimate for 2011–12 is based on the rebased GDP series and sourced from private communication with NIPFP.[10]

[9] In ascending chronological order, these are Mundle and Rao (1992), Tiwari (1996), NIPFP (1997), NIPFP (2001), which provided estimates for central subsidies in both 1995–96 and 1996–97, and NIPFP (2003).

[10] Sincere thanks to Dr Sudipto Mundle (NIPFP) for this information.

corresponding improvements in recovery rates. Subsidy payments at the all-India level remain almost unchanged at 13.5 per cent over the same time period (1994–95 to 1998–99). The vast difference between centre and all-India level estimates of subsidies (a little under 8 per cent of GDP) is indicative of the relative contribution from the centre and states to aggregate subsidy payments: 33.86 per cent and 66.14 per cent respectively, as of 1998–99.

There have been no subsequent estimates of implicit and explicit subsidies using this methodology, although an updated NIPFP study for subsidy payments in 2011–12, 2013–14, and 2014–15 is forthcoming (Mundle and Sikdar, 2019). The updated study will be based on the new GDP series (rebased to 2004–05) and provides a comparable estimate to the initial Mundle and Rao (1992) paper which estimated all-India subsidies for 1987–88 (albeit based on the old GDP series). Mundle and Sikdar (2019) estimate that all-India total budgetary subsidies declined from 12.9 per cent of GDP in 1987–88 (this is as per the new GDP series and, therefore, does not conform to the figure in Table 4.1), to about 10.6 per cent of GDP.[11] About a third of these subsidies or 3.7 per cent of GDP is estimated as being allocated to non-merit-based subsidies—indicative of the fiscal space for additional transfer payments or social expenditure, if non-merit-based subsidies are rolled back. In another recent estimation of subsidies in India, the *Economic Survey* (Vol. I) for the fiscal year 2014–15 quantified the fiscal cost of select explicit budgetary subsidies for the centre and state governments as approximately INR 378,000 crore or 4.2 per cent of GDP.[12]

Our focus is to examine the co-movement of subsidy payments in India with economic growth *over a period of time* (since 1980 to be precise), as well as the composition of subsidy payments in the same timeframe. Due to data limitations, we primarily examine trends in explicit budgetary subsidy payments made by the central government. To estimate trends in the payments of implicit and explicit subsidy payments made by the central government, and at the all-India level,

---

[11] We are grateful to Sudipto Mundle (NIPFP) for sharing these estimates through private communication.

[12] The select subsidies included those on rice, wheat, pulses, liquefied petroleum gas (LPG), sugar, kerosene, water, electricity, fertilizer, iron ore, naphtha, and railways.

we also examine trends in the co-movement of public debt (central government) and general government debt (total liabilities of the central and state governments) with economic growth. This is based on the assumption that budgetary subsidies imputed from the expenditure items in the government budget are fully reflected in debt indicators which capture the deficit financing of this expenditure. Any interpretation of our results must be subject to these caveats.

Explicit central government subsidies include subsidies on food, fertilizers, export promotion, petroleum, and other subsidies (for example, grants to National Agricultural Cooperative Marketing Federation of India (NAFED) and subsidies for the import/export of sugar and edible oils).[13] Figure 4.1 demonstrates the positive co-movement of explicit subsidies paid by the central government with GDP and public expenditure levels (figures in per capita terms and logarithmic scales) between 1980–81 and 2013–14.[14]

Between 1980 and 2013, the average ratio of subsidies to GDP was 1.59 per cent, with above-average ratios recorded consistently for the periods 1985–91 and 2008–13. This is shown in Figure 4.2. Notice that these numbers are lower than those reported in Table 4.1, since we look at explicit subsidies only. It is worth noting that the peak subsidy–GDP ratio of 2.09 per cent reached in the former period, that is, 1985–91 (the average subsidy–GDP ratio was 1.82 per cent during the same), was only crossed in the year 2008. In fact, the average subsidy–GDP ratio from 2008 to 2013 was 2.32 per cent. The trend in levels of subsidies per capita vis-à-vis that of GDP per capita (and the relative proportion of subsidies to GDP) thus indicates *positive* co-movement between the two series overall between 1980 and 2013, with a notable dip in the subsidy–GDP ratio in the post-reform decade (the average subsidy–GDP ratio was 1.27 per cent between 1991 and 2000).

[13] Petroleum subsidies were off-budget before the year 2002.

[14] Data on central subsidy payments (and its components) were obtained from the Economic and Political Weekly Research Foundation (EPWRF) Government Finances of India database and data on GDP, population, and central government expenditure were downloaded from the RBI Handbook of Statistics on the Indian Economy, 2014–15 (see Appendix 4.A2 for details). Gross domestic product data is based on the old 2004–05 series. The data is presented in constant prices (2004–05), deflated using the Consumer Price Index for Industrial Workers (CPI-IW) price index.

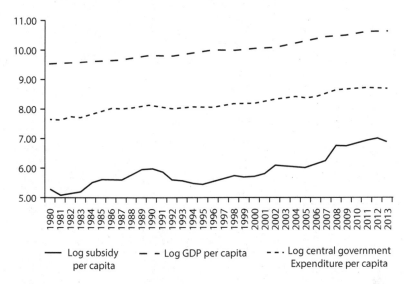

FIGURE 4.1 Trends in the Levels of Log Subsidies, GDP, and Central Government Expenditure Per Capita
Source: EPWRF (2014–15) and RBI (2014–15).

In Table 4.2, we examine the growth rate of GDP, total central government explicit subsidies and their major components, and public and general government debt (as estimates for total budgetary subsidies at the central and all-India level respectively). The category of 'major subsidies' includes subsidies for food, petroleum (after 2002), export promotion, fertilizers, and grants to NAFED for MIS/PPS.[15] Average annual growth rates for a given decade were computed by fitting a linear time trend using a standard ordinary least squares (OLS)

[15] NAFED is the acronym of the National Agricultural Cooperative Marketing Federation of India and MIS and PPS refer to Market Intervention Scheme and Price Support Scheme, respectively. The former is intended for procurement of perishable and horticultural commodities in the event of fall in market prices, while the latter is used for procurement of oil seeds, pulses, and cotton at the minimum support price (MSP) declared by the government. Procurement is undertaken by NAFED as and when prices fall below the MSP. Losses, if any, incurred by NAFED in undertaking MSP operations are reimbursed by the central government.

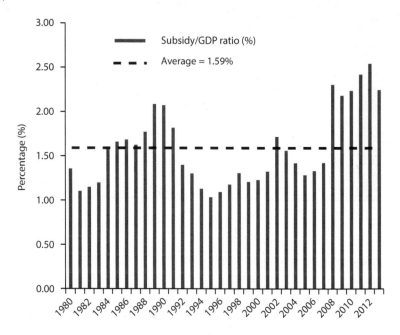

FIGURE 4.2   Trends in the Ratio of Subsidies to GDP
Source: EPWRF (2014–15) and RBI (2014–15).

regression model, the details of which are given in the Appendix. We look at 1980–9 as the benchmark period and compare it with three subsequent time periods, namely, 1990–9, 2000–9, and 2010–13.[16]

The above results indicate the following key points:

1. Growth did 'take off' in the decades following liberalization. However, contrary to popular perception, trend growth in the 1990s (post-reform) was not significantly different from that of the 1980s. Evidence for accelerated growth is found only in the 2000–9 decade, from 2003–04 onwards. This finding is consistent with that of Nagaraj (2000), Kotwal, Ramaswami, and Wadhwa (2011), and Ghate and Wright (2008).[17]

[16] When we refer to the period 1980–9, the first year refers to the fiscal year 1980–81 and the last year refers to the fiscal year 1989–90. The same rule applies to all these time intervals.

[17] These observations are further substantiated by tests for structural break post-liberalization in 1991. Table 4.A1 in the Appendix demonstrates that

TABLE 4.2 Growth Rates of GDP and Central Government Explicit Budgetary Subsidies and Debt Indicators

Indicator	1980–9	1990–9	2000–9	2010–13
GDP	2.6★★★	3.0	5.8★★★	2.0
Total Subsidies	8.6★★★	−2.2★★★	10.3	2.5
Major Subsidies	9.9★★★	−0.5★★★	10.0	3.0
Food Subsidies	6.6★★★	4.6	6.4	2.0
Fertilizer Subsidies	15.5★★★	0.7★★★	13.8	−8.8★★
Other Subsidies	2.5	−14.4★★	18.0★★	−7.5
Public Debt	6.0★★★	2.4★★★	3.6★★★	4.4
General Government Debt	7.2★★★	2.3★★★	4.5★★★	2.3★★★

Source: Authors' calculations using data cited in the 'List of Data Sources'.

Note: All variables are per capita measures. The star signs indicate the level of statistical significance with ★=10 per cent, ★★=5 per cent, and ★★★=1 per cent. In column 1, they refer to whether the growth rate is significantly different from zero, while in columns 2–4, they refer to whether the relevant growth rate is significantly different from the corresponding one in column 1.

The first column in the table gives the average per year growth rate over the period 1980–9 and whether it was statistically significantly different from zero at 10 per cent (★), 5 per cent (★★), and 1 per cent (★★★) levels. That is, here the test is if there is a positive trend. The second, third, and fourth column gives the average per year growth rates over the periods 1990–9, 2000–9, and 2010–13 and whether it was statistically significantly different from *the growth rate in the 1980s* at 10 per cent (★), 5 per cent (★★), and 1 per cent (★★★) levels. Here, the test is whether there is a trend-break relative to 1980–9. For example, in 1980–9 the growth rate of GDP per capita was 2.6 per cent, which, while not high, is significantly different from zero at the 1 per cent level. In 1990–9, the growth rate of GDP per capita was 3 per cent, which is not significantly different from the 1980s growth rate, suggesting that no trend-break relative to the 1980s was yet visible, even though the growth rate itself was significantly different from zero, like in the 1980s. In contrast, in 2000–9, the growth rate of GDP per capita was 5.8 per cent, which is significantly different from the 1980s growth rate at the 1 per cent level, suggesting a trend-break.

---

there is no evidence for a structural break post-1991 relative to growth in the 1980s, once the economic boom post-2003 is accounted for. In fact, there is evidence to show that growth 'took off' even before the reforms in the late 1980s, around 1987–88 (Bhagwati and Panagariya, 2013).

2. The decade of rapidly expanding explicit subsidy payments (1980–9) was followed by a significant deceleration in the growth of subsidies during the 1990–9 decade. A closer look at the data reveals that there was a trend-break in the year 1990, after which subsidy payments declined until 1995. This trend was subsequently reversed post-1995 (also a year of significant trend break—see Appendix, Table 4.A2): subsidies per capita crossed its 1990 level only in the year 2001, and the positive growth trend continued into the decade of accelerating growth (2000–9). In short, other than a deceleration in explicit central government subsidies in the 1990s, there is no evidence of deceleration of growth in subsidies in the subsequent period.

3. The pattern of negative growth in total subsidies in the 1990s is reflected in the decrease in the 'other subsidy' payments (and also the 'major subsidy' category, but that is not surprising). However, this trend is not echoed by the two major explicit subsides on food and fertilizers: subsidy payments on the former continued to grow at a faster rate than GDP.

4. The debt position of the central government (public debt) and the central and state governments combined (general government debt) echoes the overall trend in central government explicit subsidy payments, with accelerated growth in the 1980s, a significant decline in growth in the 1990s relative to the 1980s, and resurgence (though more contained than in the pre-reform decade) in the 2000s. We use these measures as proxies for trends in total budgetary subsidy payments made by the centre and state governments.

Table 4.3a examines the elasticity of total central government explicit subsidies and its major components with respect to GDP (per capita measures). The calculation of decadal average elasticity measures for subsidy payments (and its major components) with respect to GDP allows us to examine the co-movement of the growth rates of various subsidies and GDP. The first column gives the per capita income elasticity of a specific category of a subsidy over the period 1980–9 and whether it was statistically significantly different from zero at the relevant level. The second, third, and fourth columns gives the elasticity in the relevant period and the stars indicate the relevant level of statistical significance of the elasticity being different from that in 1980–9.

TABLE 4.3a   Elasticity of Central Government Explicit Budgetary Subsidies with Reference to GDP Per Capita

	1980–9	1990–9	2000–9	2010–13
Total Subsidies	3.29★★★	–0.71★★★	1.68★★	2.11
Major Subsidies	3.70★★★	–0.14★★★	1.62★★★	2.45
Food Subsidies	2.38★★★	1.51	0.94★	1.07
Fertilizer Subsidies	5.60★★★	0.10★★★	2.46★★★	–2.78★
Other Subsidies	1.27	–4.95★★	3.10	–4.76

Source: Authors' calculations using data cited in the 'List of Data Sources'.

Note: All variables are per capita measures. The star signs indicate the level of statistical significance with ★=10 per cent, ★★=5 per cent, and ★★★=1 per cent. In column 1, they refer to whether the elasticity is significantly different from zero, while in columns 2–4, they refer to whether the relevant elasticity is significantly different from the corresponding one in column 1.

The key finding here is that, except for in the 1990s, explicit subsidies and income have grown together. Since the elasticity can be interpreted as the percentage change in subsidies per capita when GDP per capita goes up by 1 per cent, Table 4.3a suggests that except for the 1990s when the elasticity was negative, for the 1980s as well as in the post-2000 period this elasticity is greater than 1. That is, growth in income has led to a more than proportional growth in explicit subsidies in these two periods. This can be inferred from Figure 4.1 as well—from 1996 to 2011, subsidies per capita have grown at a higher rate than GDP per capita, similar to the period 1980–9. Only during 1990–5 and 2012–13 do we actually see a dip in subsidies per capita, which are both periods of fiscal retrenchment after an economic crisis.

Table 4.3b presents the trends in the elasticity of debt indicators with reference to GDP (per capita measures) to estimate patterns in the co-movement of total budgetary subsidizes provided by the centre and state, and economic growth. These results also suggest that debt and national income have grown together, albeit in this case growth in income has been accompanied by less than proportional change (elasticity <1) in debt or total budgetary subsidies.

In order to establish whether subsidies were a binding constraint to growth in the 1980s, we need to further examine what happened to productive investment in the economy in relation to the decline and

TABLE 4.3b   Elasticity of Debt Indicators (Implicit and Explicit Subsidy Estimates) with Reference to GDP Per Capita

	1980–9	1990–9	2000–9	2010–13
Public Debt	2.21★★★	0.69★★★	0.60★★★	2.11
General Government Debt	2.66★★★	0.71★★★	0.75★★★	1.06★

Source: Authors' calculations using data cited in the 'List of Data Sources'.
Note: All variables are per capita measures. The star signs indicate the level of statistical significance with ★=10 per cent, ★★=5 per cent, and ★★★=1 per cent. In column 1, they refer to whether the elasticity is significantly different from zero, while in columns 2–4, they refer to whether the relevant elasticity is significantly different from the corresponding one in column 1.

subsequent rise of growth in subsidy payments after this period. Was the decline in the level and growth of subsidy payments in the 1990s accompanied by an increase in investment, which contributed to the accelerated growth performance observed in the following decade? To examine this, the elasticity of gross capital formation (GCF) sector with respect to GDP, central government explicit subsidies, public debt, and general government debt (all per capita measures) was calculated using a methodology similar to the one used to generate the results for Tables 4.3a and 4.3b.[18] The results are presented in Table 4.4a.

The results presented in Table 4.4a indicate that: (*i*) the level of investment has grown throughout the period of our study, with a significant increase in its growth rate in the 2000s compared to the 1980s; and (*ii*) a positive correlation was observed between investment and subsidies across all three decades. This observation is robust to the use of three separate estimates of resource diversion to competing special interests at the central and all-India level, that is, central government explicit subsidy payments, and the stock of public and

[18] *Political Economy of Development in India* examines gross *fixed* capital formation by the public sector as a measure for public investment. Following from latest data available, we use estimates of total and public sector GCF as measures for investment. Gross capital formation is arguably a more comprehensive measure than gross fixed capital formation as it measures outlays on additions to fixed assets, plus the net change in inventories. Fixed assets include plant, machinery, equipment, and buildings, while inventory includes works in process, which are partially completed goods that remain in production.

TABLE **4.4a**   Growth and Elasticity of GCF

Indicator	1980–9	1990–9	2000–9
	Growth Rate		
GCF Per Capita	4.90★★★	3.77	11.26★★★
	Elasticity of GCF with Reference to Various Indicators		
GDP	1.84★★★	1.26	1.97
Subsidies	0.47★★	−0.18	0.78
Public Debt	0.82★★★	0.82	3.15★★★
General Government Debt	0.68★★★	1.49★	2.39★★★

Source: Authors' calculations using data cited in the 'List of Data Sources'.
Note: All variables are per capita measures. The star signs indicate the level of statistical significance with ★=10 per cent, ★★=5 per cent, and ★★★=1 per cent. In column 1, they refer to whether the growth or elasticity is significantly different from zero, while in columns 2–4, they refer to whether the relevant growth rate or elasticity is significantly different from the corresponding one in column 1.

general government debt. The elasticity of investment with respect to both public debt and general government debt exhibits a statistically significant increase in the decade of accelerating growth (2000–9).[19] During this decade, total investment (in per capita terms) has in fact grown more than proportionally compared to public and general government debt, that is, elasticity is greater than one. The positive co-movement of these series was presumably driven by other economic and policy factors, but demonstrates that the increase in transfers to competing classes was actually accompanied by an *increase* in productive investment during India's growth transition over the past three decades.

We further examine these trends for GCF in the public sector to conform to the narrative in *PEDI*. These results are presented in Table 4.4b below. These results indicate that the level and growth of public capital formation has also increased significantly since the 1980s, but with a period of significant deceleration in the post-reform decade (1990–9). In particular, public capital formation 'took off' in the 2000–9 decade with evidence for a break of trend from the year

---

[19] These observations are statistically significant at the 1 per cent level.

TABLE **4.4b**   Growth and Elasticity of GCF in the Public Sector

Indicator	1980–9	1990–9	2000–9
Growth Rate			
Public GCF Per Capita	3.4★★★	−1.3★★★	9.7★★★
Elasticity of Public Sector GCF with Reference to Various Indicators			
GDP	1.17★★★	−0.38★★★	1.71★
Subsidies	0.30★	0.07	0.72★★
Public Debt	0.56★★★	−0.10★★	2.69★★★
General Government Debt	0.46★★★	−0.39★	1.95★★★

Source: Authors' calculations using data cited in the 'List of Data Sources'.
Note: All variables are per capita measures. The star signs indicate the level of statistical significance with ★=10 per cent, ★★=5 per cent, and ★★★=1 per cent. In column 1, they refer to whether the growth or elasticity is significantly different from zero, while in columns 2–4, they refer to whether the relevant growth rate or elasticity is significantly different from the corresponding one in column 1.

2002 onwards.[20] From Figures 4.1 and 4.2, and the analysis so far (see Appendix, Table 4.A2), we know that growth in explicit subsidy payments by the centre decelerated in the early 1990s, but increased significantly from 1995 onwards. Moreover, the payments of explicit and implicit subsidy at the all-India level remained steady at around 13.5 per cent of GDP in the late 1990s (1994–95 to 1998–99), accompanied by positive growth in the debt stocks of the central and state governments.[21] While the trend of deceleration of public investment in the 1990s and the accelerated growth post-2002 were presumably driven by various economic and political factors, these trends put together suggest that increased subsidy and debt financing through the late 1990s, and later in the 2000s, did not impede the growth of public investment in the decade of accelerating growth (2000–9). Table 4.4b provides evidence for a significant increase in the elasticity of public

[20] The results for a trend-break test are provided in the Appendix, Table 4.A3.

[21] It is, therefore, not surprising that the elasticity of (decelerating) public investment with respect to public debt and general government debt, which were growing in the 1990–9 decade, is negative at the 5 per cent and 10 per cent levels of significance, respectively (see Table 4.4b).

investment with respect to subsidies, public debt, and general government debt.

Even if subsidies were a binding constraint on growth in the 1980s, these empirical trends could still be plausible if there had been a substantial change in the nature and composition of subsidy payments in the 2000s to make them more productive for society. In an ideal scenario, one would examine the evolution of 'merit I' and 'merit II' subsidies vis-à-vis that of 'non-merit subsidies' to assess this possibility. One could also argue that subsidies used to correct market failures, that is, merit-based subsidies (vis-à-vis non-merit-based subsidies) may be good for economic growth. A. Kohli (2012) argues that government spending, taxes, subsidies, and so on, became more 'pro-business' or conducive for economic growth after around 1980. However, the lack of comparable and frequent observations across time on this subject, and/or an exogenous shock to the provision of merit-based/non-merit-based budgetary subsidies does not permit us to examine this analysis at present.

From the available data on central government explicit subsidies, we find that major subsidies (including subsidies for food, petrol, export promotion, fertilizers, and grants to NAFED for MIS/PPS) have increased from 84.18 per cent of total subsidy payments by the centre in 1980–9 (on average) to 95.25 per cent of total subsidies in 2000–9. The lion's share of these subsidy payments is attributed to food and fertilizer subsidies, which increased from a combined average of 66.65 per cent of total central explicit subsidy payments in the 1980s to 89.04 per cent in the 2000s. There is strong evidence to suggest that subsidies on food (wheat, paddy rice, pulses, and sugar) are subject to substantial leakages and are poorly targeted to reach the lowest income deciles.[22] Fertilizer subsidies are moreover largely beneficial to urea and phosphatic and potassic (P&K) fertilizer manufacturers as opposed to poor farmers who have more elastic demand for fertilizers.

---

[22] 54 per cent of public distribution system (PDS) wheat, 15 per cent of PDS rice, and 48 per cent of PDS sugar is lost as leakages. Households in bottom three deciles consume only 56 per cent of the remaining 46 per cent of PDS wheat, 53 per cent of the remaining 85 per cent of PDS rice, and 44 per cent of the remaining 52 per cent of PDS sugar that reaches households. Moreover, only 36 per cent of subsidized pulses is consumed by the bottom three income deciles (*Economic Survey 2014–15*, Volume I).

The *Economic Survey* (2014–15) posits that large farmers are better able to source scarce subsidized agricultural urea, forcing small farmers to purchase urea primarily from the black market, thus incurring about 17 per cent extra expenditure relative to large farmers (all-India estimate). The Survey, moreover, suggests that only about 35 per cent of fertilizer subsidies reaches small farmers, the intended beneficiaries. The resilience of food and fertilizer subsidies may suggest that *PEDI's* large farmer and urban classes are still important beneficiaries. There is thus little evidence in favour of the hypothesis that explicit subsidy payments have become more productive (in terms of societal benefit vis-à-vis the fiscal expenditure and opportunity cost of providing the same) in the 2000–9 decade.[23]

However, implicit subsidies or state-level subsidies may well be behaving differently, but due to data limitations we cannot say much about this. In this context, mention must be made of a very recent note by Mundle and Sikdar (2017) that provides some discussion of both explicit and implicit subsidies as well as state-level subsidies, although only for two years: 1987–88 and 2011–12. The note points out that budget subsidies, implicit plus explicit, amounted to 10.6 per cent of GDP in 2011–12, down from 12.9 per cent in 1987–88. The share of merit-based subsidies went up from 3.8 per cent of GDP in 1987–88 to 5.6 per cent in 2011–12. The share of non-merit-based subsidies declined from 9.1 per cent of GDP in 1987–88 to 5 per cent in 2011–12. The authors conclude that there has been some improved efficiency in this aspect of public expenditure. Further work along these lines can establish if this comparison between two years is part of a broader trend in the composition of total budgetary subsidy payments.

To conclude, the trends in explicit central government subsidies do not provide evidence in favour of what we call the 'Bardhan subsidy hypothesis', namely, that the subsidy Raj was the most important binding constraint to economic growth in the 1980s. Going back to the questions posed at the beginning of the section, we conclude that there must have been other binding constraints limiting growth whose

---

[23] This observation is not limited to central government subsidies. For a comprehensive discussion of the effectiveness of major central and state government subsidies, see *Economic Survey 2014–15* (Vol. I).

relaxation, due to the process of liberalization, contributed to the subsequent increase in average economic growth.

Admittedly, the evidence we provide does not refute *PEDI*'s hypothesis either since both growth rates and subsidies were clearly driven by other factors during the period we cover and, in the absence of an exogenous shock to the growth or composition of subsidies, we cannot make any causal inference about the impact of subsidies on growth. Nor can we rule out that reforming subsidies will not make significant differences to growth in absolute terms, as opposed to being the most important binding constraint. Also, data limitations prevent us from saying much about other aspects of Bardhan's influential argument such as whether there has been a fundamental change in the extent, volume, or nature of subsidy payments (to make them more inclusive and/or productive) once we take into account implicit and explicit subsidies as well as state-level subsidies beyond a snapshot provided by Mundle and Sikdar (2017).

★★★

Curbing non-merit-based subsidies is a bit like trying to curb pollution. No one wants to give up their own benefits, but everyone realizes that a big chunk of public resources being spent on non-merit-based subsidies cannot be good for society overall. In the current *Economic Survey* of the Government of India, there is a good discussion of reforming subsidies and making them more pro-poor. The main lesson from Bardhan's book is that reforming the subsidy Raj is fundamentally a political problem. However, our reading of the academic as well as policy literature suggests that Bardhan's important argument has not been as influential as it should have been, beyond token expressions such as 'lack of political will' or 'populism' or 'political constraints on reforms' in the context of reforming the pattern of public expenditure.

Bardhan's argument also highlights the need to think harder about policy reforms that can limit the extent of treating public funds as a 'common-property' resource that is then overused (especially by richer and more powerful groups), leading to a collective loss in terms of foregoing opportunities for increasing growth and living standards. Examples that readily come to mind include constitutional amendments that limit the government's ability to borrow, or increasing transparency in budget documents so that implicit non-merit-based subsidies or wasteful government expenditures become much more visible to public scrutiny. Similarly, while every effort should be made to direct public investment into productive channels, whether it is infrastructure, law and order, investment in human capital, or anti-poverty programmes, we should keep in mind that budgetary allocation is only a necessary condition for effective public investment. Simply pumping in more money without reforming the institutions of governance and public service provision is not going to solve the problem. In this context, the discussion in policy circles (for example, the last few *Economic Survey*s from 2014–15 to 2016–17) as to *how* best to target subsidies to the poor to raise the impact of public funds in achieving the objective of reducing poverty is very welcome. However, the scope of such discussions should be broadened to cover all other areas of public expenditure and not just subsidies.

APPENDIX

Estimation of Time Trends and Elasticities

To calculate growth rate of a variable (say, z) we have used the following standard OLS regression model:

$$\ln(z) = a_0 + b_0 * t + b_1 * t * D_{90} + b_2 * t * D_{00} + b_3 * t * D_{10} + D_{90} + D_{00} + D_{10}.$$

In the regression equation D_{90}, D_{00}, D_{10} are decadal dummy variables corresponding to 1990–9, 2000–9, and 2010–13, respectively. The coefficient b_0 gives the growth rate for the 1980s while b_1, b_2, and b_3 give the incremental growth rate for 1990–9, 2000–9, and 2010–13.

To calculate elasticity of a specific subsidy (z) with respect to per capita income (y), we have used the following OLS regression model:

$$\ln(z) = a_0 + b_0 * \ln(y) + b_1 * D_{90} * \ln(y) + b_2 * D_{00} * \ln(y) + b_3 * D_{10} * \ln(y) + D_{90} + D_{00} + D_{10}.$$

The dummy variables are as above. The coefficient b_0 in this regression gives the elasticity of a specific subsidy with respect to per capita income for the 1980s while b_1, b_2, and b_3 give the differential elasticity for 1990–9, 2000–9, and 2010–13 with respect to the 1980s.

To test for a trend-break in a variable y at time t=T, we have used the following OLS regression model:

$$\log y_t = a + \alpha * t + \beta * D_T + \gamma * t * D_T + \epsilon_t$$

D_T is a dummy that takes on the value 1 for t ≥ T, and 0 otherwise. The standard method allows for a break both in the intercept and the slope. The coefficients α and γ capture the average growth rate over the entire period, and the increase (if any) in the growth rate from time T onwards, respectively. Table 4.A1 presents the results of tests for trend breaks in GDP per capita for T equal to 1987, 1991, and 2003. The null hypothesis for no trend-break in 1987 and 2003 can be rejected at the 10 per cent level and 1 per cent level of significance, respectively (column 3).

TABLE **4.A1**   Test for Trend-Break in GDP Per Capita

	(1)	(2)	(3)
	Log Gross Domestic Product Per Capita	Log Gross Domestic Product Per Capita	Log Gross Domestic Product Per Capita
	T Statistic	T Statistic	T Statistic
Trend 1980–2013	0.028★★★	0.028★★★	0.020★★★
	(0.00)	(0.00)	(0.01)
Trend 1991–2013	0.013★★★	0.000	
	(0.00)	(0.00)	
Post 1991	−0.049	0.013	
	(0.03)	(0.02)	
Trend 2003–13		0.019★★★	0.018★★★
		(0.00)	(0.00)
Post 2003		0.068★★★	0.062★★★
		(0.02)	(0.02)
Trend 1987–2013			0.009★
			(0.01)
Post 1987			0.041
			(0.03)
Constant	9.545★★★	9.545★★★	9.567★★★
	(0.02)	(0.02)	(0.02)
Adjusted R Squared	0.99	0.99	0.99
No. of Observations	34	34	34

Note: The star signs indicate the level of statistical significance with ★=10 per cent, ★★=5 per cent, and ★★★=1 per cent. In column 1, they refer to whether the growth or elasticity is significantly different from zero, while in columns 2–4, they refer to whether the relevant growth rate or elasticity is significantly different from the corresponding one in column 1.

Tables 4A.1, 4A.2, and 4A.3 present results from the authors' calculations that are based on data cited in the 'List of Data Sources'. The methodology used for the calculation of time trends and elasticities is described in Appendix A1.

Table 4.A2 presents the results of tests for trend breaks in central government explicit subsidies per capita for T equal to 1990 and 1995. The null hypothesis for no trend-break in 1990 and 1995 can be rejected at the 1 per cent level of significance.

TABLE 4.A2 Test for Trend-Break in Subsidies Per Capita

	(1)	(2)	(3)
	Log Subsidies Per Capita	Log Subsidies Per Capita	Log Subsidies Per Capita
	T Statistic	T Statistic	T Statistic
Trend 1980–2013	0.086★★★	0.042★★★	0.086★★★
	(0.03)	(0.01)	(0.01)
Trend 1990–2013	−0.022		−0.214★★★
	(0.03)		(0.04)
Post 1990	−0.592★★★		0.020
	(0.18)		(0.13)
Trend 1995–2013		0.049★★★	0.219★★★
		(0.01)	(0.04)
Post 1995		−0.520★★★	0.043
		(0.12)	(0.15)
Constant	5.075★★★	5.248★★★	5.075★★★
	(0.13)	(0.09)	(0.08)
Adjusted R Squared	0.82	0.89	0.94
No. of Observations	34	34	34

Table 4.A3 provides results for a trend-break test in GCF in the public sector (a measure of public investment). The null hypothesis of no trend-break in T=1994 and T=2002 can be rejected at the 5 per cent level of significance and 1 per cent level of significance,

TABLE 4.A3 Test for Trend-Break in GCF in the Public Sector

	(1)	(2)	(3)
	Log Gross Capital Formation in the Public Sector	Log Gross Capital Formation in the Public Sector	Log Gross Capital Formation in the Public Sector
	T Statistic	T Statistic	T Statistic
Trend 1980–2011	0.041★★★	0.026★★★	0.041★★★
	(0.01)	(0.00)	(0.01)
Trend 1994–2011	0.023★★		−0.035★★
	(0.01)		(0.02)

(*Cont'd*)

TABLE 4.A3   (*Cont'd*)

	(1) Log Gross Capital Formation in the Public Sector	(2) Log Gross Capital Formation in the Public Sector	(3) Log Gross Capital Formation in the Public Sector
	T Statistic	T Statistic	T Statistic
Post 1994	-0.297★★★		-0.083
	(0.10)		(0.08)
Trend 2002–11		0.077★★★	0.097★★★
		(0.01)	(0.02)
Post 2002		-0.052	0.067
		(0.08)	(0.09)
Constant	13.888★★★	13.967★★★	13.888★★★
	(0.07)	(0.04)	(0.05)
Adjusted R Squared	0.90	0.94	0.95
No. of Observations	32	32	32

respectively. The trend-break in 1994 was followed by a deceleration in public investment from 1994–2001, whereas the trend-break in 2002 was followed by a period of accelerated growth.

LIST OF DATA SOURCES

- Central Government Explicit Budgetary Subsidies and its components: downloaded from the EPWRF Government Finances of India database, available at http://www.epwrfits.in/CentralFinanceTreeview.aspx, last accessed 16 July 2019.
- Gross domestic product: downloaded from the Reserve Bank of India Handbook of Statistics on the Indian Economy 2014–15, available at https://rbidocs.rbi.org.in/rdocs/Publications/PDFs/00HC398B27C6AFF47039ABE93049886B494.PDF, last accessed 16 July 2019.
- Population data: downloaded from the RBI Handbook of Statistics on the Indian Economy 2014–15, available at https://rbidocs.rbi.

org.in/rdocs/Publications/PDFs/00HC398B27C6AFF47039ABE
93049886B494.PDF, last accessed 16 July 2019.

- Consumer Price Index (CPI-IW): downloaded from the EPWRF
  Price Indices database. Time series (1980–2014) constructed using
  link factors specified in the database. The time series was subsequently re-based to 2004–05, available at http://www.epwrfits.in/
  CPI_IWTreeview.aspx, last accessed 16 July 2019.
- Gross capital formation (both total and in the public sector): down-
  loaded from the RBI Handbook of Statistics on the Indian Economy
  2014–15, available at https://rbidocs.rbi.org.in/rdocs/Publications/
  PDFs/00HC398B27C6AFF47039ABE93049886B494.PDF,   last
  accessed 16 July 2019.
- Public debt and general government debt data: downloaded from
  the RBI Handbook of Statistics on the Indian Economy 2014–15.
  Public debt is defined as per the Government Debt Status Paper of
  February 2018, Budget Division, Department of Economic Affairs,
  Ministry of Finance, available at https://dea.gov.in/sites/default/
  files/Status%20Paper%20final%2028.3.18.pdf, last accessed 16 July
  2019.

5 India's Political Economy

Has Something Crucial Recently Changed?

James Manor

The title of this chapter ends with a question mark. It follows that the answer to this question may be 'yes' or 'no', or even 'not much'. But let us consider the argument that something crucial has indeed changed in recent years, to see how far we can get with it—even though, as we shall see, there is evidence that inspires scepticism about it.

Since 1991, when economic liberalization in India began in earnest, it has often been said that no government will reverse the process. That is true. But it is also true that no government has carried liberalization forward boldly. We have not seen dramatic change on that front. But some commentators push the argument further, claiming that while ruling parties and alliances have changed, they have not differed markedly in the array of interest groups which they favour and from which they seek votes—the only difference being the Bharatiya Janata Party's (BJP's) abandonment of much hope of Muslim support. Even if they are correct—and that is debatable—these commentators overlook the possibility that while rival parties and alliances seek to cultivate roughly the same groups, to achieve this, they may adopt quite different approaches to India's political economy.

Our understanding of this has been enriched by the insights in Pranab Bardhan's 1984 classic book, *The Political Economy of Development in India* (hereafter *PEDI*). In it, he argues that all governments have based their power upon, and attended mainly to the interests of, 'three dominant proprietary classes': rich farmers; industrialists; and professionals and bureaucrats. Changes of government have not triggered changes in this basic reality.

But is this still true? When we consider what changed after 2004 and then further changes since the parliamentary election in May 2014, do we now see—for the first time—marked contrasts between successive governments: the United Progressive Alliance (UPA, 2004–14) and the BJP government since 2014?

NOMINALLY 'SOCIAL DEMOCRATIC' GOVERNMENTS IN INDIA

The Congress Party, which has ruled India for most of the post-Independence period, has long been seen by some observers and by some of its own leaders as a 'social democratic' party. This term derives from the political history of western and northern Europe, and is far less familiar in North America—or for that matter, in India. It essentially means a party that is committed to a mixed economy in which the private sector and private property play important roles, but in which the state looms quite large. The state derives revenues from taxpayers and the private sector and then uses them to create social programmes and welfare state provisions which are intended to benefit poorer, disadvantaged groups; to enhance human capital; to redistribute wealth; and to promote social justice. Social democratic parties occupy the centre-left in the political spectrum and offer a middle way between Communist parties on the left and pro-capitalist parties on the right. Many such parties have joined the 'Socialist International'. It includes Britain's Labour Party, the French Socialist Party, the Social Democratic Parties of Germany, Sweden, Denmark, and Finland, and many more—including the Indian National Congress.

Under Jawaharlal Nehru, the public sector grew immensely, although the economy remained mixed. The Congress committed itself to a 'socialist pattern of society', but much state investment was intended to assist the private, corporate sector to flourish. More crucially, in practical terms, Congress 'socialism' served the interests of landowning groups. In those days, they exercised dominance in most villages

(Srinivas, 1959),[1] and translated that into dominance over the regional units of the Congress Party's organization and thus over governments in nearly all states. Those landed groups—one of Bardhan's 'dominant proprietary classes'—distributed the lion's share of resources from the 'socialist' order to their caste fellows, increasing inequality in villages where most Indians lived (then as now). They also blocked attempts at land reform—apart from zamindari abolition in some regions—and ensured that agricultural incomes would remain untaxed.

Nehru could not force through changes that would undermine the power of the landed groups on whom the Congress then depended for election victories. One potent regional leader of those dominant landed castes, S. Nijalingappa, told this writer that he and others like him were pleased that Nehru spent so much time on foreign policy because it distracted him from left-of-centre initiatives which they opposed—and managed to thwart.[2] Nehru was the leader of the Congress, but also its prisoner. He appears to have believed that the mere existence of a large state sector would suffice to make his government 'social democratic'. He paid less attention to redistributive policies intended to reduce poverty—and had he pursued them, the landed groups in Congress would have frustrated him.

Indira Gandhi won a landslide election victory in 1971 on a promise to 'abolish poverty' (*garibi hatao*), but then did little to pursue that goal. Her son Rajiv was an extraordinarily inconstant prime minister who, halfway through his term (1984–9), reversed himself on most of the major policy initiatives that he had introduced. So under all three of these leaders, Congress was only nominally 'social democratic'. It is hardly surprising, then, that *PEDI* should have paid only limited attention to pro-poor programmes.

P.V. Narasimha Rao, the next Congress prime minister (1991–6), faced severe economic problems and thus lacked the financial resources to offer India a genuinely 'social democratic' government. But it is crucial to recognize that he liberalized the economy with 'social democratic'

---

[1] The dominance of landed castes has since diminished markedly, and the acceptance of caste hierarchies by so-called 'lower' castes, has diminished substantially. For a discussion of the implications of these fundamentally important changes for power dynamics, see Manor (2016a).

[2] Interview with author, Bangalore, 7 July 1971.

intent. In private in February 1992, he explained this very cogently, consistently, and in exhaustive detail. He was at pains to stress that 'I do not believe in trickle-down economics', and that his model was not Margaret Thatcher (a neoliberal), but Willy Brandt (a social democrat). It is important to understand that *economic liberalizers need not be neoliberals*, and that there are good social democratic reasons to liberalize in an economy where a swollen state sector has led to stagnation. That describes India's economy in 1991.

Rao stated (in strictly private discussions)[3] that he was liberalizing the economy to accelerate economic growth—because growth would eventually generate greater government revenues, and those revenues could then be used for 'social democratic' purposes: social programmes, the redistribution of wealth, and poverty reduction. He did not pursue radical, 'big bang' liberalization. The changes that he introduced were cautious, incremental, and limited (see Manor, 1995; Jenkins, 1999). They and the similarly cautious changes that later governments have introduced have left India with a *far from 'neoliberal'* order—no matter how often social scientists and journalists lazily use that word. Senior politicians and bureaucrats still retain massive powers over the economy—something that genuine neoliberals despise.[4]

For many years, it seemed that Rao's social democratic dream would never come to fruition. Even when economic growth began to take off in the late 1990s, revenues increased only sluggishly. But then in 2003, revenues began to surge—thanks to growth and to new approaches to tax collection.

The figures in Table 5.1 need to be adjusted for inflation, but it is nonetheless apparent that in the post-2003 period, state and central governments have had far more money to spend than before. Revenues

---

[3] These discussions occurred during a working week which this writer spent with Rao during February 1992. He said that he did not explain these things publicly because he believed that to do so would be to invite controversy that could impede his efforts. Interviews at the time with state-level ministers from his own Congress Party in two key states (Maharashtra and Karnataka) revealed that none of them understood why he was liberalizing—with the exception of one junior minister in Karnataka who had studied economics as a Cambridge undergraduate.

[4] Some of them are quoted later in this chapter, when the Modi government's timid approach to economic liberalization is discussed.

TABLE 5.1   Gross Revenues of Central and State Governments (in Billions of Rupees)

	Central Government	State Governments
2002–03	2,162.66	2,577.07
2003–04	2,543.48	2,899.61
2004–05	3,049.58	3,291.53
2005–06	3,674.74	3,824.58
2006–07	4,735.12	4,561.84
2007–08	5,931.47	5,218.44
2008–09	6,052.99	5,483.18
2009–10	6,245.28	5,628.97
2010–11	7,868.88	7,358.20
2011–12	9,324.40	8,620.01

Source: Reserve Bank of India (2013: Table 116).

Note: For fuller details on change over time, compare the following documents: RBI, *Annual Report 2004*, Appendix Table IV.6: Combined Receipts and Disbursements of the Central and State Governments. Available at: https://rbidocs.rbi.org.in/rdocs/AnnualReport/PDFs/38804.pdf (accessed on 28 August 2019); RBI, *Annual Report 2018*, Appendix Table 7: Combined Receipts and Disbursements of the Central and State Governments. Available at: https://rbi.org.in/scripts/AnnualReportPublications.aspx?ld=1247 (accessed on 28 August 2019).

have continued to soar since 2012, even in years when growth rates have dipped.[5]

THE UPA: INDIA'S FIRST GENUINELY 'SOCIAL DEMOCRATIC' GOVERNMENT

Not long after the arrival in office of the Congress-led UPA after the 2004 election, it began to become clear that the government might have sufficient resources to begin making Rao's social democratic dream a reality. But for that to happen, the government needed to devise and implement initiatives that would promote redistribution and make growth inclusive.

[5] For example, *The Pioneer* reported on 25 January that direct tax revenues had increased by 12.93 per cent between April and December of 2014, and that personal income tax revenues had risen by 12.62 per cent in the same period (PTI, 2015; IANS, 2015).

At that time, many commentaries were attributing the UPA's victory at the 2004 election to a revolt of the rural poor against the previous BJP/National Democratic Alliance (NDA) government's energetic pursuit of economic liberalization. This was a myth. That government had been far from energetic at liberalizing and—more to the point—at the 2004 election, Congress and its allies had done better among prosperous groups than among the poor, and better in urban areas than in rural (Manor, 2011a). In part, this happened because Congress had spent significant amounts of its increased revenues on initiatives that benefited prosperous and urban groups—continuing its tradition of efforts to please *all* interest groups. But the more dramatic increase in pro-poor programmes was a departure from that tradition. The government was thus not entirely locked into path dependency. That is, the state had a significant degree of autonomy from supposedly dominant socio-economic forces. Senior Congress leaders knew about the myth of the revolt of the rural poor, but they did not challenge it because it made them appear more humane.[6]

They set about devising an array of policies to benefit poor groups and to promote inclusive development in order to make the myth of strong support from the rural poor a reality at the next election. Steeply rising revenues enabled them to spend heavily on these initiatives. Some of them emerged from the National Advisory Council (NAC) chaired by Sonia Gandhi—most notably the highly innovative National Rural Employment Guarantee Act to which Mahatma Gandhi's name was later attached (the MGNREGA).[7] Other programmes emerged from elsewhere in the government. As noted above, substantial funds were also spent on programmes to benefit the non-poor, since the Congress still sought votes from a broad array of interests. This might suggest that it made no dramatic departure from Bardhan's model, but spending on poverty initiatives rose sharply to unprecedented levels—and that was plainly a significant departure.

In the first of its two five-year terms (2004–9), the UPA spent over US$57 billion on such initiatives, vastly more than any previous Indian government, and similar policies were pursued during its second term between 2009 and 2014. After the 2009 national election,

---

[6] Interviews with two senior Congress strategists, New Delhi, July 2004.

[7] This process is explained in detail in Chapter 2 of Jenkins and Manor (2017).

many commentators opined that these pro–poor policies explained the UPA's victory. That was yet another myth—or at least an exaggeration (Manor, 2011b). But there can be no doubt that the Congress-led UPA was the first genuinely 'social democratic' government in the history of India—and of the Congress Party. Does this not indicate that something new and quite different from Bardhan's model was afoot?

The overall result of the UPA's policies was redistributive and inclusive. This has been authoritatively demonstrated by a research team drawn from India's National Council of Applied Economic Research and the University of Maryland, USA. Among the many things that it analysed was the impact of poverty initiatives between 2004 and 2012. Investigators surveyed 41,554 households in 2011–12—the *same* households that had been surveyed in 2004–05. They found that while per capita household incomes among high-caste Hindus (the most prosperous group) had increased by 4.6 per cent per annum, significantly larger gains were made by *all* other categories. 'Other Backward Castes' (the lower-middle stratum in the traditional caste hierarchy) saw per capita incomes increase by 7.3 per cent; Dalits (Scheduled Castes) by 7.8 per cent; *Adivasis* (Scheduled Tribes) by 5.7 per cent; and Muslims by 5.4 per cent (India Human Development Survey, 2018). The last three of those groups include many of the poor*est* people in rural India who are notoriously difficult for policies to reach. Agricultural labourers, who are also very poor, saw their wages triple between 2004–05 and 2011–12 (India Human Development Survey, 2018; *The Hindu*, 30 March 2014; *The Hindu*, 5 April 2014).

Despite this, the UPA lost the 2014 national election for several reasons. A firestorm of media criticism engulfed the government after multiple scams surfaced in late 2010. A serious, pre-existing paralysis in government grew worse when those scandals left bureaucrats terrified to make decisions, lest they be misconstrued by anti-corruption investigators whom the UPA belatedly unleashed.[8] The government's problems were compounded by serious misjudgements by senior Congress Party leaders. And, of course, Narendra Modi conducted an extremely effective, lavishly funded national election campaign in 2014.

Much of the funding came from one of Bardhan's 'dominant proprietary classes': industrialists. They hoped that Modi, who presented himself as a courageous leader, would take bold steps to liberalize the

---

[8] This problem persists. See Manor (2015a).

economy. They were, however, to be disappointed. They are no longer 'dominant'—their influence on the new government was too limited to trigger such changes.

THE BJP GOVERNMENT'S FAILURE TO ACCELERATE ECONOMIC LIBERALIZATION

This brings us back to the central question of this chapter. Is there, for the first time, a marked difference between the UPA government and its BJP successor since the mid-2014 election? We must first consider a dog that has not barked, a change (noted just above) which was widely anticipated from the Modi government but which has not occurred: India has not witnessed a rapid acceleration of economic liberalization.

A brief sampling of comments from enthusiasts for liberalization in just one of the financial newspapers, the *Business Standard*, will illustrate this point. One composed: 'An obituary for economic reform' (Sharma, 22 November 2015). Another bemoaned: 'Structured Procrastination' (Bhattacharya, 23 August 2015). A third, struggling to remain hopeful, argued that it is 'too early to give up' (Prakash, 12 November 2015). This view has persisted in more recent times. On 27 May 2016, T.N. Ninan argued that the prime minister 'seems to have turned his face away from the business of introducing serious reform' and two days later, an editorial in the same paper was headed: 'Avoiding reform: Two years in, major reforms seem off the table' (Ninan, 27 May 2016; *Business Standard*, 29 May 2016).

The detailed comments by various analysts explain their case:

> There is a growing sense of disquiet and disillusionment with the National Democratic Alliance government and the lack of economic progress.... The feedback from friends and industry leaders is sombre—they sense no economic revival.... [S]ensible people are losing hope.... The PM has not taken enough of the risks needed to push structural reform. He has not used his mandate to bring about systemic change; he seems to think that tinkering with the current system of government and running it tighter is all that is needed to get India back on the growth track. (Prakash, 12 November 2015)[9]

---

[9] It may seem odd to accuse Modi of being risk averse, but there is considerable evidence to support this idea from beyond the sphere of economic policy. He refused to participate in the 2014 Lok Sabha election campaign

Another commentator argues that for Modi, 'development doesn't seem to mean growth any longer; it means distribution' (Srinivasa-Raghavan, 3 July 2015). Yet another says that 'none' of the changes in economic policy has 'been transformative in nature'. He asks: 'does the PM really believe that the reforms introduced so far are of the transformative variety?' Modi has shown

> a worrying degree of complacency in declaring ... that his government had already achieved a great deal.... Has nobody shown Mr Modi the numbers? ... [P]repare to hear the government and its backers defend weak-kneed and confused "incrementalism" as real, big-bang reform. (Sharma, 23 November 2015)

The problem may go deeper than inaccurate (or wilfully misleading) official statements on economic reform. The government may suffer from a lack of understanding of what structural change might entail.

> This government seems to either lack or (be) unable to communicate, an economic vision of what they wish to accomplish. They seem to be bogged down on clearing projects and micro details and not focusing enough on policy....Who is in charge of economic policy in the government? (Prakash, 12 November 2015)

Some argue that the government is timid because it is 'wary of taking decisions that might have an adverse political reaction.... [L]abour policy reforms promised almost a year ago have made tardy progress' (Bhattacharya, 23 August 2015). This theme is echoed by Pratap Bhanu Mehta, who was discussing both economic policy and the government's record in general:

---

in Odisha (Orissa) after a single visit because he saw during that visit that his party would lose badly there and he preferred not to be associated with the defeat. A similar aversion to risk shaped his strategy for the Delhi state election and contributed to the BJP's humiliation there. That aversion is driven by an impractical and ultimately self-destructive idea: that *nothing must go wrong* so that Modi's reputation will remain unsullied by reverses. That leads him not just into reverse but into disasters which deeply mar his reputation—as in the Delhi and Bihar state elections. But at this writing in December 2015, the aversion lives on. For details, see Manor (2015b).

Instead of boldness, we are getting timidity. There is not a single measure this government has taken or a policy it has proposed that in any way can be called bold, which involves the slightest political risk, or displays a measure of conviction…. Government is, for the most part, business as usual, even more so. (Mehta, 7 August 2015)

Much more could be cited in this vein, including the famous comment by former BJP Union minister Arun Shourie who described the Modi government as 'Congress plus a cow' (*The Hindu*, 27 October 2015). Some might argue, with some justice, that the prime minister's decision to undertake demonetization in late 2015 was a bold stroke. But it scarcely qualifies as an example of economic liberalization.

The point here is that no marked difference has emerged between that government and its Congress-led predecessor in the pace of economic liberalization.

A STRIKING DEPARTURE FROM THE UPA GOVERNMENT ON A DIFFERENT FRONT?

There may, however, be a sharp contrast in another important sphere. Some argue that the BJP government has adopted a very different approach to development in general—and more specifically, that it has abandoned the efforts of its predecessor to tackle poverty through spending on social programmes. If this is true, then we see marked differences between successive Indian governments in the interest groups that they seek to favour and cultivate. There are divergent views on this and they are worth considering in some detail.

In an analysis composed after the BJP government's 2015 budget, Jean Drèze reminded us that in the early years after Independence, economic growth and development were mainly pursued via capital investment—mostly by the government—to create infrastructure and an industrial base. He noted that it later became apparent that investment was also needed in *human* capital—in mass education, health, nutrition, and so on. Some progress was made on those fronts, but too little was done—and for that, India has paid a heavy price. The UPA government (2004–14) innovated by spending very substantial sums to address that problem.

He argued that the BJP government's 2015 budget veered back to the model from the early post-Independence years. Human capital took a back seat. The budget stressed major new investments in infrastructure, which the private, corporate sector needs in order to flourish; that investment will mainly come from *government*. Private investment is hoped for, but the finance minister said that in the new public–private partnership model, the government 'will bear a major part of the risk'. There is an uncanny resemblance here to Bardhan's description of the 1950s and 1960s: the government did not just invest in areas that would benefit private industry, but also acted as the risk absorber of last resort (Bardhan, 1984: 41–2).

Drèze then turned to more specific issues: human capital, social sector spending, and poverty reduction. He wrote that the impact of the 2015 budget in these spheres would be 'catastrophic'. Health and education 'receive unprecedented shock treatment'. Social programmes that contribute to people's productive capacity 'face severe budget cuts' (Drèze, 5 March 2015).[10] Aruna Roy added that the BJP government which made 'drastic budget cuts on all major social sector schemes including the meagre pension schemes for the elderly, widowed, disabled and other disadvantaged people is blatantly anti-poor' (Times of India, 28 February 2015).

They are arguing that there is a much greater difference than we have ever seen before between the strategies of successive governments: Modi's and its UPA predecessor. If they are correct, this marks a crucial change: renewed support from the new government for Bardhan's 'dominant proprietary classes', and a sharp de-emphasis on efforts to enhance human capital and to benefit disadvantaged groups.

But are they correct? Note once again the question mark at the end of this chapter's title. We need to consider a different perspective.

A MORE AMBIGUOUS ASSESSMENT OF THE MODI GOVERNMENT

It comes not from the BJP government or its advocates but from N.C. Saxena who, as a colleague of Drèze and Roy on the NAC, cannot

---

[10] See also, especially on the disappointments in the budget for farmers (a lack of clarity on micro-irrigation, and 'no provision for R&D or for research findings on needy farmers'), B. Agarwal in the *Indian Express* (9 March 2015).

be accused of indifference to poverty and inequality. He presents a complex narrative, attended by ambiguities.[11]

During the financial year 2014–15 (which commenced in April), spending on social sectors—on things such as food subsidies, the National Health Mission, and the MGNREGA—was indeed reduced. But in part, this was the result of a decision in March 2014 by the *previous* UPA government—*before* the parliamentary election in May which brought the BJP to power. It changed the way in which funds for social programmes flowed from the central government to the state level. They would now go to state governments' finance departments, rather than to various agencies directly in charge of social programmes. Those agencies would now have to approach finance departments for funds. It took time for actors and institutions in the various states to adapt to this change, and as a result, funding for social programmes declined.

After the May 2014 election, the new BJP government made further changes. Some of these caused still more reductions in spending on social sectors, but the picture is complicated. In financial year 2014–15, Modi decided to reduce spending on social programmes in order to reduce the central government's deficit, but this did not necessarily amount to a permanent, sustained policy change. Among the programmes that suffered cuts in funding, the MGNREGA loomed quite large. But the cuts lasted only until the minister incharge was changed. The new man argued successfully for a reversal of that decision; so before long, the new government had returned to an approach similar to that of its predecessor, the UPA. Modi may initially have sneered at the MGNREGA when he told Parliament that he was maintaining it 'as a monument to failed Congress policies' (*Economic Times*, 28 February 2015). But when disappointing monsoons left several regions facing near droughts in 2015, some BJP leaders lobbied for an increase in the number of days that poor villagers could work under the programme from 100 to 150. That proposal was not accepted, but the Modi government found the MGNREGA too useful, politically, to be scrapped.

Another quite complex set of changes had implications in the food sector. The new BJP government decided to increase the release of

---

[11] Interview, New Delhi, 19 November 2015. Saxena updated and reaffirmed these arguments in an interview in New Delhi, 29 November 2016.

foodgrains from its stocks—outside of fair price shops that operate under the Public Distribution System (PDS)—onto the open market. This lowered the overall market prices for grains,[12] but it did not entail a reduction in foodstuffs for fair price shops.

However, under the National Food Security Act, 2013, which had been passed by the previous UPA government, the total amounts of foodstuffs allocated to fair price shops should have increased drastically. The BJP government allowed only a modest increase—which can be seen as an indication of its coolness towards social sectors.

That government also decided not to buy rice from rice millers. It was abandoning a system in which much of the profit went to millers rather than to farmers. The government's aim was to benefit farmers in the long run. But in the short term, as various actors adjusted to the new process, it hurt farmers.

One further innovation—which amounts to a major structural change in the way in which funds for social sectors are disbursed—also occurred under Modi. It is at this point in the discussion that the views of Drèze and Saxena, which have been contrasted in the comments earlier, begin to converge.

The key issue here is how, *in practice*, things have changed under the Modi government. In late 2014, the 14th Finance Commission—which had been appointed by the former UPA government—submitted its recommendations to the BJP government. Its prescriptions, like those of all previous Finance Commissions, were accepted by the central government.[13]

They included a substantial increase in the share of funds to be transferred from New Delhi to state governments—or rather, to many but not all of those governments since 10 of the 29 are to receive less than before.[14] Let us examine this from Saxena's point of view. That change

[12] This change also (*i*) earned the government additional revenues, (*ii*) reduced its administrative costs incurred for the storage of grains, and (*iii*) enabled an increase in exports.

[13] For details on that process, see Manor (2015b).

[14] See Manor (2015b) for a discussion of why not all state governments will actually receive increased funds—in part because the criteria (for example, forest cover) used to determine the amounts to be devolved have changed. See also *Times of India* (5 July 2015). It reports that the Uttar Pradesh Chief Secretary foresees an overall decline in central assistance to the tune of INR 9,443

led the central government to reduce its own contribution to social programmes on the assumption (which it knew to be debatable, see p. 108)
that state governments would choose to use substantial amounts of the
untied funds that were passed to them to support those programmes.

As a consequence, in financial year 2015–16, the central government's spending on the social sectors decreased by INR 60,000 crores.
But the overall amount of government funds which were (at least on
paper) intended for those sectors increased by INR 180,000 crores. In
practice, however, this may lead to a *reduction* in such spending for two
main reasons.

First, an inevitable delay has occurred in the release of funds from
New Delhi to state governments while the latter await technical details
of the new process and adjust themselves to it. That is a temporary
problem, but it entails a temporary cut in social spending.

Second, more importantly, further reductions in such spending are
likely over the longer term because the funds that reach state governments are untied—not earmarked for social sectors—and many but
not all of those governments have tended to commit only limited
resources to those sectors.

It is thus possible to say that the BJP government has not reduced
social spending, and that the actual outlay for social programmes now
depends on decisions at the state level. But senior figures within the
BJP government who wish to reverse the increases in support for social

---

crores. West Bengal will see a net loss of roughly INR 2,000 crores—including cuts of 66 per cent in funds for mid-day meals and 77 per cent for universal education. The *Times* provides detailed figures for various government
programmes which indicate that there are gains and losses. Under numerous
headings, mostly very modest increases in funds were announced: educating
Scheduled Caste children, 'Scholarships for SC, ST, OBCs', MGNREGA,
the 'Multi-sectoral development programme for Minorities', social assistance,
the National Health Mission, and 'Housing for all'. In other areas, however,
outlays have been reduced—in one case, modestly (the National Livelihoods
Mission); in others more substantially (the Food Security Mission, Rashtriya
Krishi Vikas Yojana, the National Livelihoods Mission, AIDS control, and the
Integrated Child Development Scheme). The central government has pulled
out entirely from the Backward Regions Grants Fund and some other welfare
schemes.

sectors under the UPA are happy with the new devolutionary process because they know that many state governments will not sustain those increases.[15]

Indeed, they appear to have *intended* this change to achieve a reduction in social spending. In comments which indicate the convergence of the arguments of Saxena and Drèze, the latter makes two key points about this. First, BJP leaders ignored the Finance Commission's emphasis on 'the need for continuation of central support in some critical fields including "education, health, water supply and sanitation, child nutrition"'. Second, they did nothing that would require state governments to use some of the newly devolved funds on social sector programmes (Drèze, 2015). Drèze adds that 'there have been no social policy initiatives of any worth from the Modi government so far'.[16] BJP leaders in New Delhi find the devolution of funds to state governments highly convenient because the political blame for cuts in social spending will fall not on them but on state-level leaders. Saxena has not dissented from this interpretation.

It will take time before we see how these new arrangements work in practice. Further initiatives from the Modi government may alter the picture. So it is a little early to pass final judgement on that government's approach to social spending. But the arguments of Drèze and Saxena tend to converge around one conclusion: *in practice*, under the BJP government, far less support will be provided for social programmes than under the Congress-led UPA government which held power between 2004 and 2014.

DO GOVERNMENTS HAVE THE AUTONOMY FROM POWERFUL INTERESTS TO ADOPT NEW APPROACHES?

In his 1984 book, Bardhan argued (in effect) that governments did not possess sufficient autonomy from the 'dominant proprietary classes' to

---

[15] Others, including BJP ministers in New Delhi, have expressed worries about a negative impact on the BJP's popularity if spending on social sectors is cut. Modi's right hand man, Amit Shah, is reliably reported to share their anxiety—because reduced spending could cost the party votes. Interview with a senior advisor to the BJP, New Delhi, 8 July 2015. He reiterated this view on 11 December 2016, as the crucial Uttar Pradesh state election in early 2017 loomed.

[16] Private communication, 21 December 2015.

diverge very far from the paths that their predecessors have followed. This appears to have changed (see Chapter 6).[17] There are three things to consider here.

First, under the Congress-led UPA government (2004–14), key actors—Sonia Gandhi and the NAC, and also some assertively pro-poor bureaucrats and politicians—devised several major poverty initiatives which were decidedly innovative. Vastly more money was committed to these programmes than ever before in independent India. These actions plainly served interests other than those of the three 'dominant proprietary classes'. The UPA also introduced policies that addressed the needs of those classes, but unprecedentedly huge sums were spent on poverty initiatives.

This was not a response by the UPA government to votes from poorer groups at the 2004 election. Contrary to the media myth of a revolt of the rural poor in support of the UPA, prosperous groups had (as we have noted) backed the UPA more fulsomely at that election than had the poor. In other words, the UPA acted autonomously, not under pressure from poorer groups since their votes had not swept it to power. The UPA's pro-poor innovations were aspirational, in that they were intended to attract votes from the poor at the next election.

But the UPA's pro-poor policies were patently a departure from the practices of all previous governments (including Congress governments). The re-election of the UPA in 2009, after five years of this new approach, indicated that its senior leaders were correct in their assumption that they had sufficient autonomy to pursue this new course and that they would not suffer an election defeat as a result of a reaction by the 'three dominant proprietary classes'. It may thus be more accurate to refer to them as the 'three *formerly* dominant proprietary classes'.

Second, in the BJP-led NDA government that has held power since mid-2014, power has been radically centralized in the Prime Minister's Office (PMO). Most ministers in the central government learn what their policies are from their senior bureaucrats who transmit messages from the PMO. All key decisions are taken at the apex by Modi and his right-hand man Amit Shah, who give the very strong impression that they too feel that they have sufficient autonomy from three 'dominant proprietary forces' to govern in this assertive manner—even though

---

[17] I am grateful to the editors for raising this question.

their departure from the path trodden by their UPA predecessors bears (as we have seen) some resemblance to the approach of the governments which Bardhan analysed in 1984.

The NDA has used theatrical gestures to give the impression that it cares about disadvantaged groups such as its many acts of homage to the Dalits' icon, B.R. Ambedkar. These have been lavishly publicized by most media outlets, which the BJP strongly influences via inducements and intimidation. However, most Dalits remain unconvinced after suffering abuses at Una, Bhima Koregaon, and elsewhere. That might suggest that the NDA is siding with the 'dominant proprietary forces'. But Modi's decision to demonetize damaged the interests of one of them: prosperous farmers, millions of whom, according to his agriculture ministry, suffered grievously.

There is a third aspect to this story, which might easily be overlooked. Since the very late 1990s, power has also been radically centralized in most state governments in the federal system. In late 2016, roughly 80 per cent of Indians lived in states in which one leader exercised personal dominance or near-dominance. That trend is largely explained by the radical centralization of illicit 'fundraising' in the hands of chief ministers, who use the immense powers which they retain in the far-from-neoliberal order to issue permissions and approvals in order to extract massive 'contributions' from industrialists and investors in urban land. This enables them to disempower legislators and even ministers, and to achieve autonomy from the interests whom the latter represent. And as numerous capricious actions by these chief ministers indicate, they also retain very substantial autonomy from the moneyed industrialists from whom they receive 'contributions' (Manor, 2016b).

On all of the three fronts noted earlier, political leaders in the UPA, the BJP, and many state governments have indeed achieved considerable autonomy, so that they are not in the thrall of any 'proprietary class'.

This has implications as we seek to answer the central question in this chapter: do we now see—for the first time—successive governments in New Delhi offering strikingly different sets of policies to address fundamental issues? The Congress-led UPA and the BJP-led NDA had sufficient autonomy from all organized interest groups to adopt different approaches to public spending and to India's political economy. But were there not significant contrasts between their strategies? Did the NDA government turn its back on the approach of its predecessor, which was India's first genuinely social democratic government? And did that change entail markedly different treatment of the three 'dominant proprietary classes' by the UPA and Modi's NDA? Despite the complexities and ambiguities noted earlier, the answers to these questions appear to be in the affirmative. Bardhan may need to produce a further edition of his book to take account of this change.

III

The Dominant Proprietary Classes

Continuity and Change

6 Business Interests and State Autonomy in India

Rob Jenkins

Among the less-heralded contributions of Pranab Bardhan's *The Political Economy of Development in India* (*PEDI*), which John Toye (1988: 113) rightly called a 'minor masterpiece of compression', was its application of frameworks associated with one discipline to the study of theoretical puzzles confronted in another.[1] An example that has received at least some attention, though mainly as an isolated phenomenon, is *PEDI*'s application of economics-derived rational-choice-based analysis to the political dynamics among India's domi-nant class groups and, crucially, their engagement with the Indian state. Another instance of *PEDI*'s penchant for intellectual cross-fertilization has received less attention: its import into the study of Indian political economy of ideas derived from Theda Skocpol's (1979) comparative research on wide-ranging social transformations, as well as her work on more narrowly defined cases of policy reorientation (Skocpol and Finegold, 1982). Skocpol's findings suggested an urgent need for schol-ars to look beyond 'society-based' explanations for a country's policy

---

[1] This chapter draws substantially on material and analysis developed jointly with James Manor on the politics of India's employment-guarantee legislation, as well as from various sole-authored outputs on national and state-level land policy reforms.

or institutional framework—that is, to be more receptive to theories
of change that recognize states as themselves possessing at least partial
autonomy, temporarily or otherwise, from powerful social forces.

Three main claims were advanced by *PEDI* around this set of
issues. First, it argued that in analysing state behaviour vis-à-vis interest
formations, we must not 'ignore the large range of choices in goal
formulation, agenda setting and policy execution' available to the
'state leadership' as well as 'the powerful impulses shaping policies and
actions that are generated *within* the state' (33–4). Second, the book
highlighted the autonomy public officials enjoyed due to the structural
position occupied by the state as the key mediator between India's
'dominant proprietary classes'—industrial capitalists, rich farmers,
and the 'professional' class comprising 'civilian and military' ('including white-collar workers'). Third, *PEDI* claimed that state elites were
not driven 'merely by motives of self-aggrandizement' but by what
R. Miliband (1983) had called a certain 'conception of the national
interest', which such actors possessed agency continually to reinvent.

Given the striking increases in the wealth, stature, and influence
of India's private sector over the past quarter century—the result of a
more-or-less continuous process of pro-business, if not always precisely
market-oriented, economic reform (Kohli, 2006a)—one might expect
all three of *PEDI*'s claims concerning the agency and relative autonomy of the state to no longer apply. Public authorities have in recent
years appeared to bend over backward to accommodate the interests of
India's business community in particular. The large corporate retinues
that typically accompany India's officials to international meetings are
a vivid indication of this trend. More substantially, the increasing political dominance of industrial capital would seem to have (*i*) removed
the state leadership's agenda-setting advantages by firmly implanting a
market-centred development paradigm; (*ii*) undercut the state's ability
to act as a coalitional mediator (who needs one when a single class
dominates?); and (*iii*) robbed state elites of the Milibandian autonomy
that allowed (but did not compel) them to prioritize national interests
over sectional gains.

Despite all the structural shifts in the Indian economy over the past
three decades, this chapter argues that state elites continue to enjoy,
as *PEDI* put it, a comparably 'large range of choices' when advancing
policy agendas. State elites are capable of making significant policy

and institutional decisions that are diametrically opposed to the interests—and expressed preferences—of industrial capital. To support the
proposition that Bardhan's conception of state autonomy remains
substantially valid today, this chapter examines the changing nature
of both the state and the interest groups with which it engages. The
analysis focuses on the evolution of India's legal regime concerning
the compulsory acquisition of land for public purposes. Land acquisition is an especially suitable policy domain because it is one in which
industrial capital has been unusually united in its demands. The fate of
land acquisition legislation over the past decade, at least, demonstrates
the potential for autonomous action by state elites even under the most
challenging circumstances. Moreover, the starkly conflicting interests
between the proprietary classes represented in the *PEDI* framework—
in this case, primarily between industrial capital and rich farmers—
allows state elites to interpose themselves politically to lengthen time
horizons and expand options for political compromises.

ACTORS AND AUTONOMY

The question of how the Indian state can best be characterized has
been a longstanding concern of political economists. Like other post-
colonial states, India's has been seen as lacking in resolve—all too ready
to capitulate to powerful groups on contentious issues such as land
reform. It has also been portrayed as 'overdeveloped'[2] (Alavi, 1972),
and in some respects even 'predatory' (Lal, 1984). Other analysts have
seen India's state as founded on a shifting constellation of class interests whose mechanics constituted an 'intermediate regime' (Kalecki,
1972; Raj, 1973). The Indian state has sometimes been characterized
as a 'hybrid' (Mitra, 2011). Rudolph and Rudolph (1987) memorably
dubbed India a 'weak-strong state', one where 'demand politics' and
'command politics' remained in unsteady equilibrium. This characterization continued a long tradition of interrogating fundamental 'paradoxes' in the study of Indian politics (Weiner, 1989). The weak-strong
descriptor also captured another essential ambiguity of the Indian case:
while the state can appear inflated and ubiquitous, it often exhibits

---

[2] The classic rebuttal to Alavi's claim that excessive state power was inherited from colonial regimes is Leys (1976).

scant presence in the lives of marginalized social groups, people living in remote rural areas, or those operating in the vast informal economy (Drèze, 2002).

More recently, however, the Indian state has been described in rather stark, all-or-nothing terms—as controlled by powerful interests, impervious to fundamental change, or aligned with a particular vision of the world. Some recent characterizations have cast the Indian state as all but captured by big business and in the thrall of a neoliberal vision of development. Kohli (2012) went so far as to say that a 'state–business ruling alliance' has been constructed. The seemingly undue influence exerted by some business groups, including at the state level, is indeed a cause for concern.[3] But claims that the state has been captured, or that state elites have forfeited whatever autonomy of action over economic policymaking they once possessed, have been greatly exaggerated (Sundar, 2010). Indeed, a sizable portion of the literature on India's economic performance since the early 1990s has emphasized the capacity of the state to formulate constructive relations with the private sector (Calì and Sen, 2011). Of particular note has been research that stresses the state's ability to initiate substantial policy changes, including within institutions of multilateral governance, that have helped Indian firms to adapt to global economic interdependence (Sinha, 2016).[4] This is a far cry from a model of political influence in which reform agendas are dictated by business groups with a clear and immutable set of economic interests and policy preferences.

From the founding of the Indian National Congress in 1885, there were indications that India's emerging capitalist class would operate as a political actor. This included support for the nationalist movement as well as routine consultation with Congress on the policy positions business associations advocated in negotiations with colonial authorities. A political sensibility was also evident in the tendency for business groups to couch their economic demands on issues such as tariff levels and exchange rates in terms that would demonstrate the private sector's

[3] The role of the Adani group in Gujarat during Narendra Modi's tenure as chief minister has been a high-profile example of business–politics interactions at the state level. See Jaffrelot (2019).

[4] For a comparative perspective that stresses the importance of enabling factors, see Doner and Schneider (2000).

commitment to the welfare of the country as a whole (Mukherjee, 2009). The Bombay Plan of 1944, an economic development framework drawn up by a group of industrialists that foresaw a leading role for the private sector in independent India, was a statement of political intent as much as a strategy for economic development (Lokanathan, 1945). The backing of business groups in various parts of India for the free-market-oriented Swatantra party from the late 1950s through the early 1970s was another thread in what was to become a rich fabric of state–business relations. S.A. Kochanek's (1974) analysis of the business community's complex relationship with government actors provided empirical detail on the varying routes to influence, even as it adopted a fairly conventional perspective characterized by interest-group pluralism. This was followed by Mitra (1977), whose explanation for shifting terms of trade employed a class-analysis framework. But it was not until *PEDI*'s elaboration of the power-sharing dynamic among the three 'dominant proprietary classes' that mainstream scholars began to regard industrial capital as operating within a comprehensive model of the Indian state.

Even so, nothing like consensus has ever existed in the theoretical literature on how to operationalize the concept of state autonomy. In general, the claim that the state enjoys relative freedom of action vis-à-vis social forces—or from the political sphere more broadly—has represented a reaction against highly mechanistic models of change. Skocpol's critique of Marxist and neo-Marxist accounts of the state concerned what she considered their crude assumptions about class dominance. Such models, Skocpol argued, made it 'virtually impossible even to raise the possibility that fundamental conflicts of interest might arise between the existing dominant class or set of groups on one hand, and the state rulers on the other' (Skocpol, 1979: 27). Skocpol's use of the term 'state rulers' highlights an additional conceptual difficulty: the nature of the actors concerned. In the literature on the determinants of state action, it is not always clear who exactly—which category of individual or entity—is taking autonomous action, just as it is often not apparent whether they are acting independently of social classes, organized interests, political factions, or even ideological traditions. Fred Block (1977) sought to address some of these quandaries by introducing the notion of 'state managers'—people whose relative independence stems from their lack of involvement in capitalist relations of production, even if such individuals were members of that class before becoming state managers. For the purposes of this chapter, the term governing (or state) elites will refer to senior elected politicians from parties that have exercised governmental power and the uppermost echelons of the civil service—a usage that deviates slightly from the one adopted in *PEDI* (51).

The 'governing elites' nomenclature was used in my analysis of the politics of the early years of India's economic reforms, from the mid-1980s to the end of the 1990s (Jenkins, 1999). I argued that *PEDI*'s political economy framework could be used for analytical purposes distinct from those that were then prevalent. While the mutual-veto standoff between the three dominant proprietary classes had, for a time, halted the spread and consolidation of economic liberalization—because each group feared losing rents and relative influence from a new and uncertain policy dispensation—these very same divisions had, from 1991 onward, performed the opposite function: they undermined the capacity for dominant groups to engage in effective collective *resistance* to a reformist agenda unleashed by a determined core of governing elites (Jenkins, 1999). Arguably, some of these elites were acting in accordance with a 'particular conception of the national interest', one in which overcoming the country's indebtedness to external creditors figured prominently. There were many enabling factors that allowed this reform-sustaining political dynamic to unfold—notably, the political skill with which governing elites framed and sequenced policy decisions to further divide opponents of reform, and the scope provided by India's political institutions to achieve this and other objectives, including the involvement of India's state governments in the management of dissent. India's industrial capitalist class has changed immensely since the early 1990s, but in ways that do not necessarily undercut the periodic autonomy of the state explored in this earlier research.

It is significant that economic liberalization, at least in the short to medium term, threatened the interests of all three dominant proprietary classes and not just industrialists benefiting from protectionist trade policies or competition-stifling regulations. The professional managerial class—including managers of state-run enterprises in industries 'reserved' for the public sector—were rightly concerned about an ideology that elsewhere in the world had been associated with a movement to shrink the state. Prosperous farming groups faced the prospect of reduced subsidies and changes to agricultural markets that would damage their economic fortunes. The political packaging of reform included public claims from governing elites that the market would free farmers from the shackles of a controlled economy, and private assurances to civil service unions and members of professional associations that—in India, unlike countries that had succumbed to market fundamentalism—the state would maintain a significant presence in the broad field of economic development, including the management of programmes designed to cushion vulnerable groups from the worst effects of economic dislocation.

The Indian state's ability to sustain this economic transition in the face of daunting political odds was striking. Just a few years earlier, Harriss (1987) had argued that liberalization was all but impossible given India's institutional arrangements. But the sustainability of reform rested on more than tactical skill at navigating interest-group pressures. It relied upon an institutional structure that conferred extraordinary decision-making power on a tight circle of key officials. Economic liberalization was unleashed from the apex of the political system—first, largely at the direction of a triumphant Indira Gandhi following her return to power in 1980, and then later by Rajiv Gandhi in the mid-1980s. Prime Minister P.V. Narasimha Rao, who drastically increased the scope and pace of reform in the early 1990s, as well as the prime ministers who headed the United Front government that followed, took decisions in consultation with a relatively small group of senior civil servants. These included 'lateral entrants' from academia and international organizations (Sengupta, 2004) and 'technopols', or technocrats-turned-politicians, such as former prime minister Manmohan Singh and former finance minister P. Chidambaram (Williamson, 1994). They were, in fits and starts, collectively framing a new conception of the national interest, including a revised understanding of national self-reliance to accommodate the country's new development paradigm (Jenkins, 2004).

It is important to recall that, at the outset of the reform process, many business leaders were extremely wary of what India's new policy dispensation might mean for the fortunes of their firms, their industries, and indeed the country's economic outlook more broadly. However, to remain on good terms with governing elites who had

committed themselves to liberalization, while also articulating boundaries past which economic reforms should not stray, many business
leaders and commentators stated their support for internal, but not
external, liberalization, or for financial-sector liberalization to make
capital more easily available, while insisting on the need for barriers to
entry for competing firms (Kochanek, 1996).

In the nearly three decades since then, the private sector's increasing
influence over policymaking has not merely been a reflection of the
leverage that money can buy via campaign contributions (and outright
bribery). The ideological hegemony of market-oriented thinking is an
important part of the story. One channel through which business influence on core state institutions is apparent is the growing role played
by private-sector actors and media organizations in shaping India's
rapidly evolving foreign policy. S. Baru (2009) saw a rapid increase in
direct participation by business leaders, as well as considerable evidence
that they were having an impact. Influence over foreign policy is in
part a reflection of media-ownership concentration among a limited
number of corporate entities. But just as importantly, an intellectual
transformation has taken hold among governing elites, in which the
private sector is regarded as essential to building India's national power.
This exemplifies the way in which governing elites may be operating
on the basis of a radically new 'conception of the national interest'—
one in which promoting the fortunes of industrial capital is no longer
regarded as taking sides in the perpetual struggle among the dominant
proprietary classes, but rather a means of advancing India's strategic
position and long-term goals.

Thus, while state actors and India's business class have closely aligned
interests and operate within an increasingly shared strategic worldview,
to call their relationship an 'alliance' is a stretch. If it *is* an alliance, it
is one of convenience. Defections by either side take place with some
regularity. It is certainly not an exclusive relationship. Either way, Baru
(2000) argues that such alliances are more evident at the state level than
in national politics and policymaking.

That the state can act with relative autonomy, even as it continues
to be closely intertwined with business actors, is an idea found in a
number of existing studies. R. Mukherji's account of the emergence of
economic liberalization in India, for instance, assigns a key role to economic ideas—particularly policy and institutional analyses framed by

experts appointed to government-created commissions, committees, and advisory boards (Mukherji, 2014). The wide-ranging and almost non-stop deliberations between senior civil servants, technopols, and lateral entrants within the economic bureaucracy have allowed India to develop policies adapted to its unique circumstances, rather than to rely on prefabricated frameworks imported from international institutions. This, Mukherji has recently argued, is a pattern that has persisted for the entire post-reform period. As a result, 'powerful social forces', for all their influence, 'cannot totally undermine hegemonic policy ideas within the state' (Mukherji, 2017: 54).

E. Chatterjee's research on the evolution of India's electricity-sector reforms draws attention to an equally relevant aspect of how state autonomy has been maintained: the ambivalent relationship between business and the bureaucracy. On the one hand, '[t]he central state's pro-business turn is visible in the power sector, with corporate lobby groups, personnel and energy capitalists increasingly brought into the policy process in New Delhi' (Chatterjee, 2014: 213). On the other hand, India's '[b]ureaucrats retain suspicions about business, due in part to past experience with private energy players' (213). The policy agenda is thus 'market-oriented but state-led' (214). Chatterjee argues that even as '[c]ertain technocratic elements at the apex of the Indian state have unsystematically increased their functional autonomy', the state remains 'fundamentally plural' and 'unevenly embedded'. The result is that '[c]loser business links have been forged, but there is still no neat capital–state nexus: the state remains the sector's prime mover, thanks to energy security, redistribution and employment concerns, and the (perceived) unreliability of the capitalist class itself' (209). Sunila Kale's research on electricity-sector policy in India, which stresses historical path dependence to explain inter-regional variation in the nature and success of reform, also highlights key aspects of autonomous state action, notably, the sense in which India's federal division of power invests state governments with varying degrees of what Michael Mann has called 'infrastructural power' (Kale, 2014: 10).

To a considerable extent, the rationale for these independent actions has been to ensure the political survival of the very pro-business reform agenda that has become dominant in Indian policymaking circles and in public discourse more generally. The need to take forceful action to forestall a backlash from rural India—whether among landless agricultural labourers or communities threatened with large-scale land alienation—has animated key legislative changes of the past dozen years. K. Polanyi's insight that the modern market economy is historically rare and politically fragile has been internalized by an important segment of India's governing elites (Polanyi, 2001). The country is still at an early stage of its transition to a market economy (and perhaps market society, to use Polanyi's terminology), and the threats to its continued development are substantial. As Polanyi argued, market societies are far from self-regulating.

Bardhan himself has been critical of theories (both Marxist and neo-Marxist) that regard 'state autonomy' as a means by which the state disentangles itself from the dominant class in order to prevent profit- and rent-seeking interests from destroying capitalism itself (Poulantzas, 1972). Yet, as we shall see, India's governing elites, often acting in concert with social movement actors, have shown themselves capable of taking countervailing actions. Sporadically, they have adopted a longer-term perspective on development.

LAND ACQUISITION AND INDIA'S BUSINESS CLASS

Land acquisition is a particularly significant policy domain in which to examine state–business relations. It is an arena in which an exceptional state interest—in private property necessary to fulfil public aims— is involved. This is expressed in the idea of 'eminent domain' itself. Regulating land transactions, erecting tax systems based on land, and assuming ownership or stewardship of land has traditionally been a prerogative of states in most parts of the world and almost everywhere among modern states. Maintaining the state's discretionary power over compulsory acquisition was, moreover, not only of direct relevance to the state's self-image, but also directly beneficial to the private-sector actors with whom state officials have routinely colluded in the process of acquiring land. In other words, there tend to be very strong incentives for states not to enact rules that undercut the legal basis for this form of dispossession. And, yet, in India, that is precisely what governing elites did.

The Right to Fair Compensation and Transparency in Land Acquisition, Rehabilitation and Resettlement Act, 2013 (LARRA), was among the last major laws passed by the Congress-led United

Progressive Alliance (UPA) government of Prime Minister Manmohan Singh. The UPA governed India from 2004 to 2014, but LARRA was passed just eight months prior to the 2014 general election, in which the UPA government was swept from power by the Bharatiya Janata Party (BJP), whose leader, Narendra Modi, became prime minister.[5] Along with the National Food Security Act, 2013 (NFSA), also passed during the UPA's final months in office, LARRA was one of the several rights-based laws—including the Right to Information Act, 2005 RTIA, and the Right of Children to Free and Compulsory Education Act, 2009 (RTEA)—passed during Manmohan Singh's decade in power.

A set of rules, procedures, and oversight structures was defined by LARRA to govern the forcible acquisition of land by the state, as well as the responsibilities of specific government and private entities to those individuals and groups affected by the exercise of this power. Three features of LARRA should be noted at the outset. First, the Act took the unusual step of recognizing that state-facilitated development initiatives can deeply disrupt the basis of social, economic, and political life for entire communities. Thus, LARRA fundamentally changes the frame of reference used when considering effects: compensation is to be awarded not just to individual landowners, but to stakeholders in the local economy more broadly, including those reliant for their well-being on the economic activities associated with existing land-use patterns. Second, LARRA specified several citizen-initiated procedural mechanisms through which the state, in theory, can be compelled to fulfil particular economic rights. For instance, the 'views of the affected families' must be included in a Social Impact Assessment (SIA) report, and non-governmental actors must be involved in appraising the SIA report. The Right to Fair Compensation and Transparency in Land Acquisition, Rehabilitation and Resettlement Act called for local 'consent' when land was to be acquired for private companies or public–private partnerships. Citizens would participate in Rehabilitation and Resettlement Committees and in social audits. Third, LARRA created a set of purpose-built institutions to carry out

---

[5] The BJP won enough seats to form a parliamentary majority on its own, but remained nominally a part of a coalition known as the National Democratic Alliance (NDA).

functions identified in the Act: not only the local bodies mentioned above, but also a National Monitoring Committee for Rehabilitation and Resettlement and a Land Acquisition, Rehabilitation, and Resettlement Authority for each state.

The politics surrounding LARRA's passage in late 2013 were complex and revealing about the character of the Indian state and the dynamics of India's policymaking processes. The strong cross-party support for LARRA also reflected the widespread sense that the Land Acquisition Act, 1894 (LAA), introduced by the British colonial government (though amended periodically after Independence in 1947), was unable to afford the protections demanded by citizens of a sovereign democracy. Moreover, mushrooming protest activity against land acquisition orders across India was causing political instability and prompting potential investors to reassess the worth of the property rights they had negotiated with the state. A 2013–14 study, which identified a total of 252 land-related conflicts, found that a quarter of India's districts experienced a significant level of land-related conflict, and that a majority of the most contentious cases involved the compulsory acquisition of land by state agencies (Society for Promotion of Wasteland Development & Rights and Resources Initiative, 2014). A major contributor to the frequency and intensity of protest was the Special Economic Zones Act, 2005, the implementation of which involved large-scale acquisitions mainly on behalf of private-sector firms.[6]

But even as LARRA came officially into force on 1 January 2014, both the Act itself and the model for extending rights that it represented continued to be matters of intense public debate. This was partly an artefact of timing: LARRA entered the statute books just as India was gearing up for a general election, one in which the effectiveness of the UPA government's rights-based approach to addressing poverty became a subject of considerable contention.[7] Substantial overhaul,

---

[6] The role played by the Special Economic Zones Act, 2005—particularly its implementation and the political reaction thereto—in creating the conditions for the passage of LARRA eight years later is discussed in Jenkins, Kennedy, and Mukhopadhyay (2014: chapter 2).

[7] The contours of the debate over rights-based approaches are reflected in two competing assessments: Drèze and Sen (2013) are largely sympathetic, while Bhagwati and Panagariya (2013) are highly critical.

if not outright repeal, of LARRA was a priority for business groups that had aligned themselves closely with the BJP. That LARRA was a target for much of India's business community, as well as many political leaders from within and beyond the BJP, was evident from the harsh condemnation of the Act's structure, concept, and provisions voiced in the pro-Modi business press. One commentator referred to LARRA as 'India's Law from Hell' (Nayyar, 2014). During the campaign, LARRA was held up as a symbol of what business constituencies saw as bureaucratic obstacles to investment, and which the BJP quietly promised to remove.

In India, the formidable regulatory hurdles that confront firms seeking to purchase or lease land for industrial purposes have been a perennial complaint among both domestic and international businesses and business associations. In some instances, states have competed with one another for inward investment by promising expedited access to land—for production facilities, for energy and transportation infrastructure, for housing developments and other amenities required by future workers and managers, and so forth (Dutta, 2009).

Industry groups were concerned about the LARR Bill, introduced in Parliament in 2011, long before it became law, though up until the last moment it was hoped that inertia would halt the Bill's progress until it lapsed when Parliament was dissolved. Similar legislation promoted by the UPA government during its first term had lapsed in 2009 in precisely this fashion. For many Congress Members of Parliament (MPs), a passive abandonment of the Bill was more attractive than having to take a stand that, inevitably, would alienate important constituencies. Still, business took the renewed threat seriously. For more than two years, from late 2011 through late 2013, India's three premier business federations—Associated Chambers of Commerce and Industry of India (ASSOCHAM), Confederation of Indian Industry (CII), and the Federation of Indian Chambers of Commerce and Industry (FICCI)—submitted memoranda to parliamentary committees and made detailed presentations to informal groups of MPs and party leaders, outlining the allegedly prohibitive costs that would be incurred, and the potentially huge delays to greenfield projects that would result, if the new legislation were enacted (*Hindu Business Line*, 2011; FICCI, n.d.).

Upon assuming office in May 2014, the Modi government targeted LARRA revision as a symbol of its reformist intent and its ability to carry out its campaign promises. The options available included outright repeal of LARRA, national legislative amendments regarding specific provisions within the Act, the framing of regulations to counter the Act's effects, and/or having state governments take the initiative on reform, whether through regulation, legislation, or a combination of the two. Despite Modi's lack of a majority in Parliament's upper chamber, the Rajya Sabha, the business constituency that helped to get the BJP elected as well as the network of like-minded intellectuals that had gravitated towards the party in the years preceding Modi's election pressed for decisive action on land policy at the centre, rather than leaving the matter up to state governments. The strong preference was for amending (or, if possible, even repealing) LARRA through parliamentary action.

The Modi government thus introduced the LARRA (Amendment) Bill 2015, a series of exemptions from LARRA's two defining procedural requirements: (*i*) that projects involving the acquisition of land be subjected to an SIA (and a defined process for conducting, disseminating, and acting on the SIA); and (*ii*) that under the conditions stipulated in the Act, public authorities seeking to acquire land must obtain local 'consent'. These proposed exemptions were framed so broadly (applying to projects that sought to, among other things, promote 'rural infrastructure') that critics feared any project could conceivably evade the landowner protections that were at LARRA's core.

Hoping to win support from non-NDA parties for its plan to amend LARRA, the Modi government sought to involve state governments in the reform effort. This was because several state governments were governed by regional parties. To the extent that they had complaints with LARRA—which was promising to undercut a major source of illicit income and campaign finance—and then voiced these complaints in centre–state consultations, these state-level ruling parties could push their MPs in New Delhi to support—or at least not block—amendments to LARRA. The policy inputs provided by state governments (many ruled by Congress and other electoral rivals of the BJP) to the consultation process organized by the central government's Ministry of Rural Development (MoRD) during the latter part of 2014 revealed a range of complaints about LARRA, which (it is worth underscoring) came into force just months earlier (Jenkins, 2017). Despite these complaints, resistance to the Modi government's LARRA Amendment Bill turned out to be one of the few issues that brought opposition parties together—divided as they were on many other economic policy issues, some regional parties being considerably to the left of Congress. The opposition was also emboldened by the resistance to amending LARRA expressed by organizations affiliated with the BJP—notably, groups closely linked to the Rashtriya Swayamsevak Sangh (RSS).[8] This was all against the backdrop of growing civil society activism that sought to associate the Modi government's attempted roll back of community protections under LARRA with what movement leaders portrayed as BJP's pro-corporate, anti-poor bias.

As the difficulties facing the Modi government's reform effort began multiplying—including complaints from business leaders from India and abroad that the government lacked the perseverance necessary to execute politically fraught reforms (CNBC: *Money Control*, 2015)— Congress and regional party MPs, including their representatives in the Rajya Sabha, sensed an unparalleled opportunity to embarrass the new prime minister, who had personally aligned himself with LARRA reform in high-profile public speeches in early 2015 (*Economic Times*, 2015). The Modi government resorted to issuing an executive 'ordinance' to bring the LARRA Amendment Bill's provisions temporarily into effect. Such ordinances lapse if they are not followed by affirmative parliamentary action, according to a specified timeframe, though renewals are possible.

In August 2015, when the last of its successive ordinances was due to expire, the Modi government announced that its efforts to pass the LARRA Amendment Bill, to which it had made revisions in a failed effort to win over fence-sitters, had come to at least a temporary end (*The Hindu*, 2015). The political protests had grown too debilitating, and the prospects for support in the Rajya Sabha dimmed considerably following BJP's poor showing in the Bihar state assembly election of 2015. Throughout 2016, the Joint Committee of Parliament examining the government's LARRA amendment bill continued to deliberate, though the testimonies and

---

[8] This included both the Swadeshi Jagran Manch, an economic policy forum focused on preserving India's 'economic sovereignty', and the Bharatiya Kisan Sangh, the Sangh Parivar's official farmers' association (*Indian Express*, 2015).

written inputs from experts, including from private-sector actors, remained confidential.[9]

The land acquisition policy battle has not yet ended. And other constitutive elements of state power—including the judiciary, which has passed several orders curtailing the ability of public sector entities to evade the protections provided by LARRA—are becoming increasingly relevant. Indeed, a key facet of how state power is organized in India is the existence of a federal system. The impasse reached by the Modi government's reform efforts, once it became clear that the Rajya Sabha would block any substantial legislative amendments, underscored the extent to which the private sector's capacity to continue influencing land policies will increasingly depend on its ability to engage with state governments, which possess significant rule-making authority on land-related matters. India's Constitution leaves it in the hands of the president (acting on the advice of the prime minister) to determine whether, for subjects that the Constitution assigns jointly to the central and state governments, a state law that contradicts elements of a federal law can still stand (Verma, 2014). Article 254(2) permits state governments to pass statutes on matters contained in the 'Concurrent List' of competencies. Because Item 42 on the Concurrent List includes land issues, this has opened the door to a state-by-state approach to amending LARRA. At this writing, state-level legislation that effectively amends provisions within LARRA had been enacted in three states—Rajasthan, Gujarat, and Tamil Nadu—while in several others, including Telangana, Jharkhand, and Maharashtra, similar measures were under consideration.

OTHER POLICY DOMAINS

Land acquisition policy is a good case, though not the only one, of the Indian state undertaking substantial actions that contradict the expressed preferences of one of the dominant proprietary classes—in this case, business leaders from almost every sector. Other manifestations of state autonomy, however, have been of little direct concern to industrial capital. One of these was the UPA government's passage in

---

[9] One of the justifications for extending the committee's term was the lack of full response from state governments (*Firstpost*, 2016).

2005 of the Mahatma Gandhi National Rural Employment Guarantee Act (MGNREGA). The passage of MGNREGA—and its durability under Modi, who expressed public contempt for MGNREGA but, as with LARRA, has been unable to abolish it—is another example of the capacity of the Indian state, under certain conditions, to act with relative autonomy vis-à-vis dominant social forces. In this case, substantial decision-making autonomy could be discerned in the willingness of the leaders of the UPA, which included a cross-section of regional, centrist, and left parties, to override the objections of the agricultural communities represented by *PEDI*'s rural rich category.

Mahatma Gandhi National Rural Employment Guarantee Act guaranteed every rural household 100 days per year of paid employment on local public works projects. The projects were to be approved by and executed under the authority of village-level elected councils. Village councils would also be responsible for holding public audits of the funds expended and physical assets created, the purpose being to reduce the incidence of corruption. Groups representing medium and larger farmers—those that rely more heavily on hired labour—generally opposed the idea of guaranteed rural employment for a good reason: it would provide alternative employment opportunities, and thus increase wage-bargaining leverage, for members of the agricultural working classes, who also tend to come from non-elite social groups, particularly Dalits and Adivasis. That MGNREGA was enacted over the objections of often prosperous landowning groups is a vivid demonstration that public authorities in India continue to pursue crucial human development goals in the face of opposition from powerful political interests. A state completely dominated by a nexus of social and business elites—one with little cognizance of the need to build support for both the state and its emerging development paradigm—would surely not have embraced the rights-based model that produced not only MGNREGA, but also RTIA, the Forest Rights Act, 2006 (FRA), RTEA, NFSA, and indeed LARRA itself. These and other laws have sought to make both growth and governance more 'inclusive', providing significant opportunities for poor people and their allies to make an impact within state structures (Jenkins and Manor, 2016).

Indeed, the way MGNREGA came into being demonstrates that infiltrating government institutions to steer policymaking in a preferred direction has not been the sole preserve of elite interests. During the

UPA government, the National Advisory Council and the Planning Commission served as important institutional channels of influence for a range of non-elite groups. This 'porousness' of the Indian state can provide social activist formations, working with and on behalf of poor and marginalized communities, the ability to shape important dimensions of the country's development paradigm. Networks of civic engagement that span the state-society divide (Evans, 1997) can be used to advance counter-hegemonic agendas.

The rights-based approach represented by LARRA and MGNREGA affects the nature of the Indian state in other ways as well. The networks through which these laws were conceived and enacted have become strengthened and deepened as a result of the opportunities provided by the laws themselves. The institutions and procedures encoded into the design of much of this rights-based legislation allow coalitions of (current and especially former) civil servants, movement leaders, and policy experts, as well as sympathetic cabinet ministers and MPs, to exert leverage on public authorities to deliver on policy commitments. In fact, a notable characteristic of India's rights-based development model in recent years has been what might be termed 'the institutionalization of grievance'—that is, the creation of legislatively created spaces in which popular discontent with specific manifestations of state failure are actively encouraged. The desire to create institutions that could fuel and channel discontent, in the interest of holding public officials to account, informed the complex administrative architecture that underlies much of the legislation passed during the UPA era (Jenkins and Manor, 2017: Chapter 2). Membership in local-level oversight bodies and state-level monitoring committees are roles that provide civil society activists opportunities to obtain government-held information, question field-level implementation officials, deliver pointed commentary through the media and in local public fora, and even spur collective action by otherwise unorganized workers themselves.

The purpose-built governance mechanisms built into both MGNREGA and LARRA—whether for public auditing of expenditure or participatory methodologies to assess the likely impacts of land acquisition—are efforts to improve programme performance and to bring people directly into the process of minutely scrutinizing the work of officials. This is part of a longer-term trend in India, and elsewhere, of democratizing, or at least substantially disintermediating, processes of public accountability (Goetz and Jenkins, 2005: Chapter 3). The objective has been to construct, within each legislative act, precisely articulated procedures that can replenish and expand the political energies and capacities of non-elite groups. The architects of the UPA government's rights-based laws knew from hard-won experience as field-level activists and administrators that their participation and accountability mechanisms would perform these roles imperfectly, at best, and much worse than that most of the time. Yet, as Drèze has argued in the case of MGNREGA, '[t]he process of mobilising for effective implementation of the Act also has much value in itself, as an opportunity for unorganised workers to organise' (Drèze, 2010: 513). Thus, MGNREGA was envisioned as part of a strategy of political mobilization—a means of continuously encouraging what Drèze and others have called 'democratic struggle' (Drèze and Khera, 2014). This is an incipient shift in the character of the Indian state that holds open the possibility of preserving, or possibly even expanding, its relative autonomy from socially and politically dominant constituencies.

None of this implies that the political influence of organized industry, or indeed other powerful groups, is on the wane. Indeed, the result of the 2014 general election increased the direct access of business interests to government policymaking, not least through the appointment to key posts of several economists sympathetic to the laments of business stakeholders concerning regulatory burdens and policy instability. The Modi government dismantled both the NAC and the Planning Commission, replacing the latter with NITI Aayog, or the 'Policy Commission'. It is not at all obvious, however, that the current constriction of policy space for progressive activists is permanent, or that recent institutional reforms will squeeze out pro-poor policy-making over the longer term. This is in part because of the precedent established by MGNREGA and other rights-based initiatives that poor people and civil society groups working on their behalf have a legitimate claim to participate directly in governance activities formerly assigned to state agencies alone.

★★★

This chapter has argued that India's policymaking processes continue to be characterized by a substantial degree of state autonomy. Autonomy in this usage refers to the capacity and willingness of ensembles of actors acting within state structures to define rules and deploy resources in a manner contrary to the expressed preferences of members of the dominant coalition, which in India includes elements of the private sector. Big business, like other groups operating in India's complex polity, is both an organized lobby and a leading class formation, whose aspirations to social status and ideological hegemony are key drivers of its actions, just as they are for other groups. In recent years, this class-for-itself dimension of industrial capital has undoubtedly gained influence over the country's policy agenda as well as its political vision. Under the NDA government, there has been increased and more systematic access for the private sector, and at earlier stages in the policy review and formulation process. It is through close partnership with government agencies, for instance, that the CII, FICCI, and KPMG have collectively played a highly visible role in monitoring reform activity across India (KPMG et al., 2015). But this trend has not prevented the Indian state from taking autonomous action to advance its conception of the national interest—and in the process ensuring that new opportunities to engage in rent-seeking behaviour are introduced (Chandra, 2015). Changes to the legal framework governing compulsory land acquisition represent a significant case of relative state autonomy from dominant class interests.

That LARRA was passed, over the vociferous objections of virtually every section of India's business community, including some of its most well-networked industry associations and politically connected conglomerates, is significant. This is not to imply that India's capitalists have been politically neutered. Indeed, other objectives of industrial capital coincide more closely with the emerging vision of governing elites. It should be noted, however, that there are divisions within the business community—by sector, scope of operations (national versus regional), exposure to global markets, and so forth—that shape the direction of policy, while also providing leverage to officials, elected and bureaucratic, whose time horizons and commitment to a shared vision of national purpose are longer and larger, respectively. A similar dynamic is at work with respect to MGNREGA and the powerful rural interests opposed to its enactment, implementation, and expansion.

State autonomy in the cases discussed in this chapter was not obtained primarily through 'insulation' of officials from dominant interests, whose perspectives and representatives are disproportionately represented in both formal decision-making institutions (for example, cabinet meetings) and informal deliberative and transactional spaces (for example, negotiations over the terms of donations to political parties). Rather, a zone of policy autonomy was carved out, in part, through the cultivation of countervailing influence from representatives of non-elite groups. The channels through which non-elite perspectives were articulated, and the justifications offered, differed across the two rights-based initiatives discussed in this chapter, and varied over time as well. But in both cases, policy positions were expressed not just in terms of material welfare, but with respect to the political inclusion of poor and marginalized people as well. In both the MGNREGA and LARRA cases, governing elites worked to amplify the voices of less-privileged people. Tactical alliances between leading governing elites and social movement groups provided some of the leverage that allowed the state to take policy actions contrary to the expressed preferences of powerful constituencies.

Bardhan himself has acknowledged the growing importance of social movements and other grassroots political phenomena in a number of writings since *PEDI* was published. His perspective on their significance has been characteristically subtle—grasping both the potentialities and the pitfalls. In 2005, Bardhan noted with appreciation the techniques used by the Rajasthan-based Mazdoor Kisan Shakti Sangathan (MKSS), for instance, when he discussed his 'economists' view' of corruption and how it could be combatted (Bardhan, 2005a). Recognizing the role played by social movements, including the (MKSS), in pushing for MGNREGA and attempting to make it function more effectively, Bardhan was among the 'leading economists' who issued a statement in 2014 calling on the Modi government to improve and increase resources for MGNREGA, rather than restricting its scope or starving it of funds (critics called them a group of '*mis*leading economists'). In his updated reflections on *PEDI* published in this volume, however, Bardhan cautions that movement activism can often devolve into obstructionism, including reflexive opposition to large-scale land acquisition for industrial or infrastructural purposes—a trend that LARRA is often seen to have abetted.

In his chapter, Bardhan also highlights the crisis of legitimacy faced by the Indian state, including the market-led development paradigm it has promoted for the past three decades. In the main case presented in this chapter, governing elites demonstrated a rare capacity to address a crucial—and highly visible—dimension of this legitimacy crisis: the alienation of people's land by business interests, abetted by state power. They did so in the face of strong opposition from industrial capital. A similar dynamic characterized the passage of MGNREGA. Both public statements and second-hand accounts of private deliberations indicated that policy action was informed by a desire to prevent further erosion of the state's legitimacy as a protector of ordinary people facing economic—and in some cases physical—dislocation due to rapid economic and social change. The rights-based laws passed during the UPA government were not merely a case of contingent partisan alignments allowing one interest formation temporarily to outflank another on a specific policy matter—one where processes of implementation would again favor the powerful. There was, rather, a distinct sense that these initiatives were being undertaken in pursuit of the 'national interest', which was variously expressed but nevertheless rooted in a belief that it was necessary to preserve and renew public trust in the state, particularly in terms of its approach to global market integration.

That these considerations were aided by sustained engagement with activist groups working on behalf of non-elite groups does not indicate the further erosion of the state's monopoly over rule-making. Rather, it represented a reconfiguration of the state, and in some respects an enhancement of its capacities. The activist groups that played such a major role in the enactment of LARRA, MGNREGA, and other rights-based legislation had their policymaking capacities enhanced and their voices amplified within state institutions, including parliamentary committees, and through sustained engagement with the Supreme Court-appointed commissioners charged with monitoring government compliance with court orders issued in the landmark Right to Food lawsuit filed in 2001. These and other trends have reduced the likelihood of the state's decision-making machinery being captured by one or more dominant classes, and increased the chances of the state continuing, at important junctures, to transcend political alignments.

7 The Second Dominant Proprietary Class

Rich Farmers and the Political Economy of Indian Development

John Harriss[1]

At around the time that *The Political Economy of Development in India* (*PEDI*) was first published in 1984, the rich farmers of India had begun exercising the power of their numbers in striking public demonstrations, using the weapons of *rasta roko* (blocking of roads and railways) and massive political rallies. Pranab Bardhan had already noted 'the increasing incidence and effectiveness of farmers' agitations in different parts of India' (Bardhan, 1984: 57), but he also thought they were relatively weak by comparison with what he called 'urban lobbies', because of the money power of the latter. A few years later, it seemed possible to some observers that this view might have to be corrected. As the news magazine *India Today* reported (30 November 1987):

> Momentous happenings are taking place in the otherwise placid Indian countryside. Consider these events: a nobody becomes the messiah of farmers in western Uttar Pradesh: in Maharashtra, the chief minister succumbs to a 'rasta roko' agitation organised to demand a better price

[1] I am grateful to Pranab Bardhan for his helpful comments on an earlier version of this chapter.

for cotton: the Gujarat Government gives in to several demands after a year-long stir: in Karnataka, farmers will form a new political party.

Consider also that next March, Delhi will probably see the most amazing demonstration of farmers' unity ever. About five million people, backed by organisations in 14 states, will declare India's ryots 'debt-free' and demand a better price for their produce. If this show of strength comes off, it will mark a watershed in national politics.

In the event, the show of strength did not quite come off on this scale, but about half a million farmers did 'camp in New Delhi's stately core' (in the words of *New York Times*, 28 October 1988) in October 1988, until 'the stench became too much to bear and after a week, the Rajiv Gandhi government bowed to [a] 35-point charter of demands that included higher remunerative prices for sugarcane and waiving of electricity and water charges for farmers' (*Times of India*, 16 May 2011). It did indeed seem to observers at the time that the mobilizations of farmers—in what were called 'new farmers' movements'—marked a watershed in national politics. They seemed, very strikingly, to bear out Bardhan's analysis of the part played by the second dominant proprietary class in the political economy of Indian development—for all the qualifications that he entered about their clout—through making heavy demands upon the state for subsidies in various forms.

But then, in the course of the 1990s the farmers' movements, though they did not altogether fade from view, no longer appeared to play nearly such a prominent role in Indian politics. As *Times of India* said (16 May 2011), following the death in 2011 of Mahendra Singh Tikait—the man who had caused those many farmers to occupy the capital city in 1988—'over the last decade or more, he faded from public memory'. And it is likely that many scholars broadly agree with the argument put by Atul Kohli that over the period since the publication of Bardhan's analysis there has come about 'a basic realignment of state and class forces' in which 'the Indian state and big business groups ... [have] solidified their political and economic alliance' (2012: 3). The suggestion is—though it is not expressly stated by Kohli—that while the political economy of Indian development may once have been determined by the compromise of power between the state and the proprietary classes, there is now a narrow ruling alliance of state and big business (compare Jenkins, Chapter 6). If we accept this argument, for the moment, then what has happened to the rich farmers? Is the decline of the farmers' movements an indication that the rich farmers no longer exercise the influence that they once did? If so, then why should the needs and interests of cultivators (and notably those of the rich farmers) continue to account for a very significant share of India's still very high subsidy bill?[2] It is widely considered that Indian agriculture has been in crisis, and even the apparent resurgence of growth after about 2004 seems not to have had much success in relieving agrarian distress. What does all this have to say about the role of the rich farmers? These are questions taken up in this chapter. Following Bardhan's example, I will first briefly review trends in the agricultural economy, and in policy towards agriculture; then consider what has happened to the rich farmers over the last 30 years; examine trends in farm politics; and conclude with observations on the current political economy of development in India.

INDIAN AGRICULTURE AFTER 1980

In the early 1980s, at the time Bardhan was writing, agriculture still contributed between 35 and 40 per cent of gross domestic product (GDP). Its share had fallen to about 25 per cent at around the turn of the century. By 2013–14 the share of agriculture in GDP was less than 15 per cent, though the sector still employed more than 50 per cent of the labour force (*Economic Survey 2013–14*). Bardhan noted that the estimated agricultural growth rates of more than 2 per cent per annum in each of the two periods that he considered (1950–51 to 1964–65, and 1967–68 to 1981–82) were not significantly different, in spite of the introduction of Green Revolution in the second of them (sometimes referred to as the 'early green revolution phase'). Though different scholars have come up with varying estimates of the rate of growth of the agricultural economy since then, most reckon that the 1980s (which may be referred to as the 'late green revolution phase', the period from 1981–82 to 1991–92) saw higher rates of growth than before, and higher rates of growth than in the period following the inception of India's economic reforms in 1991—at least up to

---

[2] On developments in India's subsidy regime since *PEDI*'s publication, see Chapter 4.

about 2004.[3] A. Panagariya (2008) disagrees about the trend, finding the highest growth rate of agricultural output (at factor cost) in the period 1988–2006, of 3.4 per cent (though only 2.3 per cent for the period 2000–6). His calculations seem to be an outlier.[4] Most scholars reckon that the period from about 1997–98 through to 2003–04 was a difficult one for Indian agriculture, with growth rates of around only 0.5 per cent per annum, probably deserving the description of 'crisis' (used, for instance, by so serious a scholar as A.Vaidyanathan in 2006), though it is also clear that the agricultural economy has seen healthy growth in the more recent past. The *Economic Survey 2014–15* had it that '[t]he agricultural sector registered an annual growth of 3.8 per cent per annum in value-added in the decade since 2004–05' (Vol. II: 75). After 2012, however, there were several poor monsoons and the agricultural growth rate dropped again. The Government of India's *Economic Survey 2015–16* shows that growth in agriculture over the whole period since 1992–93 has seen at best only a marginal upward trend, accompanied by high volatility from year to year. The *Economic Survey 2017–18* offers no more positive a view.

The ideology of the farmers' movement, articulated notably by Sharad Joshi (leader of the Shetkari Sanghatana, organized especially in Maharashtra), described the main cleavage in Indian politics in the early 1980s as being between 'Bharat' and 'India', or the country versus the city. It was forcefully argued then, as it had been earlier by Charan

---

[3] R. Ramakumar's calculations of an index of agricultural production, using Ministry of Agriculture data, show an annual growth rate of 3.10 per cent for 1949–50 to 1964–5; 2.30 per cent for 1967–8 to 1980–1; 3.40 per cent for 1981–2 to 1991–2; 1.59 per cent for 1992–3 to 2010–11 (2014, Table 1)—and less than 0.5 per cent per annum for 1992–3 to 2002–3. G.S. Bhalla and G. Singh's calculations (2009) of the annual compound growth rate of the value of agricultural output depict the same trend. Mahendra Dev has said that the growth in GDP in agriculture 'recorded the highest growth rate of more than three per cent per annum during the 1980s', and that there was 'significant deterioration since the mid-1990s' (2009: 23). Jens Lerche, however, has calculated averages of yearly growth rates of agricultural GDP at factor cost of 1981–2 to 1990–1: 3.8 per cent; 1991–2 to 1996–7: 4.9 per cent; 1997–8 to 2003–4: 0.5 per cent; 2003–4 to 2011–12: 2.9 per cent (2013, Table 1).

[4] Lerche's calculations alone (see note 3) lend some credence to Panagariya's analysis.

Singh, that the exchange between the agricultural and urban industrial sectors was heavily biased in favour of the latter, though as Bardhan pointed out in *PEDI*, the evidence then available on the terms of trade (TOT) and on inter-sectoral resource flows did not bear out this claim. He pointed out, too, that 'the administered purchase price has been well above the weighted average cost of production ... since the mid-sixties for wheat and since the mid-seventies for rice', also noting that the principal beneficiaries had been rich farmers in Punjab, Haryana, Uttar Pradesh (UP), and Andhra Pradesh. His argument was in line with that advanced by A. Mitra (1977) that the state tilted the terms of trade in favour of the agricultural sector, coupling this benefit with other direct subsidies to agriculture, in order to win the political support of the surplus-producing farmers.

Recent evidence points in the same direction. Data presented by Mahendra Dev show the terms of trade moving towards agriculture in the 1980s, and being favourable to agriculture from about the time of the inception of India's economic reforms in 1990–91 (2009: 25). A more recent analysis from the *Economic and Political Weekly* Research Foundation (EPWRF) (Krishnaswamy and Rajakumar, 2015) shows that the trends in the TOT, according to three different series, saw even an accelerated improvement in favour of agriculture after 2004–05.[5] In the period from then until 2013–14, the compounded annual growth rate of agricultural prices of 10.7 per cent was more than twice of manufactures at 4.7 per cent. The same analysis shows that one cause for TOT remaining in favour of agriculture was the continuous rise of procurement prices, well ahead of the wholesale price index for all the major farm crops (except for cotton) over the last 20 years, and at a higher rate than the costs of production.

Favourable terms of trade did not, however, arrest the increasing inequality both within the rural economy and between the rural and urban economies. The latter trend lends credence to the impression that the agricultural economy is being discriminated against, the evidence on relative prices notwithstanding. The EPWRF then also makes the vitally important point, as did Bardhan, that increasing procurement prices benefit only a small proportion of all Indian cultivators, the vast majority of whom depend upon foodgrain purchases for most of the

---

[5] See also *Economic Survey 2014–15* (Vol. II, 75).

year. Indeed, according to the High Level Committee set up by the Bharatiya Janata Party (BJP) government in August 2014 to restructure and reform the Food Corporation of India—which makes purchases from farmers at administered prices—only 6 per cent of farmers in 2012–13 sold any foodgrains to procurement agencies (*The Hindu*, 17 February 2015).[6] It is a fair bet that a high proportion of them still came from Punjab, Haryana, western UP, and Andhra Pradesh. It seems, then, that it is all too likely that the agricultural economy as a whole can be doing quite badly but that the rich farmers can still do well. I will return to these points, about the significance of the continuing sharp inequalities in rural society in the next section of the chapter.

Growth figures aside, Bardhan noted in 2009 that 'the agricultural sector is in bad shape' (2009: 31), and both the then prime minister and deputy chairman of the Planning Commission, in speeches made in June 2010, expressed regret at the low rates of growth of the agricultural economy. Why hasn't the agricultural economy done better? Thirty years ago, *PEDI* 'repeatedly emphasise[d] the importance of public investment for agricultural growth' (14). It went on to say: 'Public management of agricultural infrastructure is as (in the short to medium run, probably more) important as public investment' (15). Both points still stand. P. Balakrishnan, for example, has noted that public capital formation in agriculture has been declining for 25 years (*The Hindu*, 14 February 2015); and the *Economic Survey 2013–14* pointed out the long-run trend for public expenditure to cede its share in total gross capital formation (GCF) in agriculture to the private sector. The *Survey* argued, too, that 'quality of public GCF, which is largely directed toward subsidies, is also of concern' (Vol. II: 153). The *Economic Survey 2014–15* argues that '[g]iven the vast investment needs of the sector,

---

[6] Ramakumar and Bakshi (2015) report that the Situation Assessment Survey carried out by the National Sample Survey Office (NSSO) in 2013 shows that:

> Only 31 per cent of paddy farmers and 39 per cent of wheat farmers were even aware of the MSP [minimum support price] scheme. Worse, only 13.5 per cent of paddy farmers and 16.2 per cent of wheat farmers sold their harvest to procurement agencies. The reason: shortage/unavailability of procurement agencies and local purchasers. In fact independent village surveys conducted by the Foundation for Agrarian Studies, Bengaluru, have also demonstrated that actual prices received by farmers were lower than MSP.

greater public investment would only help increase private investment' (Vol. II: 81). The *Economic Survey 2015–16*, on the other hand, drew attention again to *PEDI*'s point about the management of agricultural infrastructure, arguing:

> [T]here are issues of expansion in irrigation and its efficiency, growth of capital formation in the sector has been declining and there is volatility in the markets, especially of prices, altering and distorting cropping patterns of some crops. This suggests that for the agriculture sector to achieve a target of 4 per cent, a significantly different approach has to be followed. (99)

Vaidyanathan, in his analysis of the crisis of Indian agriculture of 2006, made the same arguments that Bardhan had in 1984. He noted 'a slowdown in investment, especially public investment, in the agricultural sector' (2006: 4011), but argued forcefully that more investment alone would not solve the problems of Indian agriculture. What is needed, he said, is a whole range of institutional and policy reforms— the transformation, indeed, of public management of agricultural infrastructure—so as to establish 'an environment that enables and induces users of land and water to make more prudent and efficient use of these resources' (2006: 4014). In 1984, *PEDI* had said that the purpose of the emphasis that it placed on the importance of public investment in agriculture was 'not merely to contrast this with the usual liberal emphasis on favourable price policy for farm products and the usual radical emphasis on land reforms, but more to link up with the larger questions ... of the political economy of public investment and the nature of the state'—that were, of course, the focus of the book. It went on to show that the burdens on the state for underwriting extensive subsidies that benefited especially rich farmers (subsidies of output prices and subsidies to reduce the costs of key inputs of fertilizers, water, electricity, diesel fuel, and credit) reduced the revenues that might have been reinvested in public capital formation in agriculture. While supporting this argument, more than two decades later Vaidyanathan went further, arguing that 'government policies for pricing of water, electricity, fertilizers and credit ... induce demand growth far in excess of available supplies ... and encourage inefficient use of scarce agricultural resources' (2006: 4013). The longitudinal studies of a region of northern Tamil Nadu, over the 1980s and into the 1990s, brought together by B. Harriss-White and S. Janakarajan (2004), provide ample empirical backing for Vaidyanathan's argument. More recently, noting that '[a]lmost all of the increase in total fixed capital investment [in agriculture] in the 2000s came from private sources', R. Ramakumar says that a great deal of this investment has gone into the exploitation of groundwater. And experience has shown that unregulated expansion of groundwater irrigation leads to mining of the resource—or 'inefficient use of scarce resources' (2014: 13).

It has long been argued that Indian agriculture suffers from what A. Gulati—one of the most forceful and influential of the critics of the policies that successive Indian governments have pursued in regard to agriculture—calls the 'subsidy syndrome'. He has consistently expressed both the view that 'subsidies on key inputs have lost their rationale and are now crowding out productive investments, damaging environment, accentuating inequity and promoting inefficient cropping patterns', and the argument that 'raising the prices of these inputs is only a partial solution' (Gulati and Sharma, 1995: A101). Whether the solution must begin with 'liberalising the output markets'—as Gulati argued—remains controversial and there are good reasons for supporting Ramakumar's argument that 'non-price factors—inputs, technology, institutions and infrastructure … significantly determine growth in farm output' (2014: 16). But this is not the place in which to engage in the debate over agricultural policy. The point is that subsidies remain a critical feature of the sector, as they have done pretty much from the time of the emergence in the 1960s and 1970s of what P.B. Mehta and M. Walton refer to as the input provision model for Indian agriculture: 'a specific political economy of agriculture … fundamentally organized around a combination of state-mediated provision of inputs … and guaranteed markets' (2014: 28). Even now it is argued in the *Economic Survey 2013–14* of the Government of India that '[o]ne of the major reasons for the increase in the centre's fiscal deficit after 2008–09 has been the build-up in subsidies …. [which have seen a] sharp increase … from 1.42 per cent of GDP in 2007–08 to 2.26 per cent in 2013–14 (RE)'. And at this time, subsidized food (as much a subsidy of surplus-producing farmers as of consumers) and fertilizer subsidies accounted for almost two-thirds of all the subsidies explicitly listed in the Budget. *The Economic Survey 2014–15*, in advocating the shift away from subsidies to productive investments, notes that 'public expenditure on agriculture is only one-fourth of expenditure towards food and fertilizer subsidies' (Vol. II: 89).

In sum, the lack of public investment in agriculture, poor management of agricultural infrastructure, and public expenditure on subsidies that benefit disproportionately wealthier farmers in particular parts of the country—Punjab, Haryana, western UP, and coastal Andhra Pradesh, which are the main suppliers of the Public Distribution System—remain as much of a problem now as when Bardhan wrote in 1983–84. These observations would seem to suggest that the power of the second dominant proprietary class of Bardhan's model remains significant.

WHAT HAS HAPPENED TO THE RICH FARMERS? INDIA'S AGRARIAN STRUCTURE TODAY

Bardhan argued that 'except in localized pockets of North and central India, the class of landlords which is uninterested in profitable cultivation, but primarily involved in usury and speculation, enjoying the status value of large landed estates and the social power of domination over a retinue of bonded labourers—the class usually described in the Indian literature as "semi-feudal"—has largely disappeared' (Bardhan, 1984: 48). Ignoring the fiercely contested 'mode of production debate' of the 1970s, he argued that agrarian capitalism was by then well established, especially in the better-irrigated tracts. *Political Economy of Development in India* took as its working definition of 'rich farmers' those with holdings of 4 hectares and more,[7] and referred to evidence that those with such holdings accounted for 19 per cent of the rural population, 60 per cent of the cultivated area, and 53 per cent of crop output in 1975.

According to the Agricultural Census of 2010–11,[8] holdings of 4 hectares and above now account for only 4.95 per cent of the total, and for 31.8 per cent of the operated area. According to the 59th Round Report of the National Sample Survey (NSS), ownership holdings of 4 ha and more in extent already accounted for only 3.6 per cent of the

---

[7] This is certainly only a rough way of defining the class, because so much depends on land quality, water availability, and the crops that can be cultivated.

[8] Available at http://www.agcensus.nic.in on 17 February 2015.

total in 2003–04, having made up just under 8 per cent (7.87 per cent) in 1982. These observations might seem to suggest that the 'rich farmers', as Bardhan defined them, are not as significant as they were when he was writing. But over the last 30 years, it is quite clear that there has been considerable further fragmentation of landholdings. According to the Agricultural Census, the small and marginal holdings (those of up to 2 hectares in extent) accounted for 74 per cent of all operated holdings in 1980–81 and 85 per cent of them in 2010–11. The 59th Round Report shows that in 2003–04 small and marginal holdings (defined in the same way) already accounted for 90.4 per cent of all ownership holdings in the country (up from 81.3 per cent in 1982). V. Rawal's analysis (2008) of data from the 59th Round shows that 31 per cent of rural households across the country as a whole owned no land at all, and another 30 per cent owned less than 0.4 hectares, while only 5.2 per cent of households owned more than 3 hectares (though those owning 3 hectares and more accounted altogether for 43.6 per cent of the cultivated area). The absolute numbers and the relative share in the rural population of households without land had been increasing—perhaps by as much as six percentage points since 1992—while inequality in land ownership had also increased. The share of the rich farmers amongst all rural households has declined over the last 30 years, and their share of the operated area with it, but given the extent of fragmentation of holdings overall inequality has increased.[9] It must be noted that this rise in land-holding inequality and increased landlessness are not due to any grand development of capitalist agriculture, but are mainly down to the facts of population growth and the consequences of divisible inheritance.[10]

[9] Of course, no one village study can be taken as 'representative', but the findings of Ramachandran, Rawal, and Swaminathan (2010) in a careful study of Ananthavaram, Guntur District, Andhra Pradesh, are characteristic of findings in some other longitudinal village studies. In 1974, households owning 10 acres and more (≥4 hectares) accounted for less than 5 per cent of all households in the village, but owned more than 50 per cent of the land owned by village households. By 2006, the same figures were 1.4 per cent and 25.6 per cent. But landlessness in the village and the extent of inequality in land ownership had increased sharply.

[10] Pranab Bardhan and co-authors demonstrate, in a study of the evolution of land distribution in West Bengal over the period 1967–2004, that the effects of land reform were negligible by comparison with those of population growth (Bardhan et al., 2014).

Their share of all landholdings has declined, no doubt, and many of the 'rich farmers' may not be very rich at all in absolute terms, but data from detailed village studies in many parts of the country confirm that there remains considerable concentration of economic power in rural India. A study, for example, of household incomes in 13 of the villages studied by the Project on Agrarian Relations in India of the Foundation for Agrarian Studies in Karnataka, Andhra Pradesh, Maharashtra, Rajasthan, UP, and Madhya Pradesh found both that 'the distribution of household incomes was highly unequal in all villages' and that 'the gap between socio-economic classes in terms of income was huge. In every village, there was a small class of landlords, capitalist farmers, and rich peasants whose mean incomes were more than 10 times that of manual worker households. This class has clearly made substantial gains from the process of high economic growth in India during the neo-liberal period' (Bakshi, Das, and Swaminathan, 2014). On the other hand, according to the Foundation's calculations from its village surveys in Andhra Pradesh, Uttar Pradesh, and Maharashtra, it was virtually impossible in 2005–06 for the marginal and small land-holders, operating up to 2 hectares—which means all but about 10 per cent of rural households—to earn an income sufficient for family survival from cultivation alone. Bhalla has gone further, arguing that 'the hard fact is that the typical household operating a holding of less than 4 ha [accounting for 96 percent of all farm households] cannot cover actual expenses out of the combined income from crop cultivation and animal husbandry' (2014: 15),[11] which also suggests the gap that exists between the rich farmers (the remaining 4 per cent of rural households) and the rest. The economics of crop cultivation in India remain precarious for a majority of farmers, as the Situation Assessment Survey for 2013 conducted by the NSSO clearly demonstrates (Ramakumar and Bakshi, 2015).

The survival of many people in rural India depends upon their hiring out their labour and/or on engaging in some kind of non-agricultural activity, typically involving self-employment. Bakshi, Das, and Swaminathan (2014), in their studies of household incomes, found

[11] Ramakumar and Bakshi (2015) report from the 2013 Situation Assessment Survey that the 69.4 per cent of agricultural households possessing less than 2.5 acres of land had average household incomes that were less than their average consumption expenditures.

that on an average households reported incomes from at least three sources.[12] Village studies from across the country confirm these points, and there can be no doubt of the greatly increased importance, over the last 30 years, of migration from villages for work, including both rural–urban and rural–rural migration, commuting from villages, and short- and longer-term circular migration. There are different estimates of the absolute numbers involved, ranging from 30 to 100 million.

As people from many rural households have had to move out of their villages in order to find work, so the rich farmers—as *PEDI* already noted—have invested outside, and in different types of non-agricultural activity: 'moneylending, trading, transport, and other businesses and services. This kind of portfolio diversification has made these families less susceptible to the vagaries of agricultural production, apart from strengthening their urban political and economic connections' (Bardhan, 1984: 48). These trends have gone further over the last three decades, and they mean that the gap between (urban) 'India' and (rural) 'Bharat' that was such an important part of the ideology of the farmers' movements is no longer deep in most parts of India. There can be a few rich farmer families where some members do not belong to the professional and business classes.

Now, as J. Lerche has argued in a preliminary study of patterns of agrarian accumulation:

> The big capitalist farmers from the agriculturally most developed states are in a league of their own. In the last decade they have shown their economic strength by seeking out cheaper additional lands for their ventures outside their home states where land is expensive and land ceilings sometimes are too vigorously implemented for their taste. For example, farmers from Punjab, Haryana and west UP have been buying up land in the state of Chhattisgarh and abroad, e.g., in Georgia, and Ethiopia; while Kerala farmers have been leasing land in neighbouring Karnataka, especially for growing vanilla. (Lerche, 2014: 15; sources given in the original)

He goes on to say that less is known about accumulation by agricultural capitalists outside of agriculture, though studies from different parts of

---

[12] See also Mahendra Dev (2009: 27): '[E]ven an average farmer household is not able to earn from cultivation half of the income needed to cross the poverty line.'

the country show up the significance of state-related accumulation (for example, Pattenden's [2011] evidence on the revenues from their 'gatekeeping' activities that accrue to big farmers in Karnataka);[13] education and urban/overseas jobs (see Jeffrey, Jeffery, and Jeffery, 2008, on the investments of Jat farmers in western UP in education and government jobs); trading, agro-processing, and moneylending (see studies by Harriss-White, 2010); as well as through land sales. In some states, in the South and West, agricultural capitalists have also moved into industrial production—the Patels of Gujarat, Reddys of coastal Andhra, and Gounders of western Tamil Nadu are notable examples—though Lerche points out: 'There is no neat fit between agricultural development and industrial investments' (2014: 26).

All of this is to say that over most of the country, there have been strong tendencies over the last 20 years or more for both the rural rich and very many small peasant farmers and landless labourers to turn outside their villages. As one ethnographer has put it, 'more and more people are losing interest in village affairs' (Singh, 2005: 3173), while the sociologist D. Gupta suggests that there is a sense in which the Indian village is 'vanishing'. He also argues that '[w]hat land reforms and land redistribution could not do, demography and sub-division of holdings has done to land ownership. Where are the big landlords? There are some, but they are few and far between' (2005: 752). The evidence referred to above shows that this is at best a partial truth. Certainly landlordism of the semi-feudal type has largely disappeared, exactly as *PEDI* argued. It is also true, as I pointed out earlier, that both census and NSS data and village studies, show the declining numbers and declining share of all landholdings owned by those who can be called 'rich farmers'. But it appears also to be the case that inequality in land ownership has increased, and there can be no doubt of the continuing significance of the power of the larger landholders, perhaps especially where there is an overlap of class and caste power, as Jeffrey and his

---

[13] Pattenden defines 'gatekeeping' as 'the act of channelling formal and informal resources between the state and society for private economic and political gain'. He argues that 'whilst traditional forms of control over the labouring class have been eroded, gatekeeping increasingly allows the dominant class to exert a more subtle form of political control, which in turn facilitates processes of accumulation' (2011: 164).

co-authors (2008) show with regard to the Jats of western UP. There is evidence, no doubt, of the 'declining power of caste hierarchies' and of what sociologists have long described as 'dominance' (Manor, 2010). Though V.K. Ramachandran and his co-authors, for instance—*contra* Gupta—describe the continuing presence of those whom they consider to be 'landlords' in villages in Andhra Pradesh, they also note 'a certain loosening of the traditional social grip of the landlords' (2010: 28), in line with the notion of the decline of 'dominance'. But the idea that control over land is no longer significant as a basis of status and of both economic and political power is misleading. Maybe 'dominance' is no longer of much account in the village, but those who have been rural power holders have often secured the reproduction of their power regionally, partly by means of the diversification of their economic interests—as Jeffrey and his co-authors show with regard to the Jats in western UP (see Harriss, 2013, for some elaboration of these arguments).

FARMER POLITICS

But are not the arguments that have just been advanced falsified by the evidence of the decline of the 'new farmers' movements', of which so much—for good or ill—was expected in the later 1980s? In an article published in 2005, G. Omvedt provides a historical sketch of the movements, arguing that '[a]s a whole the farmers' movement … has found itself in a period of decline in the 1990s and the early years of the new century … Splits and ideological uncertainties have affected all organisations' (2005: 187). Several factors account for this, including personality clashes between different leaders, and then in the 1990s a major split over liberalization and globalization. Sharad Joshi of the Shetkari Sanghatana, based in Maharashtra, came out boldly in support, while Professor Najundaswamy of the Karnataka Rajya Rayatu Sangha (KRRS) became one of the darlings internationally of the anti-globalization movement. The strength of the Bharatiya Kisan Union of Mahendra Singh Tikait has withered away, though it still survives as a farmers' organization.

Studies of the KRRS by Pattenden are particularly illuminating. Whereas the movement was represented within the anti-capitalist globalization movement as 'a mass movement … organized at grassroots in a decentralized way, and opposed to all forms of domination, including casteism and patriarchy', Pattenden found that 'at its social bases [it] has usually been controlled by dominant caste men often engaged in perpetuating caste- and gender-based forms of domination' (2005: 1979). The KRRS's international allies in the People's Global Action network were mostly uninformed, for example, 'about the abuse of Scheduled Castes (SCs) by higher caste village members' in places where the KRRS was strong (2005: 1979). And even whilst it was becoming one of the darlings of the anti-globalization movement, the KRRS was rapidly losing support in Karnataka. In the village that Pattenden studied, up to the mid-1990s large numbers of people were mobilized by the association, which they had been 'prepared to die for':

> Some had regularly attended meetings in the village and nearby city; many had spent time in prison; most had attended rallies. In 1987, soon after the first wave of mobilisation had swept through the village, 50 per cent of the village's inhabitants had attended a mass KRRS rally in Hubli. Fifteen years later, in February 2002, scarcely 20 people from Panchnagaram [the name of the village] travelled to Bangalore to demonstrate at the threatened hikes in electricity costs. (Pattenden, 2005: 1980)

All the conditions in the village that had been conducive to KRRS mobilizations started to break down in the middle of the 1990s. The intensification of commercial agriculture in the 1980s had created circumstances that provided for cross-class mobilization and the burying of caste and class differences by conflict between the peasantry generally and the local state and merchants. At the same time, the profitability of agriculture had given the richer peasants time for engaging in mobilizational activity. The decline in the profitability of agriculture after the early–mid-1990s changed all of this. Non-agricultural activities and incomes became much more important, and those more influential people who had been the local leaders of the KRRS became interested in 'gatekeeping activities' instead—roles in which they mediate between other people and the state, and are able to use the roles to secure resources for themselves (for example, from the allocation of ration cards). In sum, '[t]he sense of togetherness that had accompanied the KRRS's rise had been replaced by a growing social fragmentation with people "looking after themselves"' (2005: 1982)—so that collective action has become increasingly difficult.

S.S. Jodhka (2006) reports similar observations from Punjab: in the context of the crisis of agriculture in the state, agricultural households have become increasingly diversified, the landowning classes have become increasingly differentiated, and the farmers' movement has been fragmented (there were then 10 different organizations in Punjab claiming to represent farmers' interests).

Alongside the declining influence of the 'new farmers' movements', however, there has come about what Y. Yadav (1996) referred to in the mid-1990s as India's 'second democratic upsurge', associated with the rise to power of backward caste leaders and their followings—most strikingly in Bihar and UP, where it involved especially the Yadav caste cluster. This very significant social and political development of the last 30 years was at least partly anticipated by *PEDI*, which referred to the formation of what Bardhan called 'larger caste affiliations', or 'aggregative castes', which he thought were being strengthened by electoral politics. He went on: 'These affiliations and the associated network of patriarchal and patrimonial ties are also useful tools of class hegemony for the rich farmers, who can exercise their economic and cultural domination even without well-knit class organisations and even when they are geographically dispersed' (Bardhan, 1984: 50)

This describes fairly well what L. Michelutti (2008) has analysed ethnographically and historically in her study of the formation of the Yadav identity and its politics; while J. Witsoe's examination (2013) of the politics of Bihar under Lalu Prasad Yadav shows how the political mobilizations of Other Backward Castes (OBCs) in the state serves the interests of rich farmers. It is important to note, as well, that at least one amongst the farmers' movements—Tikait's Bharatiya Kisan Union—was instrumental in the mobilization of a Jat identity, which has contributed in turn to the rise of communalism in western UP. Research by Ramakumar shows the interrelations between the revival of *khap panchayats* (lineage panchayats) in Jat villages in UP, and both the formation of a Jat identity and the mobilization of the Bharatiya Kisan Union (BKU). They have more recently become vehicles for the spread of communalism (Ramakumar, 2016). As scholars such as Z. Hasan argued in the 1990s, the construction of the Jat peasant identity by the BKU opened up spaces conducive to the development of communalism (Hasan, 1998).

For all that, the rich farmers' movements no longer have the power that they seemed to have in the late 1980s to early 1990s, therefore, agricultural interests—which may be articulated through caste politics—can still exert a great deal of influence in the politics of major states. Rich farmer lobbies can invoke large numbers behind them, given the continuing large share of the labour force that is engaged in agriculture, even as they appropriate the lion's share of the subsidies. A striking example of this was in the way in which Y.S. Reddy ('YSR') succeeded in tapping the widespread anger felt in Andhra Pradesh over the agrarian crisis to defeat Chandrababu Naidu in the state legislature elections of 2004; and he began his term in office as chief minister dramatically by issuing orders to provide free electricity to farmers within seconds of his swearing in. Subsequently, the YSR government issued a waiver on outstanding agricultural loans, provided for input subsidies, and made heavy investments in irrigation. As an editorial of the *Economic and Political Weekly* noted, 'this served two purposes, implementing the traditional agenda that only a massive exploitation of water resources could address the problems of agriculture and simultaneously oiling the wheels of patronage' (*EPW*, 2009: 5). The 'wheels of patronage' very often worked to the advantage of rich farmers from amongst the Reddys.

The political significance of agricultural interests is also reflected in decisions of the central government to implement agricultural loan waiver schemes, first in 1990–91 and then again in the central budget for 2008–09. Though many small as well as big farmers may have benefited in the short term from being relieved of their debts, over the longer run these schemes have been damaging to the interests especially of small and marginal farmers. Following the implementation of the scheme in 1990–91, rural banking institutions reduced their lending to small borrowers, who became increasingly reliant on private moneylenders—some of them, of course, rich farmers—over the succeeding years (EPWRF, 2008).[14] As Mehta and Walton say, governments, both in the states and at the centre, have relied on populist

---

[14] These points are demonstrated through the comparison of findings of the All-India Investment and Debt Survey of 2013 with those of the same survey conducted in 1992. Ramakumar and Bakshi (2015) report that the share of debt from informal credit sources increased sharply, while 'the share of debt outstanding from commercial banks fell from 33.7 per cent to 25.1 per cent for rural households'.

approaches to the rural economy. This has proven fairly successful as a political strategy in spite of relatively weak results in regard to the performance of the agricultural economy, income growth and poverty reduction (2014: 44–9).

FARMERS AND THE POLITICAL ECONOMY OF DEVELOPMENT IN INDIA TODAY

The events of the last 30 years, and the policies with regard to agriculture pursued by successive governments of India, suggest the continuing relevance of *PEDI*'s analysis. There are good reasons for supporting Kohli's view that it is now the narrow alliance between state and big business which determines the pattern of Indian development, and the agricultural economy—given its shrinking share in GDP—perhaps no longer exerts the drag that it once did on overall economic growth. In Marxian terms 'the agrarian transition to capitalism' has been bypassed (Lerche, 2013). But the dominant partners have still had to make compromises with rural interests for electoral reasons—as the agricultural loan waiver of the 2008–09 budget starkly demonstrated, and more recently the concessions that Narendra Modi had to make in 2015 over the changes that his government sought to bring about in the Land Acquisition Act.[15] The controversy provoked by the attempt of the government to relax certain provisions of the Act, partly, at least, in order to facilitate the acquisition of agricultural land for business purposes, is a reflection of the political salience today of land as real estate. Struggle over land acquisition has become the key battleground of rural India, of much greater significance than the 'classic' agrarian conflict between land and labour (Levien, 2013). So concerned was he over the way in which his government appeared to be blatantly 'pro-business' that the prime minister devoted much of one of his monthly *Mann Ki Baat* radio addresses, on 22 March 2015, to defending the government against the charge that it was 'anti-farmer': 'I have heard the rumours being spread', he said, 'that Modi government is passing a law, which will provide less remuneration to the farmers and

---

[15] The Right to Fair Compensation and Transparency in the Land Acquisition, Rehabilitation and Resettlement Act, 2013, passed into law by the United Progressive Alliance government (see also Chapter 6).

they will not receive the full compensation. My dear farmer brothers and sisters, I cannot even think of committing this sin.'[16] Modi is also unlikely—given the rich farmers' continuing influence in the politics of major states, such as in Andhra Pradesh—to commit the 'sin' of doing anything very much to cut the subsidies from which they benefit. Given that Modi is generally seen as being closely allied with particular corporate interests, the urgency of his defence against the charge that he is 'anti-farmer' partly counters Kohli's argument about the changed character of the Indian state.

Prime Minister Modi's efforts to defend himself and his administration against the charge of being 'anti-farmer' became subject to increasing challenge with the resurgence of rural protest. Journalists wrote of a prolonged demonstration in 2017 by farmers from Tamil Nadu, in New Delhi, that the last time the capital had seen such an agitation was in 1988; while of Maharashtra, it was said that not since an agitation in 1982 organized by the Shetkari Sanghatana, 'has there been a united farmers' action on the scale that the state witnessed in early June [of 2017]' (Bavadam, 2018). There were large-scale agitations in Madhya Pradesh, Punjab and Haryana, Rajasthan, UP, and elsewhere. In March 2018, there took place a remarkable 'Long March' of 40,000 or more mainly small farmers and landless peasants, many of them adivasis, from Nasik to Mumbai, a distance of 180 km. Their demands were for the waiving of farmers' bank debts, and for the payment of minimum support prices at the level (1.5 times the cost of production) recommended by an official committee headed by the eminent scientist M.S. Swaminathan, as well as for the proper implementation of the Forest Rights Act, supporting the rights of forest dwellers. In October 2018, a demonstration of large numbers of farmers in Delhi led to violent clashes with the police. Many thousands more, both farmers and labourers, from all over the country, organized by over 200 farmers' unions, marched through the streets of the capital at the end of November in 2018. Rural distress was a major issue in the critical state elections that were taking place at the same time in Telangana, Madhya Pradesh, Rajasthan, and Chhattisgarh (Jebaraj, 2018).

The social base of the protest movements of 2018 may have changed a little from those of the 1980s—though even then, the commercial

---

[16] Quoted in Sen (2015).

farmers had some success in securing support from farm labour for their cause. The demands that are being made, over prices, remain the same. And it remains the case that the rich farmers of a few states benefit most from the agriculture-related subsidies that successive central governments have not succeeded in reducing at all significantly. These subsidies contribute substantially, in turn, to the persisting fiscal deficits that remain a constraint in India's economic development. Explicit subsidies for agriculture stuck at about 1.5 per cent of GDP through the 1990s. They were then reduced to 1 per cent of GDP by 2004, but subsequently rose again—most dramatically in 2008 because of the loan waiver (Mehta and Walton, 2014: Figure 24). These explicitly budgeted subsidies include neither the economic cost of water, nor the costs of agriculture's share of electricity subsidies. Yet, as Bardhan pointed out and as many others have argued over the years, the use of public resources for these subsidies may be seen as being at the expense of public investment in agriculture, which has for long been neglected—with adverse consequences for the agricultural economy as a whole, if not for the rich farmers who are their principal beneficiaries.

8 All Shook Up?

State Professionals in the Reform Era

Elizabeth Chatterjee

Pranab Bardhan's slim masterwork *The Political Economy of Development in India* (hereafter *PEDI*) is best remembered for its contention that by the early 1980s the state's room for manoeuvre was severely constrained by competition between three dominant classes: rich farmers, big business interests, and white-collar 'professionals'.[1] The core of the latter 'third dominant class'—and thus the focus of this chapter—comprised skilled employees within the public sector itself, the state professionals on whom the political elite had to rely to implement their policy decisions.

Even as the book was published in 1984, liberalization was beginning to reshape the country's political economy. Three decades on, economic reforms have ostensibly undermined the economic, ideological, and policy dominance of the Indian state. The orthodoxy among the business commentariat is that the state has been 'gradually moving out of the way—not graciously, but kicked and dragged into implementing economic reforms' (Das, 2006: 3). This chapter uses *PEDI*'s original

---

[1] While concentrating on *PEDI*, where appropriate I also draw for clarification on Bardhan's related political economy writings from the same period. I am grateful to the conference participants at All Souls College, Oxford, for their thoughtful comments.

analytical categories to examine the empirical basis for this assumption: has the bureaucracy in India, and the public sector that provided its primary source of rents, really undergone a reluctant sea-change since 1984?

This chapter shows, first, that the public sector has proved surprisingly resilient. There have been striking continuities in the upper bureaucracy's absolute size and salaries, and the scarcity value of their education. The public sector's economic contribution has also declined only slowly, even as its role has changed to more explicitly support the private sector (see Chapter 6). This corroborates Bardhan's interim conclusion, from the epilogue to the book's expanded edition of 1998: 'one should not exaggerate the extent of shift in the basic political equilibrium' (Bardhan, 1998: 130).

There have been significant changes nonetheless. In 1984, Bardhan took pains to distinguish his elite public sector professionals from the largely unskilled mass of 'the salariat', a mainstay of existing political economy theories. Though this distinction was seen as somewhat quixotic at the time, this chapter suggests that it provides useful insights into the transformations of the public bureaucracy in the liberalization era.

Today elite bureaucrats, already the most contentious inclusion among Bardhan's three dominant classes, no longer resemble a dominant class. This is less due to any diminution in the structural importance of the public sector, as is commonly assumed, than because their cohesion has waned both internally and vis-à-vis other elite groups. The twin sources of its rents—scarce education and control of state resources—have helped to *fragment* the third dominant class. While some professionals have lost out from liberalization, other segments, especially central government technocrats, have tentatively embraced aspects of the reforms. Bardhan's professionals thus no longer appear to behave as or consider themselves a class. Their fragmentation has facilitated the increased room for manoeuvre of Bardhan's potentially autonomous 'state elite', the national political leadership, at least in some sectors.

At the same time, further obstacles to liberalization have arisen from another quarter of the public sector, as Bardhan's updated analyses have acknowledged. Socio-economic change has bolstered a rather different state class: the amorphous mass of petty state functionaries and those aspiring to join their ranks. This group has at times helped to block or undermine implementation of the state elite's liberalization project in sectors where the discretion of 'street-level' bureaucrats is key, especially at the level of India's provincial states. The salariat is not a new dominant class, however, being both irreconcilably differentiated internally and a junior partner in an alliance of convenience with 'political middlemen' (who also played little role in Bardhan's 1984 analysis).

Together the ambivalent fate of the fragmented professionals and the petty state class help to explain the halting and uneven trajectory of liberalization in India. Even if the coherence of the old 'third dominant class' has been a casualty of liberalization, bureaucrats remain a crucial set of actors in the game of conflict and cooperation that continues to define India's political economy.

THE THIRD DOMINANT CLASS

Today, *PEDI* is often treated as the archetypal society-centric theory of the Indian state (although this is a partial interpretation at best; see Chapter 1 and Chapter 6). Bolstering the impression that Bardhan's state was compromised was the composition of his third class of 'professionals', the most complex and controversial of his dominant groups.[2] As J. Toye noted (1988: 113), the tripartite schema was a masterful synthesis of two rival political economy paradigms: the Indian scholarship on urban–rural conflict developed in reaction to M. Lipton's (1977) urban bias thesis (Bardhan, 1998: 54–5), and the 'rent-seeking society' theory of competition over bureaucratic rent creation and distribution. The concept of the professionals fused both lineages.

Nominally, Bardhan's professionals were the broad urban elites. The class's *proprietary* nature rested on their scarce 'property': their 'human capital in the form of education, skills and technical expertise', from which they were able to extract rents in both the public and private sectors, reinforced by exclusivist upper-caste networks and cultural traits (51–3).[3] This was evidenced both by the bureaucracy's diversion

[2] A. Rudra (1989) and J.D. Pedersen (1992) both disagreed that the professionals constituted a dominant class, for example, seeing them as merely a co-opted junior partner.

[3] This echoed Raj (1973: 1191) on the 'quasi-rent' extractable from knowledge and skills, as Bardhan (1993: 342) acknowledged.

of investment away from mass education in order to 'protect their scarcity rent', and their bitter resistance to reservations in medical and engineering schools.

In practice, though, Bardhan's analysis focused on public sector professionals—and, accordingly, so does this chapter. The *dominant* nature of this 'new rentier class' rested on their location within the state, which provided direct, monopolistic control of resources from which they were able to multiply their rents (52). Their dominance was therefore inextricably bound up with the Indian state's developmental project. Nationalizations, new regulations, the growth of the defence establishment, and endemic overmanning were all 'used largely to expand the job prospects and security of the professionals and white-collar workers' (58), creating 'a whole army of salaried parasites' (62). The novelty came in Bardhan's fusion of both dimensions: human capital with rent-seeking. While other Indian marxisant scholars had bracketed 'the salariat' with the petty bourgeoisie (Raj, 1973; Patnaik and Rao, 1977), Bardhan excluded the mass of low-level state employees from his skilled professional class.[4]

Thanks to their location within the state, public sector professionals were not simply amanuenses of the other classes. All but the largest businessmen had to 'approach these dispensers of permits and licences essentially as supplicants', while resenting the bureaucracy's power and wastefulness (58). There were thus 'sufficiently antagonistic conflicts of interests' between bureaucrats and the capitalist class to ensure that the former was not theoretically reducible to vassals of the latter (51). In a later piece responding to Rudra (1989), Bardhan clarified that public sector professionals had 'acquired powers which are not just of a junior partner in the ruling coalition' or the chauffeur for other class interests: 'the chauffeur has also acquired some share in the ownership of the car' (Bardhan, 1989a: 155–6). Is this still true today? The next section answers this question by considering the three pillars of the professionals' distinctiveness outlined here: their skills, rents from public sector control, and antagonistic relations with other classes.

---

[4] Rudra (1989) drew a somewhat similar distinction between the 'intelligentsia' engaged in 'the sale of mental labour' and the state's Class IV manual workers (see also Béteille, 1989), but differed from Bardhan in seeing the intelligentsia or professionals as a junior class and denying that human capital was a 'property' that could generate surplus in its own right.

THE PROFESSIONALS' SURPRISING RESILIENCE

Whether the professionals are a dominant class or mere 'chauffeurs' for others 'is a matter of empirical judgment', Bardhan wrote a quarter-century ago (1989a: 156). This section shows that the quantitative changes that the last three decades have brought to the size, salaries, and control of state resources of the public sector professionals are often overstated. In the face of ostensible state rollback, the continuity is striking.

Figure 8.1 suggests an ambivalent picture of the public sector professionals' fate. In absolute terms, the bureaucracy has shrunk, but only slightly: *Economic Survey* data shows a decline of 12 per cent from the peak of 19.56 million in 1997 to 17.61 million by 2012, a figure still higher than the 16.87 million employees of 1984. In relative terms, though, the size of the bureaucracy has decreased by more than a third,

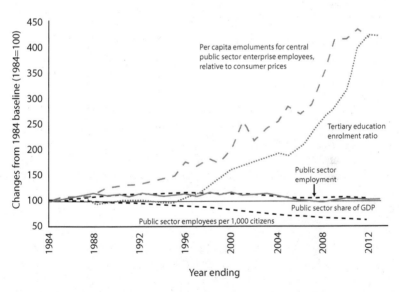

FIGURE 8.1   The Professionals since 1984: Change in Key Indicators
Source: Data from the Department of Public Enterprises (emoluments versus all-India consumer price index); National Accounts Statistics, various years (public sector share of GDP); *Economic Survey of India*, various years (employment); World Bank's World Development Indicators (tertiary education).
Note: All indicators are indexed to 1984 = 100.

from 22.71 for every 1,000 residents in 1991 to 14.65 two decades later; excluding the railways and post office the central government's share stood at only 1.39 in 2014, one-fifth the ratio of the United States of America—hardly the bloated state with which India is often associated (Government of India, 2015: 24).

Aggregate size is a crude indicator of the public sector professionals' power, however. The structure of the Indian bureaucracy is a steep pyramid. Most employees are low-level, semi-skilled workers such as office peons and drivers, not Bardhan's skilled professionals. As R. Nagaraj (2017: 163) notes in one of the surprisingly few recent studies of Indian public sector employment, senior civil servants ('gazetted' Class I and Class II officers) make up only around 5 per cent of the total at the central level. This proportion has remained fairly constant since the early 1990s, though the number of Class I officers has risen from 1.8 to 2.9 per cent in that period. The elite Indian Administrative Service (IAS), upon which existing scholarship disproportionately focuses, is even smaller, maintaining a strength of around 5,000 officers. Size-wise, the professionals appear to have remained a select and relatively stable group, any decline in their size merely mirroring the slow shrinking of the bureaucracy as a whole. There are regional variations in the bureaucracy's grip, however: though the IAS's authorized strength has actually grown since 2000, 29 per cent of positions remained vacant by 2012, a decline especially striking in several poorer states alongside pro-business Maharashtra and Gujarat (Krishnan and Somanathan, 2017).

We see apparent continuity again when turning from size to salary considerations, the legal face of the subsidies that the public sector professionals can command.[5] The growing burden of salary demands

---

[5] Assessing salary changes is made all the more complex by the difficulty of accessing wage data, especially in the states. Higher civil servants also accrue a range of non-salary perks such as subsidized housing and education, pensions, and job security, making any inference from salaries alone difficult to sustain. Pensions—that is, *deferred* payments—have become particularly important, shifting the financial responsibility for professionals' costly rents to future administrations. Wages declined from 92.0 per cent of total central compensation in 1950–1 to 69.43 per cent in 2004–5, while retirement benefits rose from 8 per cent to 30.57 per cent over the same period (Anand and Chaudhury, 2007: 3226). In 2004, however, traditional defined-benefit pensions for central government staff were ended.

was noted by *PEDI*; by some accounts, the civil servant wage bill had become the single largest item of government expenditure by the 1990s (Das, 2013: 25). This has continued: examining the Sixth Pay Commission award, Nagaraj (2017: 165) found that real wages rose by 7.9 per cent annually between 2005–06 and 2011–12, compared to per capita income growth of 6.8 per cent over the same period.

Strikingly, in the liberalization era, the upper, 'professional' bureaucracy has succeeded in extending its advantage over the lower tiers. While in the 1930s India's senior bureaucrats earned far more than their equivalents in the United States of America, Japan, or Poland, by the 1980s the indexed value of their real earnings had dropped sharply. Meanwhile, the lowest-earning public employees' earnings rose disproportionately (Potter, 1996). This 'progressivity in the public sector wage-setting mechanism' did not survive the economic reforms of the turn of the century (Nagaraj, 2017: 165). Since the 2000s, the gap between the highest and lowest salaries has widened again: pegged at 1:10.7 from the Fourth Pay Commission, it rose to 1:12 by the Sixth. Again, this suggests that the professionals' influence has remained relatively stable in the face of anti-bureaucratic discourses.

Turning towards less direct sources of subsidies, from the limited empirical data it is more difficult to establish whether the rent-seeking opportunities open to these groups have decreased. We can hypothesize, though, that if their dominant position rested on their location within an overweening state, any decline in the relative economic dominance of the public sector is likely to have reduced their importance relative to other classes (even if the actual magnitude of rents increased with economic growth). Figure 8.1 shows that the public sector's share of gross domestic product (GDP) has declined, but only since 2003 (it peaked in 2000; see also Nayar, 2009); and after the global economic downturn from 2008, this share stabilized at a slightly higher level than that in 1984.[6] After decades of underperformance, many central public sector enterprises began to outperform their private counterparts in the years after 1995–7, albeit more through benign neglect than coherent national strategy (Mohan, 2005; Khanna, 2015). Thus, more

[6] The decline appears to have accelerated again since 2014, although the government's recent decision to shift from calculating GDP to gross value added makes direct comparison more difficult.

opportunities to extract rents from 'old-fashioned' state intervention may have remained open than is usually recognized.

At the same time, even after economic liberalization industrial and commercial interests continued to depend on bureaucrats' regulatory discretion and public financing. Liberalization has created new and potentially even more lucrative rents from new forms of licensing (such as leases and concession agreements), re-regulation, and acquiring and selling inputs such as land (Chandra, 2015; Harriss-White, 1996a). Between 2003 and 2014 in particular, growth shifted to favour 'rent-thick' sectors such as utilities and raw materials from which senior bureaucrats especially stood to benefit alongside well-connected industrialists (see Chapter 11). India's gradual liberalization has therefore preserved a much more statist system than is often acknowledged, so partially preserving the privileged location of state professionals—and thus arguably helping to secure their otherwise counterintuitive support for reforms (Jenkins, 1999). 'What has changed?' Nagaraj's survey asked; examining such indicators, he concludes: 'Not very much' (2017: 175).

FRAGMENTATION OF THE THIRD DOMINANT CLASS

Yet, there are countervailing trends which suggest that the professionals' apparent resilience according to some quantitative indicators has been accompanied by significant qualitative changes in this group's coherence and distinctiveness as a (dominant) class. Theoretically, Bardhan's public sector professionals could draw on dual sources of rents: scarce skills and their location within the state. In practice, segments of the professionals are differently able to leverage rental income from these sources. As Bardhan had earlier speculated:

> In the class of professionals, although the bureaucrats will resist encroachments on their license-dispensing leverage with supplicant businessmen and on their other sources of corrupt income, the growing managerial and technocratic elite will expect to benefit from the increasing policy emphasis on technological improvement and professionalization of management. (1988b: 223)

Accordingly, already in 1993, he detected 'a perceptible change in the attitude of the bureaucracy... particularly in the higher echelons' as they reluctantly admitted that the state had overextended itself (1993: 350–1).

As Bardhan predicted, although bureaucrats are apparent losers from the state's declining direct control over the economy, not all segments of the professionals have consistently resisted liberalization. The premium accorded to the professionals' property—their knowledge, information, and networks—has proved more or less resilient in the liberalization era. Figure 8.1 implies that professionals no longer monopolize tertiary education, given the explosion in enrolment since 2006. The upper-caste elite that Bardhan discussed in 1984 has lost the most visible battle to protect its exclusivist 'meritocracy', illustrated by the extension of reservations to Other Backward Classes (OBCs) in public universities and the bureaucracy from 1990. Yet, at the same time underinvestment in primary education persists, and the quality of tertiary education remains dubious, even while demand for skilled personnel has rocketed. Revisiting India's 'tortuous transition' in 2009, Bardhan noted that structural change in India had been 'skill-biased … increas[ing] the rate of return to post-secondary education' and the scarcity value of those with technical skills and qualifications (2009: 32).[7] Those with access to the best technical education and the best professional networks, still often drawn from prosperous and well-connected groups (Jeffrey, Jeffery, and Jeffery, 2008), therefore, continue to find themselves in short supply and high demand.

Some segments of the professionals have been primary beneficiaries of this unusual growth trajectory. Specialist technocrats, such as senior employees of state-owned enterprises or infrastructure ministries, possess fungible skills, expertise, and networks that are highly valued in the private sector (where, of course, caste-based reservations do not apply). Many technocrats are recruited by private firms or offered generous board memberships upon their retirement. To compete, per

---

[7] In India labour-intensive manufacturing has not grown swiftly enough to compensate for the decline of agriculture, leaving the majority of employment in the traditional, low-end service sector, while skill-intensive sectors such as pharmaceuticals and software have expanded rapidly (Bardhan, 2009: 31). A substantial debate in economics rages around the thesis that 'skill-biased technological change' increases wage inequalities, however. For evidence that in the 1990s, unlike the 1980s, technological change was indeed skill-biased in India, see Berman, Somanathan, and Tan (2005).

capita emoluments for the employees of central public sector enterprises grew four times faster than the all-India consumer price index between 1983–84 and 2011–12, rising especially fast in the late 2000s as unskilled workers were shed (see Figure 8.1). This means that the 'status and standard of living' of the most technically and managerially skilled segment of the professionals is no longer 'directly dependent on their continued control of the public means of production', as J. Waterbury's comparative study of public sector managers recognized two decades ago (1993: 264). The technocrats' opportunities to extract rents from the state has already risen as key appointments increasingly go to specialists, scientists, and professional economists. Because they stand to benefit from the increasing demand for their expertise and competence, the technocrats are not necessarily hostile to economic reforms. Though civil servants remain strong enough to block private sector outsiders from entering into the rigidly seniority-based bureaucratic hierarchy, lateral entry on a contract basis has been approved in principle, and if widely implemented would mark a revolution.

Generalist bureaucrats fare somewhat less well in this competition. Bardhan hypothesized that both the urban professionals in general and bureaucrats in particular favoured 'a strong centre' (1988b: 223–4), but this is a battle that they have lost. The decline of the bureaucracy has been most pronounced at the central level, falling by 22.7 per cent between 2001 and 2012 to only 14 per cent of total public employment. As transfers—the key mechanism for exerting political control over individual bureaucrats—are more frequent at the subnational level (Banik, 2001), elite bureaucrats have become more reliant on political patrons for their advancement, the 'political middlemen' accorded little space in Bardhan's 1984 analysis (see p. 170–2), even as the population they seek to govern becomes increasingly articulate and media-sensitized. One officer-turned-academic accordingly predicts that 'the IAS will continue much as it is, albeit with gradually waning influence' as '[p]ressures from below and from above will increasingly constrict [its] zone of discretion' (Krishna, 2010: 442).

Nonetheless, as the previous section showed, senior bureaucrats have remained resilient and even enjoyed salary buoyancy (especially taking other perks and job security into account). Far from offering solid resistance to liberalization, even elite generalists have thus cautiously welcomed liberalization. Das (2005) reports that while only a minority of senior IAS officers favoured economic reforms in 1991, by the end of the decade more recognized that liberalization left their position relatively intact—and even offered new rewards. As the Standing Conference of Public Enterprises, an industry group, glossed the history of liberalization: 'The highly professionalised sector took no time to adjust itself to the transformed environment. It was only looking forward to the new change as it felt fairly strangulated in the regulated economic regime of the yesteryears' (SCOPE, 2010: iii).

Perhaps realizing the direction of travel, some IAS officers appear to be rebranding as specialists. Until the 1980s, most had studied humanities subjects, but the majority of the 2001–5 batches held professional degrees—engineering, medicine, business, and law (Benbabaali, 2008). Today's IAS officers are also rewarded at key promotion stages for specialization (Ferguson and Hasan, 2013). Reinforcing this idea of a split in the bureaucracy, a recent empirical study of transfers suggests that there are two routes to promotion for individual IAS officers: technical ability and identity-based loyalty to political patrons (Iyer and Mani, 2011). In their memoirs, managers of central public sector enterprises similarly distinguish their service as disinterested 'technocrats' leading these firms from their work as mere 'bureaucrats' in the ministries (Kapur, 2015: 200). The recommendations of the Seventh Central Pay Commission illustrate this tension between technocrats and others: although at the time of writing, the report is still being contested, it marks a sustained attempt to undermine the dominance of generalists over control roles and to substitute performance-related pay for the longstanding tradition of seniority (Government of India, 2015).

At the same time, as their internal coherence has declined, the professionals' external boundaries have become more porous, weakening the distinctiveness of the group's composition and class interests. By the end of the 1980s, Bardhan recognized that the professionals were 'increasingly invaded by the educated children of the rich farmers and industrialists and traders' (1989a: 156). The professionals' class interests and lifestyles have, therefore, become more similar to those of some segments of the other two dominant classes, so that together they may be merging into 'an assertive new burgeoning "middle class"' (Bardhan, 1993: 349; see also Chapter 9). In particular, the relationship between professionals and large capitalists has become increasingly simpatico, as Bardhan recognized in his 1998 epilogue: 'Some of the new entrepreneurs, belonging as they do to the families of senior bureaucrats, army officers and other members of the professional classes or sharing ties through education in elite engineering and business schools, have forged new links between the bureaucracy and private capital' (Bardhan, 1998: 131).

This undercuts the class antagonisms that provided a key criterion of their distinctiveness in 1984 and, again, weakens public sector professionals' inclination and ability to block the policy manoeuvres of other classes.

Liberalization is, therefore, not the unilateral threat to the third dominant class that it is often portrayed to be, and their resistance to it has proven correspondingly uneven and piecemeal. In revealing the disparateness of their interests, it threatens to fragment the class: today India's elite public sector professionals evince little sense of shared identity or corporate cohesion. Even while they remain dominant by virtue of their crucial structural position within a persistently interventionist state, they no longer appear to act as a dominant *class* in Bardhan's original, active sense.

FRAGMENTATION AND LIBERALIZATION

Who have been the beneficiaries of the professionals' divisions? *Political Economy of Development in India* points us towards a clear answer: any diminution in the power of the bureaucracy is likely to benefit not only the other two dominant classes—rich farmers and wealthy businessmen—but will increase *state autonomy*. Bardhan's 'state elite'—the political leadership—is a distinct actor, strategically operating 'in a game of mixed conflict and cooperation with other groups' (1988a: 65).[8] In particular, it is troubled by classic principal-agent problems: he argued that the state elite was undermined not only by 'a lack of political insulation from conflicting interests', but also 'the strong power base of the white-collar workers in public

---

[8] Rather than a competition between three dominant classes, it may therefore be more accurate to read the 1984 volume as an account with *four* central actors. The state elite is not just another dominant proprietary class, however: it is not purely self-interested, but may hold a genuine (and ideological) 'conception of the national interest' (Bardhan, 1998: 34; see Chapter 6).

bureaucracy', on whom it had to rely to implement its policy decisions (Bardhan, 1998: 74, 51n8).

This helps to explain why the state elite may have shifted its position to favour liberalization in the mid-1980s, despite the fact that this superficially undercut the source of its own power: a reduction in the power of the bureaucracy could theoretically increase the state elite's room for manoeuvre.[9] Equally, it suggests that we might expect liberalization to have advanced furthest in sectors in which technocrats— who are more likely to be pro-liberalization, as we saw earlier—play the largest roles: in macroeconomic and trade policy, broad decisions about encouraging private and foreign investment, and on-paper welfare reforms, for example.[10] In this way, the state elite has found assistance from quarters of the senior bureaucracy in carrying forward its revised ideological project of economic liberalization, at least in some sectors and from the top down.

At the same time, those professionals who favour or tolerate policy change have also encouraged modes of reform that are not reducible to a universal model of liberalization as deregulation and state rollback. It is perhaps more accurate to see many of these professionals as pro-*reform* than pro-liberalization per se. They often appear more concerned with improving managerial competence and corporate efficiency than ideological questions of public versus private ownership. Divestment in major central state-owned enterprises has proceeded only slowly, with the state retaining majority stakes in most. Instead, the emphasis has often fallen on attempts to reinvent such enterprises through corporatization, the granting of increased autonomy, and by imposing discipline through market competition (Chatterjee, 2017a). Simultaneously, and in opposition to the notion that the Indian state is becoming uniformly 'pro-business', technical regulatory agencies such as the Election Commission, the Reserve Bank of India, and the Comptroller and Auditor General have become increasingly assertive (see Chapter 11). Such developments preserve—or even increase—the

---

[9] The argument that economic liberalization was initially the project of a relatively autonomous state leadership has fairly wide support (Shastri, 1997; Varshney, 1998; Jenkins, 1999; Mooij, 2005; Mukherji, 2014).

[10] This is an interesting supplement to Varshney's (1998) celebrated distinction between 'elite' and 'mass' politics.

importance of senior technocrats. In this way, the resilient influence and tentatively pro-reform alignment of many professionals have combined to facilitate an uneven, and still curiously state-centred, form of liberalization.

LIMITS OF LIBERALIZATION: A NEW (JUNIOR) STATE CLASS?

If Bardhan's public sector professionals have gone through a fragmentation, more effective—if scattergun—resistance to liberalization has come from a different quarter of the public sector, one largely neglected in the 1984 volume: the petty bureaucracy. As we saw earlier in the chapter, both power and jobs have shifted away from the more insulated terrain of New Delhi and from quasi-governmental organizations such as public sector enterprises to the subnational level. The largest share of public sector employment (41 per cent) now decisively lies with India's states. It is at this level that public sector employees have managed most successfully to protect their employment, although their job contracts have become ever shorter and more casualized (Nagaraj, 2017: 169).[11] This petty bureaucracy, along with the large group of aspirants seeking to join it, remains numerically significant in many states.

These are not the upper-caste functionaries of 1984. Economic growth and socio-economic change, along with the extension of reservations, has seen a colonization of the state's lower tiers by upwardly

---

[11] The shrinking of the bureaucracy has largely hit its lowest 'non-professional' tiers, such as the vast auxiliary services with which many state-owned enterprises were involved. Yet these job losses may have been exaggerated: some low-skilled jobs have been outsourced to the private sector on short contracts rather than purely cut, while others have been disguised: in 2009–10, Class IV (manual) employees were promoted en masse to Class III (clerical) status. Nagaraj (2017: 176n7) suggests that this outsourcing may explain the substantial discrepancy (21.3 per cent in 2009–10) between official and National Sample Survey statistics: the former shows a decline in public employment while the latter shows that the bureaucracy *grew* by 3.4 per cent annually across the 2000s. In explanation, he speculates that survey responses may not adequately distinguish between those employed *by* government and those providing services *for* government.

mobile groups (see Chapter 10).[12] They are often drawn from the lower castes, and Bardhan describes them in terms very reminiscent of the old 'intermediate regime' thesis: 'small and middle peasants, self-employed artisans and shopkeepers, bazaar merchants and petty middlemen, clerks, schoolteachers and service workers' (Bardhan, 1998: 136). Unlike the elite professionals, who can more readily benefit from the growth of the private sector, Bardhan notes that these 'newly emergent groups are in no mood for accepting a retreat of the state' but instead seek belatedly to capture its resources for themselves (2009: 34).

The resilience of their employment is not a simple sign of the strength of the petty bureaucracy as a new state class, however. The salariat is as internally differentiated as the diverse caste, religious, and linguistic groups from which it is drawn, making coherent class-wide action difficult. Lacking the technical skills that distinguish the elite professionals, too, its members must instead trade political loyalty for their positions. While rent-seeking may have proliferated—though good data on this is scarce—much of this is channelled upwards through the bureaucratic–political hierarchy to superiors on whom the petty bureaucrat is reliant for lucrative postings, as Robert Wade's classic studies showed (Wade, 1982, 1985). This suggests that politicians may deserve a more substantial analytical role than the 1984 volume permitted, as Bardhan's more recent analyses have acknowledged. His 1998 epilogue noted the politicization of the bureaucracy: how politicians from the newly empowered groups would transfer civil servants en masse upon taking office, doling out 'political sinecures' to 'keep the clamouring factions happy' (Bardhan, 1998: 133–4).

In this bureaucratic–political nexus, petty bureaucrats are at best a junior partner in an alliance of convenience with politicians, not a new dominant class. In fact, they are not really a distinct class at all: while Bardhan's original professionals possessed a distinguishing property and class location, it is difficult to understand this petty salariat except

---

[12] The upper castes have not simply acceded to this takeover: these new groups are still underrepresented in promotions, overrepresented in unfilled posts, and more broadly burdened with un(der)employment despite their increasing recourse to tertiary education (Jeffrey, Jeffery, and Jeffery, 2008). Meanwhile, upper-caste professionals are moving into the private sector instead, as we saw above—so arguably relocating or hollowing out state power to tarnish the prize before the lower castes take it (Bardhan, 1998: 134–5).

in reference to politicians and the other class (and caste) groups they serve. Yet, in conjunction with politicians, they are proving a crucial set of actors in the political economy of reforms in India, even if unsystematically.

While reform-minded professionals have been able to guide top-down and on-paper reforms in some sectors, in others the implementation of the state elite's policy decisions depends far more obviously on the petty bureaucracy. This group can help to block or undermine implementation of the state elite's projects in sectors where the discretion of 'street-level' bureaucrats is key. This is especially true at the level of India's provincial states, now the most important arena for increasingly regionally varied political contestation. For example, while New Delhi technocrats spearheaded an ambitious piece of legislation that did much to liberalize the power sector on paper—the Electricity Act of 2003—in many states the pricing and distribution of electricity remains highly politicized (Chatterjee, 2017b). As Bardhan has since freely acknowledged, this lower-level nexus between politicians and petty bureaucrats, far from synonymous with the original professionals, is an essential supplement to the analysis *PEDI* offered three decades ago.

★★★

This assessment suggests that the Indian system remains more statist—and correspondingly less 'pro-business'—than many scholarly interpretations today allow. Examining headline statistics, the striking feature is the *continuity* in the bureaucracy's stature and influence despite the sustained rhetorical attention to state rollback. Public sector employment has declined only slowly and salary data is ambivalent, especially when job security and other 'perks' are considered, while some bureaucrats may have been able to extract increased rents both from enlarged rent-seeking opportunities created by new regulation and from the surprisingly good performance of some state-owned enterprises.

Nonetheless, beneath this surface continuity some major changes can be discerned. The professionals have become more internally heterogeneous and incoherent, with the most technically and managerially skilled segments becoming a superficially surprising pro-liberalization constituency. They have become less easily differentiated from the other two original elites, an antagonism that was one of the hallmarks of Bardhan's original classes. Even while the state's continued importance ensures that their position remains dominant, these changes unravel the notion that public sector professionals amount to a dominant *class*. The fragmentation of the professionals has facilitated increased state autonomy, at least in New Delhi and in sectors where technocrats dominate and implementation chains are comparatively short; the interests of the more technocratic segments of the professional class and the state elite are today better aligned for 'developmental' goals (now recalibrated as business-friendly goals; see Chapter 6).

At the same time, state actors beyond the original professionals clearly deserve a greater analytical role than that allowed in the 1984 book. Especially at lower tiers of the state and in other sectors, the nexus between politicians and the petty bureaucracy frequently acts to subvert or stall reforms, and to perpetuate the networks of patronage and subsidy dispensation.

Bardhan's distinction between the elite professionals and the larger mass of the public sector salariat—and the ambivalent, complex fate of both—thus reveals a nuanced picture of the public sector's fate, and the apparent paradoxes that it has brought. On the one hand, it helps to explain the coexistence of a still-sizeable public sector with less-than-systematic bureaucratic resistance to reform. On the other, it informs India's distinctive trajectory of liberalization: 'halting and hesitant, often marked by two steps forward and one step backward', as Bardhan described it (2006: 10), and marked by the coexistence of pro-business policies with the persistence of older systems of subsidies and patronage (Chatterjee, 2017b). Even as his three dominant proprietary classes have evolved, then, Bardhan's disaggregated theory of the bureaucracy still provides a formidable tool for interpreting both the continuities in India's underlying political economy and its potential for change, however gradual, uneven, and partial.

IV

New Elites

9 Rethinking the 'Dominant Proprietary Classes'

India's Middle Classes and the Reproduction of Inequality

Leela Fernandes

India has a large middle class with immense understanding, talent, and purchasing power. In addition, a whole new class has emerged. Those who have risen from the category of poor and are yet to stabilize in the middle class, the 'neo middle class'. This class needs proactive hand-holding. Having moved out of poverty, their aspirations have increased. They want amenities and services of a certain standard. They thus now feel that Government facilities and services are not up to the mark, and hence resort to the private sector for things such as education, health and transport. This is obviously costly, putting the neo middle class into a daily dilemma. As more and more people move into this category, their expectations for better public services have to be met. We have to strengthen the Public Sector for providing efficient services to our citizens. (BJP, 2014: 17)

The post-liberalization era has ushered in an age of proliferating rhetoric on India's middle classes. Both public discourses and academic analyses have focused on questions of middle-class consumption and debated the size and cultural impact of an expanding, wealthy elite in the context of various phases of India's policies of economic reform. Meanwhile, the 2014 electoral campaign foregrounded Modi's politically astute deployment of his idea of a 'neo–middle class'.[1] In contrast to both celebratory public marketing presentations of an expanding, successful, post-liberalization middle class and academic scholarship that has reinforced conceptions of this middle class as intrinsically linked to (if not a product of) market-led growth and consumption, Modi's rhetoric captured both the limits of access to middle-class status and the continued significance of state support for large sections of the middle classes in India. His rhetoric, in effect, pointed both to the symbolic power of the promise of upward mobility that has been embodied in images of India's 'new' post-liberalization middle classes, and the limits of this promise of access as large segments of society (including the lower middle classes) have not benefited from wealth generated by new-economy jobs within the services and information technology sectors.[2] The Bharatiya Janata Party (BJP) manifesto's turn to the state (and the public sector) as a solution to the promise of access signals a central and under-analysed aspect of contemporary rhetoric and analysis of India's middle classes. There remains a significant conceptual vacuum in existing understandings of the role of the middle classes in shaping the state-led political economy of India in the post-liberalization period.

Pranab Bardhan's *The Political Economy of Development in India* (hereafter *PEDI*) in many ways seems to address a political and economic context that is very different from contemporary shifts in the political economy of India. However, this landmark text in fact provides analytical terrain that can deepen our understandings of the relationship between the state, India's middle classes, and the political economy of development. In particular, Bardhan's conception of the 'dominant proprietary classes' provides an important avenue that can begin to deepen our understanding of this relationship. Bardhan's work, written well before the current surge in public and scholarly rhetoric on the middle classes, does not explicitly focus on this social group, and there are limits to the empirical applicability of this concept to a heterogeneous group such as the middle classes. However, *PEDI* contains within it both theoretical and empirical analysis that can provide a vital

---

[1] Note that Modi in fact first used this term in the 2012 Assembly elections in Gujarat (*Deccan Herald*, 2012).

[2] I address this in Fernandes (2006).

analytical frame for understanding shifts in India's political economy in the post-liberalization period.

Bardhan's conception of the dominant proprietary classes in *PEDI* included industrialists, wealthy farmers, and the professional classes. Bardhan's discussion of the professional classes (including white-collar workers) captures a key segment of the middle classes (Bardhan, 1984: 51). His analytical lens provides the means for understanding how the upper tiers of the middle classes (English-speaking urban middle classes) have historically been beneficiaries of state resources. Consider one of Bardhan's central arguments regarding the appropriation of public surplus by India's 'dominant proprietary classes' (1984: 68). Bardhan's analysis throughout his landmark book hints at the ways in which these upper tiers of the middle classes are linked to such appro-priation—through subsidies of the middle classes that take the form of state resources channelled to the public bureaucracy, the educated elite, and public enterprise staff. As I will argue in this chapter, this argument in *PEDI* provides the analytical terrain necessary for an understanding of the ways in which the upper tiers of India's middle classes continue to benefit both from such older forms of extraction as well as new modes of appropriation in the post-liberalization period.

An analytical frame that solely focuses on the upper tier of profes-sionals and white-collar workers does not, of course, account for the much larger heterogeneous social group that constitutes the 'middle classes'. Bardhan himself addressed questions of class heterogeneity. The conception of the dominant proprietary classes itself was intended to grapple with what he described as the 'plurality and heterogeneity of these classes and the conflicts in their interests' (41), which he con-trasted with conceptions of more uniform fractions in the bourgeoisie in advanced industrial countries. He would later go on to address the porous boundaries between segments of the dominant classes, not-ing, for instance, that 'the educated children of the rich farmers and industrialists and traders' were entering the professional classes that had historically been the preserve of what he termed the 'traditional literati groups' (1989a: 156).[3]

This conception of heterogeneity needs to be expanded in order to develop an adequate understanding of the composition and politics

---

[3] My thanks to Elizabeth Chatterjee for pointing me to this connection.

of India's middle classes. The middle classes are stratified by a wide range of structural factors such as socio-economic status, caste, religion, language, and ethnicity. An adequate understanding of this social group thus requires a shift away from a focus on the middle classes as a homogeneous elite class. The lower middle classes, for instance, cannot adequately be captured by the analytical frame of the dominant proprietary classes. These segments of the middle classes may be dependent on state support but remain socially or economically marginalized. This layered stratification within India's middle classes has also intensified as previously marginalized social groups have sought access to middle class status. Thus, for instance, state policies may have helped produce emerging middle classes such as the Dalit middle classes (Pai, 2014; Srinivas, 2016). However, the structural location of these emerging middle classes does not correspond to the privileged white-collar professionals that Bardhan depicts in *PEDI*; indeed, segments of the lower middle classes may be closer in income or social status to upper tiers of the working classes. Such structural discrepancies have in many ways intensified in the post-liberalization period, as large segments of the middle classes have not benefited from new-economy jobs and as segments of the Dalit and Muslim middle classes have faced continued structural barriers to gaining public sector employment (Jeffrey, Jeffery, and Jeffery, 2008).

While the dominant proprietary classes cannot be conflated with this broader understanding of the middle classes, I will argue in this chapter that *PEDI* provides a much-needed analytical perspective that can deepen our understanding of the politics of India's middle classes in the post-liberalization period. Despite the burgeoning scholarship on India's middle classes, what is missing in this growing body of work is an analytical perspective that captures what Bardhan has called the '*domain* of class interests' (1984: 49). One of the overriding trends in scholarly work on India's middle classes has been a focus on either a culturalist or consumption-oriented understanding of class.[4] The anthropological turn in most post-liberalization studies of India's middle classes has meant that even in work that has focused on questions of inequality or power, the concept of class has been deployed as a descriptive, localized category, as the product of a diffuse set of power

---

[4] I address this in more detail in Fernandes (2015).

relations, or presented through a focus on everyday practices and strategies of mobility.[5] As I will argue in this chapter, such work generally stops short of asking how public resources are appropriated in *systemic* ways and how this appropriation of the public surplus contributes to the *reproduction* of inequality through longstanding structural processes.

This chapter will examine the possibilities of reworking Bardhan's conception of the 'dominant proprietary classes' in ways that can begin to address such systemic questions in the context of India's post-liberalization political economy. This entails a deepening of the middle class–state relationship through an analytical lens that incorporates both the extractive relationship of appropriation that Bardhan captures for the upper tiers of the middle classes (the dominant proprietary middle class) and a relationship of dependence on the state that characterizes the less privileged sections of this social group. These two faces of the state–middle class relationship also necessitate a rethinking of both the ideational and material dimensions of the middle class in the post-liberalization period. Images of a prosperous, liberalizing middle class mediate the relationship between the dominant proprietary middle class and the non-elite middle classes. Meanwhile, critiques of state investments that may benefit the middle classes (such as Bardhan's classic case of the public sector) are linked to modes of material public disinvestment tied to policies of liberalization, rather than to much-needed correctives to the extraction of resources that Bardhan analysed.

INDIA'S DOMINANT PROPRIETARY CLASSES, THE STATE, AND THE QUESTION OF THE MIDDLE CLASS

Scholarship on India rarely presented in-depth analyses of the socio-economic nature or political role of the middle classes in the early decades of the post-Independence period. B.B. Misra's early landmark study (1961) presented a rare example of work that attempted to look at India's middle class as a social group that necessitated serious empirical and analytical analysis. Misra's work did not, however, produce or intersect with scholarly trends that grappled with the nature of this social group. Analyses of socio-economic and political trends tended to implicitly invoke assumptions and claims about this social group

[5] For overviews of the scholarship, see Fernandes (2006; 2015).

through analytical concerns with modernization and upward mobility (often in relation to the potential erosion of caste). In this context, the middle classes were often a presumed political or socio-economic ideal or an assumed analytical category. The middle classes were thus characterized with a weighty significance even as they were relatively understudied as a socio-economic and theoretical subject that required sustained inquiry and explanation.

This contradiction mirrored the public-political nature of the middle classes. The middle classes have persisted as a central social group that has been marked by a paradoxical quality of intangibility and hypervisibility. On the one hand, the personification of the middle classes as the generalized expression of the Indian nation has allowed this social group to represent an elusive abstraction that seems to defy analytical and empirical precision. On the other hand, periods of national political and economic crisis or change have allowed the middle classes to take on a hyper-visible political role, often with adverse social and political implications for subaltern socio-economic groups.[6] For instance, significant sections of the urban middle classes have been imbricated in some of the more repressive political trends in contemporary India—whether through support for state repressive measure during the Emergency period or through early support for the BJP and Hindu nationalist movement since the 1980s.[7] The middle classes have thus seemed to live in a discrepant political space, claiming to represent the common national interests of a democratic India while significant segments of this social group have often been enmeshed with some of the key anti-democratic trends that have punctuated contemporary Indian politics.

A central underlying empirical and analytical question that such trends raise asks what the politics of the middle classes mean for understanding of the Indian state in general and the political economy of the state in particular. The analysis of the 'dominant proprietary classes' in

[6] For a perspective on the deleterious effects of the middle class on national political culture, see Varma (1998). Note, however, that Varma tends to conflate the middle classes with the elite sections of this social group.

[7] See, for example, Hansen (1999) on Hindu nationalism. Corbridge and Harriss (2000) have, for instance, used the term 'elite revolts' to capture this dynamic of middle-class politics.

PEDI, provides important empirical and conceptual tools that address this question. Bardhan's analysis sought to examine the ways in which specific elite socio-economic classes in post-Independence India, 'the industrial capitalist class, the rich farmers and the professionals in the public sector' (54), had effectively established networks of patronage that allowed them to appropriate economic resources from the state. His discussion of India's middle classes focuses on specific socio-economic fractions of this social group including the public bureaucracy (1984: 62), the educated elite (1984: 52), and public enterprise staff (1984: 70). Bardhan's analysis of these social segments of the middle classes outlines key features of state–middle class relations in the context of India's postcolonial state-directed economy.

Bardhan was concerned with the ways in which these social groups were operating as a kind of 'rentier class' that was effectively appropriating resources both indirectly through claims made on the state and directly as a key component of Indian state structures. As he argued:

> By managing to direct educational investment away from the masses, they have been able to protect their scarcity rent, and by acquiring license-giving powers at various levels of bureaucracy some of them have increased their capacity to multiply their rental income. (1984: 52)

Central to this understanding is the idea of middle-class formation as a state-produced category through material processes of class formation rather than an elite group that performs a primarily ideological role through its claims of serving as representative and purveyor of the idealized vision of the Indian nation.[8] The middle classes then are not simply by-products of state economic policy. On the one hand, they represent an elite social group that is attempting to make claims on the state. On the other hand, they are also, in part, structurally linked to or a component of the state (as members of the bureaucracy and public enterprises). In this sense, the middle classes represent a key social force that has shaped the nature of India's political economy.

Critical discourses on the stranglehold of bureaucratic restrictions on India's economic development (in colloquial terms India's 'licence

---

[8] For a discussion of the ideological role of the middle classes, see Deshpande (2003).

raj') now abound in both public and academic arenas. However, *PEDI*'s analysis compels us to disrupt the easy conventional narrative that now persists. According to the terms of this narrative, India suffered sluggish growth in the early decades of Independence because of prohibitive state controls of the economy. Various phases of economic reforms since the 1980s have begun to lift these stifling restrictions, generating new wealth, an expanding middle class, and the promise of upward mobility. The power and force of the middle classes in this story is unleashed by a lifting of the heavy hand of a state-managed economy. What this version of history overlooks, however, is precisely the fact that the material foundation of India's now much-debated middle classes was in fact laid by the state. Drawing on a range of examples, *PEDI* points to ways in which sections of the middle classes use various kinds of everyday political power to harness resources from the state. These examples include the ability of the middle classes employed within state bureaucracies to benefit from the 'vast amounts of subsidies implicit in the overmanning at different levels of public bureaucracy' (Bardhan, 1984: 62), and the direction of state supports for higher education rather than literacy or mass education (Bardhan, 1984: 52). Such examples hint at the complex imbrication between the state and middle classes that was a defining feature of India's political economy of development. They represent a structural feature that shaped—and stunted—the trajectory of economic development in India.

The structural nature of this dynamic in the early decades of India's developmental path is best illustrated in *PEDI*'s analysis of the appropriation of public surplus by the dominant proprietary classes. Bardhan argues:

> [M]assive doses of public investment in basic industries and infrastructural facilities and public credit are crucial at the early stages of industrial and agricultural transformation, and yet pressures from heterogeneous elements in the dominant coalition for budgetary subsidies fritter away much of the public surplus. (1984: 68)

The relationship between the state and India's middle classes that emerges in the early decades of Independence is thus defined by processes of patronage and extraction that systematically draw state resources away from productive public investment.

Further, *PEDI*'s analysis raises analytical questions that have important implications for the ways in which we understand India's middle classes. Such questions begin with a focus on the discrepant relationship between the interests of the middle classes and the public's interest. India's middle classes have historically claimed the role of the public embodiment of the nation. The middle classes in comparative contexts have laid claim to public discourses of citizenship and have cast themselves in the role of the average, representative citizen.[9] In line with such patterns, India's middle classes have shaped the contours of the public sphere and in more recent decades have presented themselves as victims of subaltern social groups that have mobilized in an attempt to gain access to state resources. The conception by *PEDI* of the middle classes as a proprietary class that appropriates the public surplus disrupts the middle classes' ideological claim of the publicness of its own identity and interests. In this formulation, the middle classes, in fact, divert public resources in the service of their own private interests. In the early decades of Independence, investments and subsidies in fields such as education or public sector employment were skewed towards sections of the middle classes, an instance of what *PEDI* identifies as the 'privatization of public resources' (80). In the early decades after Independence, growth rates in higher education significantly exceeded primary education. As L.I. Rudolph and S.H. Rudolph showed, in 1955–56 the percentage increase in enrolment growth rates in higher education was 74 per cent, compared to 42 per cent in primary education (1987: 289). In 1970–71, the increase in higher education was 67 per cent compared to 12 per cent in primary education (Rudolph and Rudolph, 1987: 298). Meanwhile, public sector employment quadrupled from 4.1 million in 1953 to an estimated 16.2 million in 1983 (Potter, 1996: 159). The language of victimization that the middle classes deploy is, in this context, a political response to subordinated social groups beginning to make claims in their own interests. Indeed, as *PEDI* notes, the case of education is an illustrative example of this political dynamic. Thus, *PEDI* observes:

[9] See, for example, Owensby (1999) on Brazil and Stivens (1998) on Malaysia.

For the underprivileged social groups, education offers the quickest
route of upward mobility, a passport to the prospect of a secure job in
the bureaucracy and the professions. No wonder that some of the bit-
terest caste struggles in various parts of urban India in recent years have
been over the issues of reservations of seats in medical and engineering
schools and of jobs in the Government for lower castes. (52)

Political conflicts over reservations are, of course, now an enduring
and defining feature of democratic politics in contemporary India.
What is of significance for the purpose of this discussion is an understanding of such claims for reservations as a reflection of, rather than
a deviation from, the special-interest claims that upper-caste middle
classes have long made on state resources. The upper-caste middle
classes now depict reservation-based claims as a politics of 'vote
banks' that caters to the special interests of lower castes or minorities.
However, such claims in fact represent a set of political claims for the
pattern of the appropriation of resources from which the upper-caste
middle classes have long benefited. In other words, when subordinate
social groups make claims for state supports such as caste-based policies of reservations, they are following (rather than corrupting) the
patterns of political and economic appropriation that the dominant
proprietary classes such as the middle classes have entrenched in
postcolonial India.

This relationship raises a deeper question regarding India's middle
classes. An analysis of the middle class as a key social group that has
appropriated public resources for its private interests underlines the
significance that this social group has had for the trajectory of India's
developmental path. Conceptualizing the middle classes as a central
subject in debates over development provides an important avenue
for an understanding of the middle classes in the post-liberalization
period in India. As I noted earlier, both political discourses and
scholarly work have too easily reified a culturalist consumption-
based understanding of the middle classes that has hampered deeper
analysis of the complex relationship between the middle classes and
the post-liberalization state, and that has often overstated the dis-
continuities between the structural nature of this relationship in the
pre- and post-liberalization phases of India's political economy of
development.

INDIA'S MIDDLE CLASSES AS A PROBLEM FOR THE POLITICAL ECONOMY OF DEVELOPMENT IN POST-LIBERALIZATION INDIA

Conventional portrayals depict the new middle class as a social group that is now tied to the expansion of private capital and new economy jobs rather than the old state-dependent middle class. The political and cultural entrepreneurs that publicly speak for this social group (whether in the media or through more typical forms of associational life such as newly emerging civic organizations) also explicitly argue that the new middle class embodies this kind of break from past dependencies on the state. This aura of discontinuity has been refracted through academic work that has focused on middle-class consumption and consumerism.[10] More significantly, such discourses invent two separate economies and portray the middle classes and subaltern social groups as discrete objects within each realm in contemporary India. The middle classes inhabit an economy that is defined by the retreat of the state and consumer-led growth.[11] Subaltern groups such as the urban and rural poor are located within a framework of development that is marked by dependencies on state supports.[12] Since such discourses dissociate the middle classes from state-led development, shifts of state resources and developmental priorities and policies from the urban and rural poor to the middle classes can occur by stealth. Atul Kohli, for instance, has noted the connection between declining public investment in the 1990s and declining revenues caused by tax concessions

[10] Such scholarship has focused the study of the middle classes through empirical and theoretical analysis of the media (such as the role of advertising and television images) on the shaping of middle class identities (Juluri, 2003; Mankekar, 1999; Mazzarella, 2003; Rajagopal, 2001) and consumerism (Lukose, 2009; Srivastava, 2014).

[11] I develop this argument at greater length in Fernandes (2009).

[12] There is of course a sub-narrative in which this middle-class-fuelled economic growth allows the state to respond to problems of poverty. This idealization of middle class oriented development is not limited to India. See, for example, Mead and Schwenninger (2002) for an array of writings by economists and analysts who make a case for global middle-class-oriented development.

given to the rich and middle classes (2012: 116). Or, to take another example, new middle-class visions of urban development have often meant that infrastructural development and resources have increasingly begun to benefit the urban middle classes in the post-liberalization period. Such transfers of resources from the poor to the middle classes can encompass a wide ranging set of examples, from the use of space through evictions of street vendors or squatters (Bhowmick, 2002) to the transfer of groundwater from rural areas for urban consumption (Janakarajan, 2004; 2008). The 'rentier' nature of the middle class has thus become a more complex process that involves indirect modes of appropriation of public resources in the context of the changing relationship between the state and private capital in the post-liberalization period. The appropriation of resources through dominant models of urban development may, for example, occur indirectly through state supports of private industry (through public–private partnerships).

Applying *PEDI*'s conception of the middle class as a dominant proprietary class in the post-liberalization period nevertheless provides critical conceptual tools that can allow for an understanding of India's post-liberalization middle classes as part of a (continued) state-led project (and problem) of development rather than as an expanding consumer group that has naturally been produced by economic growth.[13] Consider, for instance, the ways in which increasingly assertive middle-class demands in local municipal council resources direct local state resources towards upper-middle-class conceptions of urban development.[14] Recent work has called attention to ways in which relationships of patronage and state-directed patterns of land usage have provided the means for highly lucrative financial deals that benefit both local state officials and private developers and that serve the residential needs of sections of the middle classes (Levien, 2013). Such patterns of urban development have been accompanied by a range of

[13] Political scientists have shown that various phases of liberalization have been led by the state in India. On the role of the state in the 1980s, see Kohli (1990). On the reforms in the 1990s, see Jenkins (1999).

[14] Middle-class claims on civic and urban development resources have a long history stemming back to the colonial period, pointing to the importance of adequately accounting for continuities in the state–middle class relationship in India.

new middle-class practices and forms of civic and associational life in which new middle-class groups have made assertive demands on the state (for example, in conflicts with street vendors and demands for urban beautification programmes). These emerging civic groups have thus seized on these new economic and political opportunities to pressure the state for support. Such practices are examples of the continued appropriation of public surplus for private interests that already characterized state–middle class relations when *PEDI* was published three decades ago. Grand visions of urbanization are entrenched in middle-class-oriented visions of cities, and public surpluses needed for public goods such as infrastructure continue to be extracted by the proprietary control of old and newly emerging dominant classes—including sections of the privileged middle classes. This kind of analysis, stemming from Bardhan's work, compels us to think about the middle classes and the politics of inequality and exclusion in post-liberalization India as more than just a simple story about a neoliberal shift to privatization (with the attendant trappings of middle-class consumerism).[15] The middle classes instead play a more complex—and historically continuous—role in the structural appropriation of public resources for private interests.

BEYOND THE PRIVILEGED MIDDLE CLASSES: THE COMPLEXITY OF CLASS INEQUALITY IN CONTEMPORARY INDIA

The concept of the dominant proprietary classes provides critical conceptual terrain for an understanding of the socio-economic reproduction of the middle classes. However, the middle classes also represent a highly differentiated social group in ways that necessitate a rethinking of the category of class. The middle classes are a highly stratified social group that range from the dominant elites that Bardhan describes to significantly less privileged members. Internal differences of caste, religion, region, language, and socio-economic status necessitate a sharper

---

[15] Scholarship that is critical of 'neoliberalism' often overlooks the role of the state and a more complex understanding of dominant elites, as well as historical variations that are not reducible to a simple model of a neoliberal shift. I analyse such trends at length in Fernandes (2018).

delineation of which sections of the middle classes can be adequately explained as part of the dominant proprietary classes. The dominant middle classes that Bardhan's work depicts largely correspond to upper-caste, urbanized, English-speaking middle classes who have historically benefited from access to subsidized higher education and access to secure public sector jobs. These are, in fact, the same sectors of the middle classes that are now cast as the 'new' middle classes in liberalizing India. The 'newness' of the middle classes represents an ideological construction of middle-class identity in the post-liberalization period rather than a description of new entrants to middle-class status. Public and political discourses that emerged in the mid-1980s and intensified in the 1990s centred on the production of a new middle class identity that was explicitly associated with support for policies of liberalization in India. As I have argued elsewhere, the urban, English-speaking middle classes played a central role in defining this image of a new liberalizing middle class (Fernandes, 2006). Bardhan's conception of this section of the middle class as a dominant proprietary class continues to hold both empirical and analytical significance in the post-liberalization period, but in a distinctive way that departs from *PEDI*'s original conception. The largely urban, professional, and white-collar dominant class has in effect crafted a new identity that reflects its support for India's state-led project of liberalization. However, as I have noted earlier, the appropriation of resources now occurs through complex configurations of reliance on both state resources and private capital. On the one hand, the new middle class in effect has ideologically supported policies of liberalization that have increased the role of both Indian and global capital. On the other hand, as I have shown in the previous section, this middle class has continued to appropriate state resources. The dominant role of this section of the middle class is thus both ideological and material. This new middle class claims to represent the middle classes in general even as large segments of the middle classes do not have immediate access to the benefits of liberalization (such as high-paying new-economy jobs).

The middle classes in fact consist of a vast array of lower-middle-class individuals who may press for their share of the public surplus but who in reality are marginalized through layered forms of social stratification that shape their social location. For instance, vernacular or rural middle classes, emerging Dalit middle classes, and sections of the Muslim middle class may seek access to a resource such as education. However, such strategies of upward mobility do not translate into the socio-economic status possessed by the dominant sections of India's middle classes. For instance, as both governmental and academic research has shown, Dalit and Muslim middle-class individuals may simply be trapped in states of unemployment or underemployment, and may be casualties of the networks of patronage that continue to permeate state institutions.[16] Dalits and Muslims may attempt to use the pursuit of formal or higher education as a strategy of class mobility only to find that such strategies do not translate into employment (Jeffrey, 2010). Meanwhile, middle-class individuals who have managed to gain a small foothold within new-economy jobs also use a range of credentialing strategies designed to realize the promise of post-liberalization middle-class identity, only to find that there is limited upward mobility for lower-tier white-collar workers (Fernandes, 2006). The internal differentiation and stratification within the middle classes is thus complex and fragmented in distinctive ways in the post-liberalization period. In the case of unemployed Dalit middle-class individuals, stratification within the middle classes is produced by poorer classes attempting to gain middle-class status. In the case of middle-class individuals who have gained access to new economy jobs, but without the kind of promised upward mobility associated with white-collar work, there are distinct forms of stratification that are intensified in the post-liberalization period. In this context, the category of 'white-collar worker' becomes increasingly stratified, given the vast discrepancies in income and wealth between the upper tiers of new-economy jobs on the one hand and lower-level office or clerical workers on the other.[17] Social factors such as language, ethnicity, and caste may intensify and deepen such forms of stratification by posing structural barriers to upward mobility within middle-class employment. For instance, middle-class individuals may find that structural discrimination based on caste prevents them from upward mobility associated with high-paying new-economy private sector jobs.[18]

[16] See, for example, Government of India (2006); Srinivas (2016).

[17] I discuss such distinctions at length in Fernandes (2006).

[18] See Upadhyay's (2007) discussion of caste discrimination within the information technology (IT) industry.

In the post-liberalization period, Bardhan's critique of the public sector as the primary mode of middle-class extraction requires a reconceptualization that accounts for nuances in the middle class–state relationship. Shifts in the post-liberalization period have lessened the significance of public sector employment in terms of both size and as a marker of status.[19] In terms of size, public sector employment in both governmental and industrial occupations have steadily declined since the 1990s. Employment in governmental occupations declined from approximately 19.5 million in 1991 to just under 17.5 million in 2011; organized public sector employment declined from approximately 19.5 million to just under 17.3 million. However, the impact of this downsizing of public sector employment must be understood largely in terms of its effects on the lower socio-economic strata of public sector employees. Given that the non-elite middle classes are often more dependent on state employment than the upper tiers of the middle classes who have been able to transition to more lucrative new-economy private sector jobs in the post-liberalization period, the restructuring of the public sector has reduced the security of less privileged middle-class individuals without unsettling the primacy of the dominant proprietary professional middle classes (see also Chapter 8). Meanwhile, as R. Nagaraj has argued, while large landowners and regional elites have engaged in a 'pragmatic use of the public sector [that] seems to be almost entirely driven by electoral calculations', the broader segment of middle classes has resorted to individualized strategies using patronage networks with a 'hope to secure individualized gains from a plethora of sub-optimal government welfare programmes, however meagre they might be' (2015: 450). Thus, the primary effect of cutbacks in the public sector has been to reduce the socio-economic insecurity of less privileged sectors of the middle classes rather than to correct the extractive dominance of the proprietary classes.

It is this complex form of internal differentiation—along with the attendant political alienation and socio-economic anxieties—that Modi's 2014 election campaign was able to tap into. It is thus noteworthy that the delineation of this 'neo-middle class', with which I began this chapter, is centred on both the promise of public services

---

[19] Ganguly-Scrase and Scrase (2008) provide a rich analysis of middle classes in the public sector in Kolkata.

and the public sector, even as Modi pledged that he would deliver on the benefits of a continued and intensified process of liberalization. The BJP's manifesto in effect was holding out the promise of access to membership in the dominant proprietary classes, which significant sections of the middle classes do not in fact have, while continuing to uphold the policies of liberalization that the dominant segments of the classes endorsed.[20] His conception of the 'neo-middle class' was thus an effective discursive strategy that produced an ideational definition of the middle classes that linked the dominant and less-privileged sections of the middle classes.

The internal differentiation within the middle classes requires a rethinking of the concept of the dominant proprietary class. This reconceptualization requires an understanding of the ways in which the structural and ideational processes of class formation are enfolded within a distinctive interactive process in the making of middle-class identity. Consider, for example, the case of the lower middle classes. In terms of income or social location, the distinction between the 'middle classes' and the 'working classes' may be negligible. Lower middle classes who are underemployed or employed in low-paying clerical workers may occupy the same economic status as unionized workers in the industrial sector. Yet, social conceptions of the status of 'manual work' versus 'educated' workers may produce deep-seated forms of social stratification between these social groups. Such forms of distinction may be intensified when individuals from subordinated caste groups deploy education as a form of social mobility, heightening distinctions around social conceptions of labour and the meaning of social capital associated with education (even when such distinctions do not translate into economic gain).[21] This paradox is one of the defining features that is specific to middle-class formation. The political power of middle-class identity derives from this

---

[20] Since the election, Modi has also begun to muddy the distinction between the two languages of the economy that I have discussed earlier. His public rhetoric has returned to earlier languages of state-led development yet collapsed these languages with a normative support for policies of liberalization.

[21] See Jeffrey, Jeffery, and Jeffery (2008) for a useful ethnographic account of such distinctions.

very sense of ambivalence (Wacquant, 1991). The ideational force of 'middle-class' status harnesses the aspirational dispositions of less privileged sections of the middle classes even when these segments are structurally constrained by the reproduction of socio-economic inequality. While an extensive discussion of the political conse-quences of these internal contradictions within India's middle classes are beyond the scope of this chapter, Modi's deployment of the idea of the 'neo-middle class' is an example of the political significance of the contradictions that are inherent in the discrepancies between the prosperity of the dominant proprietary middle classes and the less privileged middle classes.

'THE DOMAIN OF CLASS INTERESTS': FUTURE SCHOLARLY TRAJECTORIES AND THE IMPORT OF *THE POLITICAL ECONOMY OF DEVELOPMENT IN INDIA*

While Bardhan's conception of the dominant proprietary classes necessitates a rethinking of the boundaries, internal contradictions, and dynamics that shape middle-class formation, it nevertheless marks an avenue for much-needed theoretical and empirical research on con-temporary India. As I have noted already, much contemporary research on the middle classes in India focuses on questions of consumption, income, and cultural identity. The question of 'class' within the middle class more often than not serves as a descriptive marker of privilege, identity, or upward mobility. What is missing in such scholarly work is an analytical understanding of the '*domain* of class interests' (Bardhan, 1984: 49). That is, what is missing is an understanding of class analysis as a means of examining both how public resources are appropriated in systemic ways and how this appropriation of the public surplus contrib-utes to the *reproduction* of inequality through long-standing structural processes. Such an approach belies easy dichotomies between state-led development and the age of neoliberal economics, and ultimately pro-vides an indispensable analysis of the ways in which class structures the political economy of development in India.

In the context of United States scholarship on India, for instance, the analytical space for an analysis of the domain of class interests has been a long-disappearing feature of knowledge production in the field of

South Asian studies.[22] While early decades of scholarship on India were often marked by assumptions of Indian exceptionalism that presumed that cultural identity rather than class was the foundational underpinning of the political economy of India, there remained a strong trend in the study of political economy that centred on questions of class and the systemic analysis of structural inequality.[23] In more recent years, dominant scholarly trends in political science in the United States of America have been far removed from any serious consideration of class analysis, as most scholarly work on Indian political economy has been premised on the normative belief in the benefits of policies of economic liberalization.[24] Meanwhile, work that has addressed class and socio-economic inequality (particularly in the post–liberalization period) has focused on the micro-dynamics of power relations produced by strategies and policies of economic development. Influenced by the Foucauldian turn in anthropological and cultural studies of power and inequality, such work has eschewed systemic, structural analyses of political economy as outmoded approaches.[25] The result is that there has been a growing closure of analytical space for scholarly work that seeks to understand the linkages between macro-policies on the one hand and the micro-dynamics of power and exclusion on the other. Such an understanding requires *a theory of interests* (rather than a particular methodological or disciplinary bent) that invests the category of class with analytical import rather than mere description. It is, then, the force of this theory of class interests which lies at the foundation of Bardhan's *PEDI* and which provides a path for an understanding of the inequalities, exclusions, and forms of appropriation that continue to structure the political economy of development in India.

---

[22] For a discussion of such trends, see Herring and Agarwala (2008).

[23] See for example Rudolph and Rudolph (1987) and Chakrabarty (1989) for different variants of arguments of Indian exceptionalism. For work that centred questions of class, see Byres (1981) and Patnaik (1976).

[24] For an exception to such trends, see Kohli (2012).

[25] In the study of middle-class politics, for instance, Bourdieu's work has heavily influenced anthropological research on class distinction. However, such research tends to dislocate Bourdieu's analysis of distinction from his theoretical investment in analysing broader, systemic forms of class structuration.

10 Malgudi on the Move[1]

Bardhan's Political Economy and the Rest of India

Barbara Harriss-White, Muhammad Ali Jan,
and Asha Amirali

Towards the end of his ground-breaking book on the dominant coalitions of capital—*The Political Economy of Development in India* (hereafter *PEDI*)—Pranab Bardhan writes of 'lower class interlopers' (1998: 79): 'Over the last two decades or so, all over this vast subcontinent, scattered signs of a great deal of ferment and stirring have been discernible. Much of this is still incoherent, unorganised, impulsive and primordial in forms of expression' (Bardhan, 1998: 82). It still is. At this point in the book, Bardhan is thinking as much of politics as of political economy but it is the political economy of this ferment that we will develop here.

Bardhan's thesis is that India's lacklustre performance in the 1970s and 1980s was driven by the encroachment onto state autonomy of three proprietary classes—agricultural, industrial, and the professional proprietors of human capital (39)—which proceeded to joust

---

[1] Malgudi is a fictional small town in *mofussil* India, in which several of R.K. Narayan's novels and short stories are set. Mofussil means provincial, as in 'mofussil towns'—though mostly rural.

over scarce resources in a way that retarded productive infrastructural investment and growth. This, however, does not tackle the origins of the ferment of 'subordinate classes' (77). To supply this missing element means shifting focus to the complementary plot of *PEDI*: the contribution of the wrong kind of growth—unequalizing growth (8)—to the widespread and persistent poverty and poor human development that Bardhan recognized in 1984 and surely still laments to this day.

Shifting focus to the rest of India (RoI) means we have to examine the inability of the dominant coalition to account for what Prabhat Patnaik (2011) has called the Perverse Transformation—the failure of Bardhan's industrial propertied class and the professional holders of human capital to generate employment for the wage workers, tenants, and impoverished micro-propertied rural producers, who quit agriculture in part or in whole, but in droves (Sen, 2002; Government of India, 2007; Chapter 7). Why 95 per cent of all Indian firms employ fewer than five wage workers; why the average labour force per firm dropped during the era of liberalization from three in 1990 to two in 2011; why the commonest form of livelihood is self-employment or own-account enterprise; how growth can be accompanied by failure to accumulate; why even now the unregistered, informal economy dominated by own-account enterprise still contributes a larger share of gross domestic product (GDP) than does the corporate sector, and the extent to which this RoI is in contention or contradiction with Bardhan's dominant proprietary classes (DPCs).[2]

To explore these mostly unregistered 'lower class interlopers', the actual bedrock of India's economy, we also have to examine the state outside the limits of its own reach. When India's competitive advantage results from the state's long-standing refusal to register and regulate so much of the economy, we need to ask whether, as Bardhan wrote, '(t)he autonomy of the Indian state is reflected more often in its regulatory (and hence patronage-dispensing) than developmental role' (1998: 39). Whose interests have been served not just by the state's failure to adequately provide for, or to develop, most peoples' capabilities (Sen, 1999), but also by its deliberate regulative failure (Chibber, 2003; Dasgupta, 2016; Wielenga, forthcoming)?

[2] For a discussion of these questions and of the evidence to answer them, see Harriss-White (2012).

These are important questions first because, as Bardhan has observed elsewhere (1989b), macro political economy sets parameters for understanding specific micro-outcomes. Second, the incorporation of the RoI may result in new conclusions overlooked by a political economy confined to the DPCs.

We argue that understanding India's low-skilled, high-poverty, and unequal growth hinges on developing explanations of the political–economic dynamics of classes and economic activities that are not accounted for by Bardhan's DPCs. They lie 'below' them, clustered in strata of non-monopoly capital, petty production/self-employment, and wage labour. They live and work in the informal economy, with trade being the largest component. Empirical research on class formation across India and the interlinkages between the RoI, the state, and large capital also demonstrates that the DPCs are less internally homogenous than Bardhan had theorized and that their fortunes are deeply intertwined with the RoI. If there is such heterogeneity *within classes* in India, then can heterogeneity *within the class-coalition* be a privileged factor in explaining growth and stagnation, as Bardhan argues? We argue that explaining India's growth and development must account for this 'messiness', and to the extent that the state is responsible for growth (as Bardhan strongly assumes it is), it is clear that the RoI's linkages and interests vis-à-vis the state compromise its capacity and autonomy at least as much as—if not more than—the DPCs.

Addressing these questions of political economy outside Bardhan's coalition, our chapter falls into three parts. First, what has happened to Bardhan's proprietary classes and how their roles in the development of the rest of India have been understood? In particular, were Bardhan's DPCs too internally coherent? Second, how has the RoI been theorized in class and non-class terms? Third, how does non-apex capital work on the ground, what difference does it make that capital is not 'seamless', what do the local seams look like, and how do the power relations of the Indian economy and state work locally?[3]

---

[3] We will not address how the proprietary classes broke the logjam of Hindu growth rates; see other chapters in this volume. We also lack space to examine either the Labour question or the Classes of Labour question (see Lerche, 2011).

DEVELOPMENT OF THE PROPRIETARY CLASSES AND THEIR IMPACT ON THE REST OF INDIA

Given how well populated the field of Indian political economy is—and how central *PEDI* has been to this scholarly field—it is significant that little has been written explicitly about the proprietary classes' effects on smaller-scale fractions of capital. Here we examine how the proprietary classes have developed before turning to their effects.

The First Proprietary Class: Apex Industrial Capital

Though the informal processes of liberalization and deregulation had begun decades before the 1991 reforms (Dasgupta, 2016), a number of remarkable transformations have occurred subsequently in the way components of the dominant proprietary coalition evolved and in their relationship to the state and the non-dominant classes. In particular, big capital has seen dramatic change in both its internal composition and its relationship to the state. First, its sectoral composition has been transformed from one dominated by capital goods industries such as textile, iron, steel, and paper to one in which information technology (IT), media, pharmaceuticals, and entertainment have prominent roles. This is a world apart from Bardhan's original DPCs (Damodaran, 2008: 3). Concomitantly, there has been a great turnover in the number of big businesses at the top, with many new entrants into the top 20 between 1969 and 2000 (Mazumdar, 2011: 37–8). Finally, the shifting caste composition of the big business houses has started to undermine the extraordinary domination of the historically mercantile (bania) castes, with the entry of Brahmins and even people from middle castes and from agrarian backgrounds—especially at the regional (state) level (Baru, 2000).

But big capital has also been shifting its business strategies since the time of *PEDI*'s publication—J. Harriss had already pointed to industrialists in Coimbatore setting up smaller unregistered production units due to the advantages it brought in diversifying their investment portfolios, as well as the lower labour costs due to casualization and the evasion of other regulative laws (1982: 951). Not only is the control of production through small-scale enterprise, diversification, the pre-emption of regulation, and lower labour costs important in itself, but this direct, micro-scale investment also helps big capital gain other advantages of small scale such as tax concessions and access to cheaper credit (Mezzadri, 2010: 502). These practices have proliferated after the period covered by *PEDI*, to the point where a large number of small-scale enterprises are fictitious entities created through the fragmentation of the accounts of larger units seeking the advantages of smallness. At the extreme, they exist on paper alone (as in Ruthven's 2008 study of the Moradabad metal cluster; see also McCartney, 2013: 247).

However, not only have large firms expanded through spawning smaller units, but what has been even more widespread is the practice of larger firms' outsourcing or subcontracting parts of their operations to other firms (Harriss-White, 2003: 40; 2017). By a range of different means such as credit and raw material supplies, parent firms are able to reduce their costs but still ensure timely supplies. D. Haynes (2012) has shown how sub-contracting by larger firms has more than a century of ancestry. Even during Jawaharlal Nehru's leadership, the consolidation of larger units was the exception that proved the rule. In fact, liberalization has led to the consolidation of entire industrial clusters through a combination of local accumulation, outsourcing by larger companies, and the establishment of smaller units by large capitalists in which the role of state policy and promotion has also been crucial (for example, Tewari, 1998; Chari, 2004; Mezzadri, 2014). Overall, the increasing nexus between the state and big capital has helped business houses to wrest many benefits from the state while increasingly informalizing parts of their businesses to disempower labour and reap the additional advantages of smaller scale (Kohli, 2012).

The Second Proprietary Class: Agricultural Capital

But the nexus between big business and government does not mean that the role of Bardhan's second proprietary class, the agricultural bourgeoisie, has atrophied. Its trajectories are elaborated elsewhere in this volume (see Chapter 7). While the populist 'peasant movements' of the 1980s have lost much of their force, the plethora of subsidies and benefits they managed to secure continue to account for a considerable share of the national budget. Most research shows that these transfers overwhelmingly benefit the 'rich peasant'/capitalist farmer stratum of agrarian society and constrain fiscal space for more urgently needed public investments in agriculture (Vaidyanathan, 2006). In more advanced agricultural regions where growth is concentrated, capitalist farmers have prospered disproportionately; and in capturing state resources, they have made substantial gains when other regions and the rest of the social structure of agriculture have faltered (Lerche, 2015).

While the second dominant proprietary class requires more careful research than is currently available, a few trends, teased from both general data and case studies, are relevant here. First, the continuing importance of agricultural subsidies has been accompanied by a decline in the overall contribution of the sector to GDP. Second, the transfer of subsidies has not been accompanied by any substantial gains in revenue collection from agriculture, which continues to be a tax-free haven for rich 'farmers'. Third, while some inputs and commodity markets are controlled, directed, or parametrically regulated by the state production decisions, the control and deployment of labour and rental contracts (*de facto* if not *de jure*) are unregulated or regulated through institutions of custom. Fourth, many from the 'middle-caste' capitalist farming class have diversified into the non-farm economy, straddling the rural–urban divide. Finally, agriculture is the frontline of the conflictual labour processes that perpetuate the mass rural poverty and low levels of human development regretted by Bardhan (1998: 8).

The Third Proprietary Class: Owners of Human Capital[4]

For Bardhan, the 'professionals' (disproportionately Brahmin and upper-caste) were no mere 'auxiliary class', necessary to the reproduction of society but not materially productive. On the contrary, they were in conflict with both fractions of apex private capital, successfully kept education away from the masses, protecting the rents derived from their precious human capital, and frittering away state resources in current expenditure (Bardhan, 1998: 51–2; 61–2). But since 1984, the bureaucracy (entry to which is vital to lower-caste aspiration) has entered a slow decline and started to vernacularize—especially in the lower levels and the provinces. Education has also started to obsess mofussil India. Rural Dalit families go into debt to educate their

---

[4] On the professionals as a DPC, and the rise of middle classes, see Chapters 8 and 9. On India's rural middle classes, see Aslany (2019).

children privately in English (Heyer, 2014). While India's dominant industrial proprietary class generates growth that is famously 'jobless' (see Chapter 2), a large new class (though like Bardhan's other DPCs not a class in Marx's sense) is deploying its human capital throughout the economy.

Defined in terms of assets and income, numbering anywhere from 50 to 200 million and growing rapidly, the educated middle classes are an element in the structure of accumulation driving it through consumption—Weber's 'styles of life'. These middle classes are mostly urban, 'ideological' groups, expressing dominant ideas but occupying intermediate, and often contradictory class locations. On the one hand, they overlap with the bourgeoisie (business families, informal capitalist firms owning and/or managing financial, manufacturing, service and commercial property); on the other hand, they align socially with the aristocracy of 'labour' (the salariat accounts for a quarter of all employment) and with the self-employed (over half of all livelihoods).[5] They also include the ancillary classes: not only the bureaucracy, but also the 'capability-rich' professions (law, medicine, and education).[6]

Yet, novel as they are, India's middle classes have strengthened many features of the country's pre-liberalization economy. They have generated domestic incentives for the expansion of a capitalism biased towards the provision of *services*. These services are in turn polarized between capital- and labour-intensiveness, with one powering exports and the other livelihoods. While capital continues to benefit from state subsidies—prime among which is tax evasion—labour-intensive activity is left to fend for itself in the informal economy. Not socially exclusive, but internally differentiated, and straddling the contradiction between the economics of markets and the politics of democracy (Jodhka and Prakash, 2015), the middle classes express contradictory political demands. While the upper-caste middle class is retreating into private 'gated communities' and commercial and leisure spaces in the cities,[7] the lower-caste middle class in cities and small towns aspires to wrench state patronage away from upper-caste control. Even in a

---

[5] By no means all of whom will be middle-class in income terms.

[6] For a full discussion, see Jodhka and Prakash (2015).

[7] Of course, the state led the way: many early 'gated communities' were residential colonies for state employees.

neoliberal era, they continue to call for and benefit from an economically interventionist state (see Chapter 9). They need its jobs and they
need the bridging networks that support the expansion of minimally
regulated/informal enterprise.

Thus, the three DPCs have all undergone major transformations
since the publication of Bardhan's 1984 manuscript. We can now turn
to explore whether Bardhan's conceptualization of the DPCs can
withstand the inclusion of the RoI or whether it needs to be developed further to accommodate 'Malgudian' processes.

The Limits of Coherence: A Fragmentary Coalition

While it is clear that *PEDI*'s dominant proprietary classes are all still
alive, some are in better health than others. Moreover, as we try to
demonstrate, the ruling classes that *PEDI* conceptualized were more
unitary and internally homogeneous than the heterogeneous and
fragmentary coalition that emerges when economic processes in the
rest of the economy—incompletely and selectively regulated by the
state—are included.

To begin with, as N. Tyabji has argued, 'the unintegrated nature of
the economy leads to distinct cycles of accumulation', resulting in an
internally stratified business class (Tyabji, 1981: 75). Dasgupta (2016)
has confirmed the existence of waves of accumulation before and during liberalization. Not only do these distinct cycles lead to a segmentation of capital by scale, but these waves also take spatial forms in which
regional capital, localized to a particular area or state, emerges and
prospers. These emerging, stratified, and spatially viscous fractions of
intermediate capital can develop interests that are at odds with those of
national corporate capital. For example, intermediate capital benefits
from scarcities of wage goods, but national capital relies on a structure
of prices where wage goods are cheap; intermediate capital is mostly
organized through the patriarchal family, while national capital has a
corporate management structure.

Alongside these processes, the continued vernacularization of the
state has also helped many of these capitalists to wrest advantages from
the 'local' and 'regional' state, sometimes at the expense of national capitalists who—for both their sources of capital and markets for their products—operate at an all-India level (Baru, 2000: 228). Further, *PEDI*'s

coalition of internally homogeneous capitalist class fractions wresting benefits from the 'relatively autonomous' state omits the consequences for growth emerging from a finer-grained classification. In fact, it seems that many different types of capitalists are simultaneously trying to transfer resources and gain benefits by building relationships of patronage with the state,[8] which itself tends to develop more incoherently at the central level, even as its roots deepen at the local and regional level.

Likewise, even though *PEDI* points to the increasing diversification of 'rich peasants' out of agriculture and into industry, Bardhan never really asks how this affects his model. Can the prevalence of accumulation trajectories linking agriculture to trade, services, and industry still allow us to speak of industrial capital and 'rich peasants' as two distinct groups? How does the existence of multiple portfolios of investment affect the strategies of these groups vis-à-vis the state, and does it not suggest that these categories are neither watertight, nor as internally homogeneous as *PEDI* tended to imply? Would Bardhan's macro-analysis of growth and stagnation explain Tyabji's un-integrated capitalist economy and the existence of distinct cycles of accumulation, in which (relative) stagnation in certain regions and sectors may simultaneously be accompanied by accumulation and growth of new layers of the capitalist class?

To help develop answers to these questions requires moving from a bird's-eye view to a bottom-up approach to the political economy of India, building the macro-picture through interactions with the micro-studies of the RoI: the black box of the informal economy and its interactions with the formal, registered, and state-regulated one. In such an analysis, production and distribution are driven and labour is controlled by a looser class coalition than *PEDI*'s more unitary formulation—and it leads us to ask whether the RoI is more important to the trajectories of growth and to the nature and patterns of accumulation than his DPCs are, and perhaps were.

THE REST OF INDIA AND ITS THEORISTS

Most of India's economy is non-corporate, non-metropolitan, and as fugitive from the statistical record as it is from tax compliance. It is the

---

[8] See Prakash (2014) on the distinct and costly politics of patronage imposed onto Dalit capitalists.

India of the 80 per cent living in small towns and villages. Its selectively unregistered economy has long been referred to as 'informal' and more recently as 'non-capitalist', the 'needs economy', the 'reserve army', the domain of 'timepass' and *jugaad* (creative fixing), and of the beneficiaries of state resource transfers (Altvater, 1993; Chatterjee, 2008; Harriss-White, 2003; Jan, 2012; Jeffrey, 2010; Radjiou, Prabhu, and Ahuja, 2012). All these phrases and terms indicate attempts to theorize what lay outside Bardhan's central concern in *PEDI*. They take seriously the fact that India's transition to capitalism is complete, but that a large mass of small firms are obdurately staying small and that capitalism is unfolding within a historically unique conjuncture different from that of historical Europe: Patnaik's 'perverse transformation' (2011). In this section, we will consider a subset of these conceptions of the RoI: the 'informal economy'; 'petty commodity production'; 'intermediate classes'; and the non-class political economy categories of Chatterjee's 'political society' and Sanyal's zone of 'non-capital'. We argue that the informal economy provides the key to understanding the distinctive features of Indian capitalism, as well as a more realistic picture of the processes producing not only growth, but also stagnation and poverty. These include the continuous reproduction of petty commodity production and the often blurred boundaries between this and disguised forms of wage-labour. But the RoI is also the domain of a loose coalition of small-scale capitalists whose organizational structure is embedded in local social and political institutions such as caste, gender, and religion, and whose distinct location in the economy allows it to survive and sometimes compete with big capital. Understanding their internal composition as well as their strategies of accumulation provides clues to the processes of growth and stagnation in the Indian economy better than the relatively coherent classes of *PEDI*.

India's Informal Economy

A majority of India's economy is composed of small firms that are 'unincorporated household enterprises differing from formal enterprises in terms of technology, economies of scale, use of labor intensive processes, and virtual absence of well-maintained accounts' (Kulshreshtha, 2011:S123). Despite the fact that many are unregistered, numerically they are thought to overwhelm any other size category of firms. They account for the major part of GDP and between 86 and 93 per cent of all jobs.[9] In the 1970s, early theory saw the informal sector as a transitory phenomenon to be absorbed by the formal sector once the structural transformation to capitalism was over. More complex views emerged in the 1980s and 1990s, suggesting that informality was not transitory because (*i*) it was functionally necessary for capitalist growth and (*ii*) firms chose informality in order to reduce the cost of doing business. Most recently, scholars have defined informality in terms of the employment relation, drawing an analytical boundary encompassing all those in unprotected, non-state regulated employment, including self-employment (Chen, 2007). It is, therefore, part of the economy containing a great deal of inequality as well as being the seat of labour-intensive growth and poverty.

Despite statisticians persistently regarding the informal economy as a residual, all attempts to estimate it confirm that it is massive and growing rather than shrinking—about two thirds of GDP and almost all livelihoods today. Moreover, A. Sinha and C. Adams' computable general equilibrium model of the Indian economy, distinguishing formal and informal activity and sectors, showed that in the late twentieth and twenty-first centuries it has been this sector that has driven the combination of fast growth and the expansion of employment/livelihoods of low productivity (Kulshreshtha, 2011: S132; Sinha and Adams, 2007). So not only are features such as informality which are conventionally thought of as transitory quite durable, but they also account for both of Bardhan's themes in *PEDI*.

Non-polar Classes: Petty Production

Apart from the overwhelmingly informal economy, another durable feature of Indian capitalism is the widespread existence of petty-commodity production, trade, and services (PCP for brevity), defined as a form combining the class positions of both capital and labour within the same household or enterprise (Bernstein, 2010: 128). The manner in which PCP is integrated into wider circuits of capital, as well as its interactions with the state, applies constant pressure to differentiate. The exploitation of PCP through several markets other than labour (product, money, inputs, rental-premises, and so on) blocks the path

---

[9] This discussion of informality draws on Basile and Harriss-White (2010).

of accumulation for most, forcing them to expand primarily through multiplication (Harriss-White, 2012: 125). Inheritance and marriage exchanges, start-up loans, and occasionally savings drive this expansion (Harriss-White, 2012: 125). In India, PCP livelihoods characterize not just the majority of trade and 'small enterprises', but also the vast majority of farmers (96 per cent of all farming households) that are unable to meet their expenses through earnings from agriculture alone (Bhalla, 2014: 15). The continuum of the self-employed stretches from autonomous PCP to an unknown but sizable force of disguised wage workers, dependent on brokers or merchants for their raw materials and access to product markets, indebted to them and not free to sell their labour power (Jan and Harriss-White, 2019). Further, PCP is flexible, can characterize whole regions, crowd certain sectors of an economy, and be inserted at every stage of a supply chain alongside forms of production thought by all major social theorists (from Adam Smith onwards) to be certain to destroy it—its destruction even defining modernity in the eyes of many.[10]

The state does not lack development projects for petty production: there are many forms under titles that include agrarian populism, micro-small industry, unorganized sector reforms, micro-finance, and 'inclusive development'. But together they are underfunded, poorly resourced, and tend to languish unimplemented in the political doldrums. At the same time, the state acts incoherently to destroy petty production (through physical evictions, super-marketization, city beautification); to underpin and protect it (through social security/safety nets, some kinds of cooperatives); to tolerate it (and indirectly tax it: municipal marketplaces); or to simply sustain it through unintended or ambiguous outcomes (the National Rural Employment Guarantee Scheme might be predicted to threaten PCP by offering alternative work—but equally, if it raises the wage and thus the productive returns below which an employer cannot employ wage labour, then PCP can compete for higher returns). And the politics of PCP, dispersed between the politics of capital (farmers' movements and business associations) and that of labour, is highly incoherent (Harriss-White, 2012).

---

[10] See the discussion of petty commodification in Harriss-White (2006).

But just as the vast majority of poor households reproduce at the margins of PCP and labour, with great overlaps between them, another durable feature of capitalist development in India has been the importance of a loose coalition of 'non-monopoly' capitalists in the political economy of India, overlooked by *PEDI* in its class analysis of stagnation and which provides an alternative framing to his own. These are the 'intermediate classes'.

Non-polar Classes: Intermediate Classes and Regimes

The theoretical pre-eminence of the stratum of rich farmers[11] was released from its agricultural moorings in the thesis of Intermediate Regimes, which K.N. Raj (1973) and P.S. Jha (1980) developed from Michał Kalecki (1972). Disputing the relative autonomy of the state, their formulation had at its centre a state held hostage by the 'intermediate classes': a triad, like *PEDI*'s, of agrarian and non-agrarian agents plus 'self-employed' bureaucrats (who combined capital with their own labour in private rentier production for 'the market'), and whose interests, therefore, did not align with either capital or labour. Where *PEDI* saw the three DPCs pushing and shoving each other to feed at the state's trough, Raj and Jha saw the numerically dominant ICs able to dictate policy that provided their social overhead capital, and engaging in extensive rent-seeking. If not in classically Marxist contradiction, the ICs certainly had conflicts of interest with workers over the prices of basic wage goods, aided and abetted by the former's active defence of micro-monopolies or local, collusive oligopolies. In sectors of the economy where the ICs did not benefit from synergy with corporate capital[12] and competed with it directly, ICs made immediate profits from scarcity while corporate shareholders and managers had to follow an indirect route for their returns. Further, for the most part under- or un-regulated ICs found black activity and evasion from obligations to the state easier than did large registered enterprises.[13] Stagnation,

---

[11] See Rudolph and Rudolph (1987) on 'bullock capitalists'; Mitra (1977) on 'rural oligarchy'; and Chapter 7.

[12] Jha (1980) lists upstream benefits to ICs from iron and steel, coal, energy, transport, arms, and so on.

in Jha's analysis, could be explained by policies that favoured small-scale industry over large, thereby 'sacrificing economies of scale', and through state complicity with activities that did not count as policy. This included tax evasion—the biggest subsidy of all (Harriss-White, 2003)—as well as corruption, bribery, energy theft, and speculative profiteering under conditions of shortage (Jha, 1980).

Harriss-White (2003) and McCartney (2013) have each argued that while the formal conditions for an intermediate regime have definitively come to an end with liberalization, the intermediate classes remain powerful economically and relevant politically. Despite the multitude of federated business associations, the spaces in which policy is formulated are now less accessible to them, but through market-driven politics, deploying tactics of non-competition and market segmentation, by effectively privatizing the local state—manipulating the implementation of policy—and by defending their interests through collective action and illegal activity, 'the intermediate classes are not so much in decay as cornered and fighting' (Harriss-White, 2003: 69). Intermediate classes defend non-competition with the help of the identity-based social networks through which market exchange is organized; they defend their economic interests through corporatist associations and with the help of their social contacts in the state; they manipulate local party politics (many funding all political parties, rather than being identified with any one); they enforce market contracts through authority relations based on caste, ethnicity, religion, gender, and so on, rather than through state sanctions; they consolidate local power by engaging in small acts of philanthropy or the provision of services to people in need of them, in parallel to the transfers of the state; and they also make profit by coercion and more recently the resurgence of primitive business practices—what F. Braudel called 'elementary fraud' (1982: 55). A picture emerges of a wide variety of strategies, a great deal of messiness, regulative continuity during liberalization, and a looser coalition than the internally coherent relationships of patronage between the state and discrete classes in *PEDI*.

---

[13] See Jairaj and Harriss-White (2006) for the sectoral and assets structure of fiscal non-compliance in Tamil Nadu.

The 'Rest of India' and Non-class Political Economy

Petty commodity producers and intermediate classes are the products of capitalist teleology gone awry. Their stubborn persistence, complexity, and heterogeneity have forced theorists of capitalist modernity to rethink their theories. Partha Chatterjee's (2004; 2008) response dispenses with class altogether, drawing a line between the legally constituted domain of 'civil society' and the contingent, patronage-infused, and often illegal domain of 'political society'. Corporate capital belongs to the former, all the rest to the latter. Like Chatterjee, Kalyan Sanyal (2007) also eschews the concepts of class(es) and the messy interpenetrations of forms of capitalism. Instead, he conceives of the economy as constituted by two analytically distinct spheres of 'capital' and 'non-capital'. The former is identified by the existence of the capital's exploitation of wage labour and the drive to accumulate, while the latter is 'a complex ensemble of activities where the purpose of production is to secure one's consumption/subsistence rather than to accumulate' (Sanyal, 2007: 209). This analytical separation, like Chatterjee's, breaks the teleology of capitalist development but only through manufacturing neat binaries at the expense of analytical clarity. By positing a 'non-capital' separate from capital, Sanyal dismisses the well-acknowledged economic dependency of capital on the super-exploitation of small-scale and petty production and the gendered reproduction of labour within the family (Brenner and Ramas, 1984).

Since 1984, the political economy of the RoI has become a wide and active field. The view that small, unregistered, heterogeneous capital constitutes a non-transitory, powerful economic and political phenomenon is now widely accepted. However, it has been arrived at using theoretical and methodological routes that have produced explanations at times wildly in variance with each other. There is room for research into the evidence base of the main lines of contention.

The RoI affects the DPCs in a number of ways. First, the RoI is exploited by DPCs (subcontracting); second, the RoI is a dumping ground for surplus labour that the DPCs fail to absorb; third, in individual cases the RoI supplies entrants to the DPCs (but these are rare); but fourth, in its capacity to drive growth and jobs it encroaches on the developmental role of DPCs; and fifth, RoI competes with and can undercut DPCs (particularly big capital) through super-exploitation of labour: both wage labour (by means of casual contracts, negligent health and safety conditions, and long working hours) as well as unwaged family labour. Moreover, the DPCs affect the RoI through their failure to absorb labour in decent work; through their profiting from the structure of prices created by unregulated, casualized, cheap, rightless labour and PCP, and through their capacity to enforce exchange relations that prevent accumulation. The net balance of forces is what gives India's capitalism its distinctive character—nationally and regionally.

While RoI theories have not been triggered by *PEDI*'s themes of growth and stagnation, some implications can be derived. First, the RoI has contradictory impacts on growth. On the one hand, PCP and the ICs drive growth through their capacity to expand by multiplication and their leading role in livelihoods. On the other hand, they drag growth by their producer-interest in inflation, by the large-scale diversion of fiscal resources away from the state (Roy, 1996), and by the mismatch between bribes and the productivity of the supplier of bribes (Khan and Jomo, 2001). Second, PCP is a repository of poverty— but rather than being a launching pad for upward mobility, it is the outcome of social, political, and economic obstacles to concentrated accumulation. Last but not least, the larger fractions of the ICs—joint family businesses and petty capital—may help to impose the very conditions preventing PCPs from accumulating.

GROUND REALITIES: THE WORKING OF NON–APEX CAPITAL

In the light of political economy approaches to the RoI, we now turn to insights from empirical research. The 1998 epilogue to *PEDI*, written when the reform process had by most accounts effected substantial changes in India's political economy, noted that the composition of the dominant class coalition and intra-coalition dynamics had changed and the problems posed by politically motivated public expenditure had intensified. Some of the changes—and reasons for them—have been outlined in the section 'The Development of the Proprietary Classes and Their Impact on the Rest of India' earlier in the chapter. As Jha (2013) shows, the surge in (criminal) regional party funding and economic power weakened central power. Political assertions by lower castes, together with the establishment of kinship linkages between new lower-caste entrants to the local business economy and the bureaucracy, further eroded the 'institutional insulation' of economic decision-making. The relative power of the bureaucracy declined and smaller-scale capitalist firms emerged in large numbers (Bardhan, 1998: 131). While the empirical literature does not address the themes of growth and stagnation, we can examine the political economy effects of this decentralized accumulation.

A profusion of adjectives litter the empirical literature on small capital in India—regional, provincial, agro-commercial, informal, fraternal, bullock, intermediate, and local—but despite their differences, the trajectories of accumulation they all describe are characterized by similar features including capital's rural/'rurban' roots, the structuring roles ('seams') of caste, ethnicity, religion, family, and gender, the growing interpenetration of this capital with the local state, and the tendency of capital to expand by the multiplication of firms through marriage alliances and inheritance partitions, rather than by the centralization and concentration characteristic of 'classic' processes of accumulation. Some case material sheds light on the question of the extent to which these increasingly potent local realities qualify Bardhan's model.

By the 1970s and 1980s, scholars across India were noting the phenomenon of rich(er) agricultural households diverting profits from agriculture into trade and agro-industrial enterprise and moving from village to town. In many instances, this was a continuation or intensification of trends from the colonial period. Carol Upadhya (1988, 1997) traced the development of what she termed 'a single regionally dominant class' in Andhra Pradesh (1997: 171). Benefiting from late-nineteenth-century irrigation infrastructure, followed by periods of prosperity during World War II and the Green Revolution, farmers accumulated surpluses and moved into trade and agro-industry. It was not always a unidirectional flow from agriculture to commerce and industry. At times, profits flowed the other way because land was also a source of stability and the joint-family structure encouraged and supported diversification. However, although diversification out of agriculture had strong economic rationales, Upadhya argues that it was also aimed at enabling participation in a predominantly urban middle-class culture. The rural elite increasingly looked down upon farming and village life and aspired to urban occupations and cultural polish. Strengthening caste identity was a strategy pursued by the wealthiest members of caste groups 'to define themselves as a class apart, to pursue their interests as such, and to increase their chances of attaining political and economic pre-eminence in the region' (1997: 178). In this account, the formation of a dominant non-agrarian capitalist class in Andhra Pradesh was the combined effect of relatively low returns on agricultural investment, a strong drive to attain higher (urban) status, and the institution of caste functioning to restrict entry.

In central Gujarat, a similar process of class formation with rural–urban bridging or 'regional' characteristics was observed by Mario Rutten (1995). The Green Revolution intensified a process of accumulation amongst rich Patidar caste farmers. By the 1980s, they could invest this surplus in agro-commercial and industrial businesses. Rutten noted a marked tendency for the proliferation of small enterprises rather than the growth of existing firms. This he explained by two factors. First, state policy provided an incentive for businesses to stay small because they did not have to comply with labour laws, received subsidies, and paid lower taxes (1995: 212). Second, the socially regulated nature of the economy itself encouraged diversification: family, caste, and kin networks facilitated access to credit and marketing channels, while the joint family provided a ready-made structure over which to distribute sectoral expertise and management. Because of households' increasing spread across sectors, Rutten settles on the category of 'agrarian capitalist entrepreneurs' (234) to describe the class he was observing and concludes with the observation that '[they have] become socially and politically the most powerful group in the Indian countryside today. They dominate the various organizations at the local level and to an increasing extent, Indian state power is exercised on their behalf' (354). Since they have their fingers in the pies of industry and commerce as well as agriculture, they may not be uniformly keen on higher agricultural output prices and may be more interested in small-town infrastructural development than in rural subsidies. In short, they are likely to be located somewhere along the spectrum of informality and neither agrarian nor big business.

The emphasis on analysing capital as a local phenomenon springs from the observation that both the economy and state policy—always and everywhere—play themselves out in specific social contexts. Attention to local specificities reveals the pervasiveness of social structures such as caste, family, and gender in the formation, regulation, and consolidation of capital at different levels. It also reveals the diversity within capital itself, going beyond the divides of regional and national, corporate and non-corporate, which gives capital its distinctive social character. Harriss-White's longitudinal studies of 'local' capitalism in Tamil Nadu (2015) also trace the development of agro-commerce in and around a market town over four decades as agrarian surplus moved to trade/finance and from trade to industry (although it often flowed back to trade/finance where that was more profitable). The space of 'non-corporate' or 'regional' capital is revealed as deeply hierarchical and populated by the categories of petty commodity producers, petty traders, and 'big' capital—distinguished through scales of finance, types of organization, and castes.[14] And even within 'big' capital in the rice sector, for instance, wealth disparities between paddy producers, traders, and millers are sharp and growing. These differences are key to understanding why capital does not often pull together, how politics unfolds, and what strategies are possible for various sectors, social groups, and individuals (Basile and Harriss-White, 2000; Basile, 2013; Harriss-White, 2015).

Sanjaya Baru (2000) seeks to understand the processes not of class formation per se but of regional differentiation. The key variable for him is the emergence of a diversified rich cultivating class that made economic use of the state, political parties, caste, and family networks. This class was the product of colonial and postcolonial state policies, its development varying greatly across regions. Where it was already economically and politically influential (for example, in Andhra Pradesh and Gujarat), the Indian state intervened vigorously and effectively in its favour during the Green Revolution, exacerbating existing regional inequalities. However, emerging capitalists were unable to compete with big industrial capital for the largesse flowing from permit-raj Delhi and sought to strengthen themselves at the state level, where they could most effectively influence policy formulation and implementation. Regional parties became the vehicles through which small capital penetrated state corridors and ensured sympathetic treatment for itself.

In post-reform India, all evidence points to the fact that the symbiotic relationship between regional parties and regional capital (and

---

[14] See Srinivasan (2015) on the social fissures between PCP and wage labour in the market town of Arni, Tamil Nadu.

their funding) has deepened. Shaped by regional caste relations ranging from aspiration to physical conflict, regional/local capital reaches
towards national markets in units generally of a smaller scale than apex
capital.

The Actually Existing State Outside the Scope of Its Own Effective Reach

Both Bardhan and Mushtaq Khan (1998) have viewed the state's institutional autonomy as compromised by its need to pay a steady tribute
to the various components of the dominant coalition. Liberalization
was an attempt not so much to 'remove the economy from politics' as
to remove the state even further from the regulation of the economy,
solve *PEDI*'s problem of the proliferation of subsidies and grants, and
thereby restore some of the state's supposed autonomy. Policy has certainly changed as a result. But it now clearly favours big business, with
little formal space for non-polar classes wedged between corporate
capital on the one hand and wage labour on the other—and with especially little concern for the latter. Classes are being formed, however,
in the political space where the state's reach is weak. What is the state's
impact on class formation outside its direct reach?

The informal economy beyond the regulative state is socially ordered
through authority grounded in identity and self-organized institutions,
and governed politically by a shadow or parallel state (Harriss-White,
2003: Chapter 4). A mass of field evidence has shown how the formal
or official state that nominally governs the RoI is penetrated by private
interests and forms a nexus with local small-scale capital, which profits
from the selective and partial implementation of regulative interven-
tions. In this respect, the liberalizing impact of the neoliberal state is no
different. India's state does not deregulate so much as 're-regulate', and
to the extent that it 'retreats', it increases space for informal regulation.
It does so not just informally, but also formally and explicitly—as when
land-use plan violations and planning for violations form an integrated
system (Sundaresan, 2014).[15]

---

[15] See the analysis in Harriss-White (2008). A new study of the politics
of planning in Bangalore sees the dualism between formality and informality
as misconceived: 'private and public interest networks [produce] private and

While Akhil Gupta (1995) has characterized these relations as forming a 'blurred boundary' and stressed their porosity, Aseem Prakash (2017) has identified the frontier where economic laws that should regulate an entire territory and/or society fizzle out, and other non-state regulative practices take their place, as a distinctive political space. In the North Indian rural economy that he has studied, tenancy is still regulated through caste relations irrespective of land laws. Agricultural wages are held below the legal minimum. Migrants and low-caste workers face more severe wage discrimination than does local labour, and their rights to organize are savagely repressed. Here, no attempt is made to enforce the laws regulating production. So they are ignored.

Where agricultural land meets the expanding city, the master-plans through which land-use is regulated are besieged by insider lobbying at every stage (often by real estate speculators). Exceptions are conceded before the plan is even conceptualized, not to mention during successive rounds of modification, and so become normalized. Here the state's autonomy is at the mercy of conflicts within the capitalist class and of the use of these conflicts by local state officials, who gain money and stature as a result. The nexus between the local state and local capital is readily apparent here, though perennial conflict hardly benefits all members of the class involved.

At the first off-farm transaction that determines returns to production, sellers of the marketed surplus face the collusion of commission agents and the use of producers' indebtedness to flout the law specifying contracts and price formation. The Regulated Markets Act is implemented but it may be evaded without sanction.[16] Socially regulated exchange then displaces the legal regime. In agro-processing, 'extra-service fees' (bribes) are exacted by regulators for granting licences, flouting pollution controls, and chicanery on quality standards.

---

public interest outcomes' such that '*plan violations* and *planning for violations* support each other and form an integrated system'; public interest policy and private interest plans are continuously negotiated (Sundaresan, 2014: 297, 303). Nonetheless, the recognition of informal practice draws attention to limits of the role played by formal laws.

[16] The Haryana Agricultural Produce Markets Act, 1961, is colloquially known as the Regulated Markets Act.

A fraudulently non-compliant economy is assisted by the creation of private markets and livelihoods inside the state. In transport, this consists of an illegal economy of brokerage. On one side, liaison agents create a 'single window' for bribes; on another, a system of prepaid cards has been developed by means of which these bribes are paid and accounted for. Returns from illegal overloading are shared between owners, booking agents, commission agents, informal bankers, officials, politicians, and local caste leaders in a nexus of economic, political, and cultural power. Once more, interests in the state create illegal markets and benefit privately from them. Payment for rent and bribes can also shift from cash to goods such as luxury cars and real estate. The narrative of rents and extortion is very well known, even to the office peons. Open gloating is done with sure impunity (Prakash, 2017).

In these field studies, the state is found to be ignored, displaced, used as a nutrient base for illegal markets, and captured. In a politics of regulation in which the state does not wield monopoly power, rents are used in a process of double capture: formally independent regulators are subject to manipulation by politicians, and the state is captured by local capital. In the process, informal institutions such as the credit card for tracking prepaid bribes evolve around the formal institutions such as the weighbridge or check-post. Informal relations evolve into 'hybrid' institutions that are now deeply rooted.

The actually existing state cannot be reformed without destroying these institutions, economic flows, and livelihoods. In policy for urban and regional planning, faced with severe distortions of both intent and practice, two responses have been developed: on the one hand 'flexible' regulation, on the other, ever more detailed specification. But both approaches to the informal economy have failed to impose an alternative order on the regulative frontier. The process of enforcement is captured by local capital.[17]

More work like this is needed to check whether it is different in other sectors and regions, because the question how general such politics are is one that both policymakers and scholars of the state should care about. We see that the state's regulative autonomy is at the very least severely compromised. This carries implications for the state's developmental capacity and autonomy. Its capacity is compromised

---

[17] Champaka Rajagopal, personal communication, 2013.

by its reduced fiscal flows as firms evade taxes and levies and public resources are privatized; its autonomy is eroded by the very existence of entrenched local state-capital networks with interests separate from—and opposed to—those of planners. This shows that to the extent that development and growth are state-led, as Bardhan critically saw it, it is not the interests of his three DPCs that are responsible.

★★★

In this chapter we have explored the decentralization and fragmentation of class fractions within 'the capitalist class' that were marginalized in Bardhan's 1984 *PEDI*, their relationships to each other, and to the actually existing state. Bardhan had noted in 1998 that rich farmers were diversifying into commerce and small industry and were probably 'not averse' to less regulation (Bardhan, 1998: 131), that regional capitalists were gaining strength, and that corruption was becoming normalized. Although the literature we review is not centred on these themes, we find these processes not just well rooted in the pre-history of liberalization, but also central to understanding growth and redistributivist development in India today.

Two major conclusions emerge. First, much evidence demonstrates that a large part of India is neither purely agrarian nor industrial.[18] Through tracing processes of class formation across the country, it becomes apparent that the class categories of rich farmers, industrial capital, and professionals no longer apply (if they ever did) to the economically diversified, culturally heterogeneous, and wildly size-differentiated elements of India's capitalism. Moreover, the holders of human capital—the middle classes—are neither acting in concert with each other, nor displaying convergent attitudes and interests with other class fractions. If there is such heterogeneity *within classes* in India, then can heterogeneity *within the class-coalition* be a privileged factor in explaining growth and stagnation?

Second, we drew attention to the numerical preponderance of small-scale firms and their significant contribution to the national economy. These small labour-intensive firms of informal India are permanent

---

[18] Further research should explore the role of commerce and finance in these diverse portfolios.

features of Indian capitalism. They overlap with the casual labour force in their quagmires of poverty. They are also functionally linked to the hulking, capital-intensive firms of corporate India through practices of subcontracting and outsourcing, fraud so as to evade regulation, and illegal activity linked to party-political funding. Such links supply incentives for cooperation as well as conflict with large capital.

While in 1984 Bardhan's subaltern classes were stirring, by 1998 he could see that the lower layers of capital were growing fast. But Bardhan did not consider the possibility of their having distinct class interests in and for themselves in which the power of numbers confounds the power of capital. Nor did he consider their contradictions with corporate capital and with wage labour; let alone the capacity of the RoI to drive both growth and livelihoods. He also did not anticipate their capacity to consolidate a politics which sabotages the regulative state, while their decentralized informal-criminal activity riddles the economy and their fiscal non-compliance hobbles the developmental state. Bardhan's normative case for a state that can insulate itself from the dominant classes meets evidence that what is actually needed are interlinkages between the classes and India's states[19] of a kind that can integrate the RoI with large capital in a manner that generates growth, upgrades skills, and shifts India from a low-skill to a high-skill, job-creating trajectory. Our chapter has shown that there are enemies and obstacles to such a project both inside Bardhan's DPCs and outside in the rest of India.

---

[19] As Peter Evans (1995) and others have shown.

V

Conclusions

11 An Indian Gilded Age?

Continuity and Change in the Political Economy of India's Development

Michael Walton[1]

This chapter explores India's political economy of development. It has two counterpoints. The first is vividly illustrated by the two mansions shown in Figures 11.1 and 11.2. Cornelius Vanderbilt's house (one of many built by the Vanderbilt family) is an iconic product of the Gilded Age of the late nineteenth-century United States of America. This was a period famous for its 'robber barons', many of whom sought to preserve their fame through philanthropic ventures—extreme economic rents transformed into a resonant blend of private wealth and public-spirited foundations, which transformed the collective associations of their names. The second is the more recent house of Mukesh Ambani, India's richest man, still mainly known for his conglomerate company and private wealth, but also moving into the business of support for universities and other more public endeavours.

[1] Thanks to Pratap Bhanu Mehta and Ashutosh Varshney and to participants in seminars in the Centre for Policy Research, and the Universities of Oxford, Brown, Berkeley, and the Harvard Kennedy School. Special thanks to Pranav Sidhawi for research assistance and to Martin Chorzempa and Shreya Pandey for specific research inputs.

FIGURE 11.1   Cornelius Vanderbilt's Summer Home
Source: Felix Lipov/Shutterstock.

FIGURE 11.2   Mukesh Ambani's Mumbai Home
Source: Ashwin Nagpal/Getty Images.

The second counterpoint is Pranab Bardhan's seminal book *Political Economy of Development in India* (*PEDI*), written in 1984, to which this volume is dedicated. As Bardhan himself wrote in the 1998 epilogue to the expanded edition:

> I had described a system of political gridlock in India, originating in the collective action problems of a large, heterogeneous coalition of dominant interest groups with multiple veto powers, and with no interest group powerful enough to hijack the state … the system thus settled for short-run particularistic compromises in the form of sharing the spoils through an elaborate network of subsidies and patronage distribution, to the detriment of long-run investment and economic growth. (Bardhan, 1998: 130)

The central thesis of *PEDI* was that there were three 'dominant proprietary classes' (DPCs)—richer peasantry, business, and the bureaucracy (with the bureaucracy an interest group rather than an autonomous agent of the state). Each benefited from 'particularist' deals, but would have benefited more over the longer term—as would the broader society—with a more autonomous, developmental state. But this would have involved giving up their current 'spoils'. The political leaders and various arms of the state lacked the coordinatory and enforcement capacity to effect such a restructuring of the complex 'network of subsidies and patronage distribution', even more so as many potentially faced genuine short-term losses. Even if political elites wanted to effect systemic change, the state lacked credibility.

At first sight, these two prisms look to be in opposition with each other. Even as Bardhan was writing, the beginnings of the shift to a pro-business policy and political orientation was starting under Prime Minister Rajiv Gandhi, along with an associated growth acceleration (Kohli, 2006a; 2006b; Rodrik and Subramanian, 2005). The Indian stock market was becoming active, spurred by the 1977 initial public offering of Reliance by Mukesh Ambani's father (McDonald, 2010). Dhirubhai Ambani had successfully broken into the seemingly resilient License Raj system—a system that seemed to be the preservative of established businesses, and part of the broader gridlock that *PEDI* described.

Since the mid-1980s the Indian economy has been transformed. National income per capita is now almost four times the mid-1980s level and the official poverty measure has fallen from 45 per cent in

1993–94 to 22 per cent in 2011–12 (Narayan and Murgai, 2016). Private fixed capital formation rose from less than 15 per cent of gross domestic product (GDP) in the early 1980s to over 30 per cent in 2010 (before declining to 24 per cent in 2015). The number of Indian billionaires, resident in India, reported by *Forbes* rose from two or three in the mid-1990s to almost 100 in 2018.

This does not look like gridlock. In the domain of business—one of the three DPCs at the core of *PEDI*'s political economy—the two main themes of recent years have been India's business dynamism and the increased intermingling of political and business elites. There has been a major countervailing movement in the expansion of social provisioning, especially under the 2004–14 governments of the Congress-led United Progressive Alliance (UPA) coalition, largely sustained under the Bharatiya Janata Party (BJP) government of Prime Minister Narendra Modi since 2014. It seems as if K. Polanyi's sequential double movement is happening simultaneously in India (Polanyi, 2001; Stewart, 2010). While there are different views on the drivers and impacts of this—rights-based social democracy or opportunistic populism?—it also speaks to substantial policy initiatives shaped by the unfolding political economy (see Walton, 2013; other essays in Khilnani and Malhoutra, 2013; and Aiyar and Walton, 2015).

There has also been striking action in electoral politics. The Indian electorate has shown its enthusiasm for kicking out poorly performing incumbents—in many state elections and in the national 2014 election—and also, at times, in rewarding relatively good performance, for example, in Bihar, Madhya Pradesh, and Chhattisgarh in the past decade (even if eventually the electorate decided for change in December 2018 elections in the last two states). The electoral victory of Modi, with the BJP, was, correctly or incorrectly, seen as marking a sharp, collective demand for change especially in the realm of government action, spurred by the blend of high-profile scams under the UPA and the daily frustrations of dealing with government. Some characterized this in the well-worn trope of the rise of aspirations amongst the Indian lower and middle classes, underpinned by the experience of rising incomes and increasing state presence.

This chapter argues that an updated version of *PEDI*'s original insights remains relevant. It particularly explores the following ideas:

- The parallel between contemporary India and the US Gilded Age of the late nineteenth century is indeed striking and useful, both with respect to the manner in which wealth concentration has often gone hand in hand with extensive state-business relations, and in the 'two faces of capitalism'—*both* rent-extracting and formative of institutional change and productivity dynamics.

- While there has indeed been large-scale change in the domains of economic formation and public provisioning, to an important extent India continues to be stuck and resistant to systemic institutional change. However, the nature of this has changed: the collective action problem holding back private investment was to varying degrees 'solved' in the market reform era, at least in many states. But to a significant extent, this involved restructuring of the 'deals space' in rent-sharing relations. Collective action problems remain important both for a transition to a fully rules-based system and for broader issues of governance.

- An even more interesting parallel, or rather contrast, is with the US Progressive Era (generally dated from the 1890s to the 1920s). In the United States of America, a heterogeneous coalition of political and social movements, linked with executive and bureaucratic reforms, led to a transformation of the United States of America to what would now be called a functional social democracy, a 'Grand Bargain' that saved capitalism. However, in India, the continued prevalence of 'particularist compromises' renders similar collective action particularly hard. This is in spite of the apparent paradox that most of the Progressive Era's 'victories' are legally on the books in India.

- Indeed, the very extent of these 'victories', and the associated reach of the state, has been a source for the channelling of social energies into particularist strategies, in which interest groups seek to negotiate a better deal from a more present and resource-rich state.

The rest of the chapter is organized as follows. First, context is provided in terms of key developmental features of India with the United States of America circa 1900. Second, the Gilded Age comparison is explored, reviewing the comparative features of capitalism and the state. A third section turns to the Progressive Era response, in comparison with contemporary India. A fourth section provides a sketch of the prevailing political economy equilibrium of the past couple of decades—a suggestive update of *PEDI*. A final section offers a preliminary assessment of the recent period under Prime Minister Modi in India, including in relation to movements to make improved 'governance' politically salient.

CONTEXT: KEY FACTS IN HISTORICAL USA AND CONTEMPORARY INDIA COMPARISON

To set the stage for our comparison, we first compare contemporary India with the United States of America at the turn of the last century. Figure 11.3 indicates that the United States of America was already substantially richer than contemporary India. Only in 2012 had India caught up with the 1880 US income per capita. Forty percent of the US labour force still worked in agriculture in 1900, compared with 53 per cent in India in 2009–10.[2] However, India has been growing faster since the 1980s acceleration—and much faster in the 2000s (Figure 11.4). Moreover, Indian growth has been much less volatile: it has had very few—monsoon-induced—years of negative growth, whereas the United States of America experienced substantial fluctuations, including several years of sharp contractions (Figure 11.5).

So far this looks good for India: enjoying the potential for faster growth that catch-up allows, with much greater stability. But there is a shadow: very few developing countries have succeeded in sustaining rapid growth. The typical pattern of growth in developing countries is characterized by brief growth spurts followed by economic slow-down (Hausmann, Pritchett, and Rodrik, 2005; see also Chapter 3). Sustaining growth is a different challenge from achieving a growth spurt, requiring deeper institutional change (Rodrik, 2003). This is relevant to the thesis of this chapter: a potential cause of such failures to sustain growth is the political economy of entrenchment, which prevents the creation of the institutional bases for dynamic and inclusive growth.

A major contrast between the United States of America of the past and India now concerns the reach of the state. This has two dimensions

---

[2] Data from Lebergott (1966) and Indian National Sample Survey (2009/10).

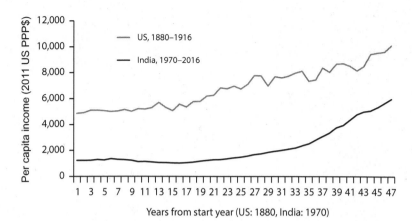

FIGURE 11.3   Income Per Capita in the United States of America
(1880–1926) and India (1970–2016) (2011 US PPP$)
Source: Maddison Project Database, 2018 version; Bolt et al. (2018).

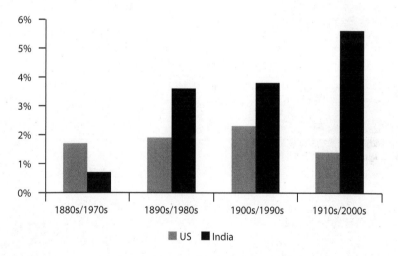

FIGURE 11.4   Average Annual Growth in Real GDP Per Capita in the
United States of America and India over Four Decades (Per Cent Per
Annum)
Source: Maddison Project Database, 2018 version; Bolt et al. (2018).

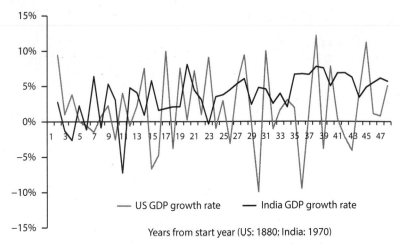

FIGURE 11.5 Annual Growth of the United States of America (1880–2012) and India (1970–2012) (Per Cent Per Annum)
Source: Maddison Project Database, 2018 version; Bolt et al. (2018).

relevant here. First, as we discuss later, the Indian state has had a full panoply of regulations of business activity since the early post-Independence period. This was vividly the case in the License Raj period up to the liberalization of 1991, but remains pervasive today. By contrast, many of the business regulations in the United States of America came in *during* the Progressive Era, following the turn of the century. There is an apparent paradox here, discussed in the section 'Updating the Political Economy Equilibrium' later in the chapter.

Second, with the exception of education, the Indian state now also has much greater reach than the United States of America then in terms of social provisioning and associated interactions with citizens. Education is an important exception, of course. Here, the United States of America was a leader, driven by local education; by 1900, enrolment in public primary education was 88 per cent with a further 6 per cent in non-public schools (Lindert, 2004). Literacy amongst adults was 92 per cent and rising by 1890 (and even amongst non-whites was 43 per cent, rising to 70 per cent by 1890). By contrast, India's adult literacy was still less than 70 per cent in 2011, and close to universal primary enrolment was only achieved in the early 2000s. However, the United

States of America had little or nothing in the way of social insurance and transfers while India has a whole range of social programmes (often poorly targeted and of low quality—but that's another story).

CAPITALIST PARALLELS: ON INDIAN AND US GILDED AGE BUSINESS TYCOONS

Comparisons with the US Gilded Age started to emerge in Indian public discourse around 2011 or so. In an opinion piece for the *Financial Times*, Sinha and Varshney (2011) said: 'Both in its rot and heady dynamism, India is beginning to resemble America's Gilded Age.' Corruption had long been a theme in India, both in the interactions between state actors and citizens and with business. It was a feature of the License Raj period, including in Dhirubhai Ambani's successful incursion into that system. What is distinctive of the more recent period is the emergence of large numbers of super-wealthy individuals, many of whom built their wealth in activities involving connections with politicians and other state actors—in land, mining, and construction, for example. More recently, James Crabtree (2018) has written a vivid account of the characters and issues in what his book evocatively titles the 'billionaire Raj'.

Here we update earlier work by A. Gandhi and M. Walton (2012) using the global database by *Forbes* on billionaires as a proxy for super-wealthy businessmen. This is, of course, only the tip of the iceberg of extreme wealth, and undoubtedly has measurement problems. But the *Forbes* team at least tries to apply a consistent method in assessing the net worth of the world's super-rich, drawing on all publicly available information. Intuitively, there is more likely to be a problem of under- than over-reporting, especially when wealth has questionable sources.

A central analytical concept here concerns that of *economic rents*— that is, returns to factors in excess of what would be obtained in fully competitive markets. Especially for wealth from corporate sources, this is an important source of private wealth. Economic rents can flow from different sources. We heuristically draw a distinction between 'extractive' rents and 'productivity-based' rents. Extractive rents involve distribution from the existing pie, achieved through favoured links with state-controlled resources, the exercise of monopolistic market power, exploitation of minority shareholders, and so on. Productivity-based rents involve returns to innovation, to the creation or discovery of new activities, before markets become fully competitive—Schumpeterian rents are a classic example. Both have been going on in India at a heightened scale since the growth accelerations of the 1980s and, especially, the 2000s. They can often be combined in the *same* business activity; we return to this idea later.

Let us look at the India data first. The emergence of Indian billion-aires is striking both over time and in international context. Between 1996 and 2003, there were between one and five billionaires in the database, and their aggregate wealth only exceeded 1 per cent of GDP from 1999. By 2018, there were 99 Indian billionaires (with residence in India), and total billionaire wealth has risen from US$3 billion to over US$400 billion (Figure 11.6). In relation to GDP, it has fluctu-ated around 10 per cent since 2010, before rising to over 14 per cent in 2018.[3] The ups and downs have tended to mirror stock market valuations, since billionaire wealth is closely linked to the valuations of listed companies. India's relative billionaire wealth is unusually high for a relatively poor country—comparable as a share of GDP to Thailand, Malaysia, and the United States of America, and greater than Brazil and Mexico (Figure 11.7).

We then use *Forbes'* description of the primary source of wealth to categorize billionaires as primarily in 'rent-thick' sectors (by which we mean sectors with likely high levels of extractive rents, owing to depen-dence on links to the state), and others where wealth is more likely to be dependent primarily on entrepreneurial activity that generates productivity gains. This is the same methodology as *The Economist* uses for its 'crony capitalism' index.[4] We here use *The Economist's* list of such sectors, including mining, commodities, finance, infrastructure, real estate, steel, utilities, and telecoms services. The index has a heuristic value, but comes with many caveats. Many billionaires expanded their wealth from diversified conglomerates—Mukesh Ambani of Reliance

---

[3] This compares a stock (wealth) with a flow (GDP) in the absence of direct measures of aggregate wealth of India and other countries. The com-parisons over time and across countries should not be interpreted as shares, but rather as indicators of the relative size of billionaire wealth.

[4] This was itself based on our earlier work, as well as that of Ruchir Sharma; see *The Economist* (2014).

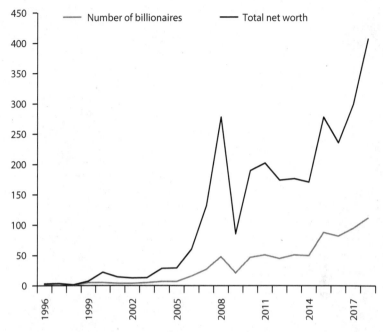

FIGURE 11.6 Indian Billionaires: Numbers and Total Wealth (US$ Billion), 1996–2018
Source: Forbes.

and Kumar Birla of the Birla group are examples. And in an Indian context, all activities involve some degree of regulatory or other interaction with the state. The information technology (IT) industry is a good example of productivity-based rents, yet has depended on (legal) support from state governments in land and tax favours, as well as having at least one infamous case of corporate corruption in the form of the Satyam scandal. Still, for what it is worth, there is an intriguing pattern (Figure 11.8). Until around 2013, over half, and in some years a much higher proportion, of billionaire wealth came from those based in 'rent-thick' sectors. In 2014, and especially since 2015, the balance has shifted, with extensive entry into the list of individuals in 'other' sectors such as pharmaceuticals, IT/software, and consumer goods, which now account for a larger fraction of billionaire wealth than the 'rent-thick' sectors.

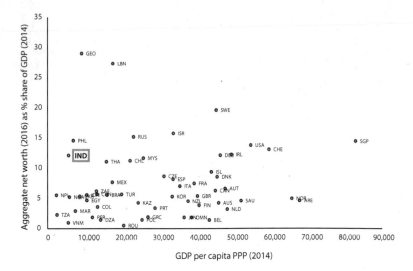

FIGURE 11.7: India's Billionaire Wealth in Comparative Context (in Per Cent of GDP)

Source: Forbes and WDI.

Note: Billionaire net worth reported in March 2016 as a ratio of nominal GDP in 2014, the latest year with actual numbers in the World Development Indicators.

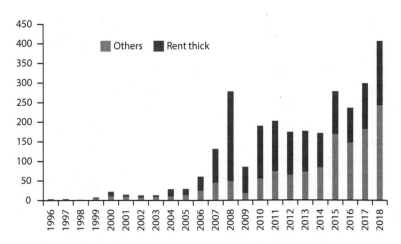

FIGURE 11.8 India's Billionaire Wealth in 'Rent-Thick' and Other Sectors, 1996–2018 (US$ Billion)

Source: Forbes and author's calculations.

While this is only illustrative, we see striking contrasts when look-ing at individuals. Vijay Mallya, in the list from 2006 to 2012, built his wealth from his father's liquor business, diversified into airlines (amongst other sectors), succeeded in running up impressive debts, became a politician in the Rajya Sabha (India's upper house), and, at the time of writing, was out of the country facing charges of financial fraud and money laundering. By contrast, the IT billionaires, such as Azim Premji, Narayana Murthy, and Nandan Nilekani (all from the same state as Mallya: Karnataka), obtained their wealth from one of India's most dramatic, productivity-based success stories. A further contrast is the infrastructure billionaires. For example, G.M. Rao and G.V.K Reddy, both from Andhra Pradesh, built their wealth from the major growth in public spending in this sector, but their companies also ran up substantial debts, mainly from state banks, and both dropped out of the billionaire list in recent years. In the same sector, Gautam Adani built his wealth (and high debts) on the back of Gujarat's construction boom, as well as having close connections to then chief minister (now prime minister) Modi (Jaffrelot, 2019).

Let us now look at the business tycoons of the US Gilded Age. Estimated wealth of the top eighteen richest around 1900 or ear-lier is given in Table 11.1—this is adjusted for inflation between 1900 and the mid-2000s. Apart from the familiarity of several of the names (from their subsequent philanthropic incarnations) there are two striking features of this list. First, there is the sheer size of the wealth—even compared to the 2018 list. John D. Rockefeller of Standard Oil and Cornelius Vanderbilt of railroad fame substan-tially exceed Jeff Bezos, Bill Gates, and Warren Buffett, the top three in 2018. Second, using the same categorization as above, the bulk of these tycoons was in traditional 'rent-thick' sectors, in contrast to today's global list, or even the more recent Indian list—though tech has become a sector where network effects confer substantial monopoly power.

This view is not just in retrospect. Gilded Age tycoons were fre-quently seen as wealthy because of 'extractive' rents, as superbly captured by contemporary cartoons. Figure 11.9 depicts the common view of Standard Oil as an octopus, with tentacles around all aspects of US life. And Figure 11.10 is a vivid representation of William Vanderbilt (the son of Cornelius) dominating railroad traffic.

TABLE 11.1   Wealth of the Richest Gilded Age Business Tycoons circa 1900 (in 2007 US$)

'Rent-Thick' Sectors		
Rockefeller	Oil	192
Rogers	Oil	39
Payne	Oil	37
Subtotal		*268*
Vanderbilt	Railroads	143
Blair	Railroads	43
Huntington	Railroads	33
Subtotal		*219*
Gould	Finance	67
Sage	Finance	43
Harriman	Finance	39
Morgan	Finance	38
Subtotal		*187*
Weyerhaeuser	Lumber and land	68
Fair	Silver and land	45
Frick	Coke	36
Subtotal		*149*
Carnegie	Steel	75
Widener	Urban transit	32
'Other' Sectors		
Field	Retail	61
Ford	Autos	54
Weightman	Pharma	44

Source: Klepper and Gunther (1996), updated by *New York Times*, 15 July 2007.

What is really interesting is the comparison between the processes at work. For the US history, we particularly draw on the wonderful history of the transcontinental railroads by Richard White (2011).

Sources of Wealth and Economic Efficiency

In both the United States of America and India, there was massive private wealth accumulation on the back of corporate expansion. While many—in the second generation of US tycoons and in

FIGURE **11.9** A Contemporary View of Standard Oil
Source: Standard Oil (via Wikimedia).

FIGURE **11.10** William
Vanderbilt and Railroad
Monopolies
Source: William Vanderbilt (via
Wikimedia).

India—inherited significant wealth, the real driver was corporate activity, not aristocratic landed wealth. Moreover, they were often highly efficient at extracting private wealth from their corporations: in the United States of America, railroad companies would suffer financial crises, but the individuals who owned them (mostly) protected their private wealth. In India, the typically pyramidal family-controlled conglomerates have 'tunnelled' resources to controlling firms, implicitly expropriating minority shareholders (Bertrand, Mehta, and Mullainathan, 2000). These companies have also done very well at getting debt from the state banking system, even if most, unlike Mallya, have not sought to avoid paying. In the United States of America, debt crises, and bondholders losing their shirts, were common (and related to the volatility seen in Figure 11.5). In India, concern over non-performing assets in the banking system has been high and rising in recent years. We have already seen that much of the corporate activity has been in rent-thick sectors, where connections matter. This has often been linked to substantial market power. And a major theme of White's assessment of the US transcontinental railways is their economic *inefficiency*, even more so if environmental destruction and social costs are accounted for (notably for the native American population and exploitation of labour, especially of Chinese workers). In India, there have been comparable concerns in many sectors—notably mining—over environmental and social costs.

Business and Politics

Relations between businessmen and politicians are central to both stories. In the United States of America, this was at the core of the approvals that railroad companies obtained for rights of way, with land deals along the railways an essential part. This involved systematic trusted networks—the railroad tycoons referred to 'friends' as a *technical* term for the many politicians in the state who could be relied upon (White, 2011). Some businessmen moved in and out of politics, including Leland Stanford, who reaped substantial private wealth from his partnership in the Pacific Railway despite being considered not too bright by his partners, and then, ironically, was the initial source of Stanford University's endowment! The railroads also effectively created the lobby system. Connections pervaded many sectors. For example, R. Menes (2006) cites cases of city-level political bosses investing in construction firms or channelling contracts to firms held by family members in early twentieth-century Philadelphia and New York.

This is all too familiar from contemporary India. Dealings with state actors are crucial to a whole range of business transactions. There are increasing overlaps, with businessmen going into politics (Mallya is just one example) and politicians going into business. This came vividly into the public discourse with a sequence of high-level scams that unfolded in the latter years of the UPA government in the allocation of the telecoms spectrum, the Commonwealth Games, and coal mining rights. Political finance is an important part of this relationship, especially as elections have become increasingly expensive. The tight legal restrictions on such finance only shift the channels outside the law. We discuss the social and political reaction to these issues in the final section of this chapter.

The Two Faces of Capitalism

A further intriguing parallel concerns what might be called the two faces of capitalism, in which rent extraction has been, to a substantial degree, aligned with productivity advances. While in both cases, there has clearly been substantial rent creation and its private appropriation, there has also been significant asset creation. In the United States of America, strategic infrastructure did get built, as the country consolidated its position of global industrial leadership. Cities became the most dynamic part of the economy in spite of entrenched corruption (Menes, 2006). In India, rent-thick connected capitalism has lived alongside a major rise in private corporate investment that has fuelled unprecedented growth (albeit in the context of an unusual 'sweet spot' in international and domestic conditions; Mody and Walton, 2012). In an analysis of overall private firm dynamics, Mody, Nath, and Walton (2011) found little evidence of concentration affecting the profit behaviour of enterprises in the post-1990 period. However, a surge in firm entry in the 1990s tailed off in the 2000s boom, especially in manufacturing. Concentration then rose, and major family-controlled business houses and state enterprises continue to dominate the enterprise landscape.

The Regulatory Contrast

There is one important contrast between Gilded Age United States of America and contemporary India. In India, the regulatory state has been a pervasive feature of the institutional context since (and before) Independence. This was dramatically true of the License Raj period, and remains substantially true for many licence requirements, despite the genuine liberalization and deregulation of 1991 and later. This is a theme we pick up in the next section. Here we suggest that, while the specific fields of interaction between politics and business are different, the underlying structural relationship of rent creation and systematic rent-sharing underpinned by political–business connections has strong parallels. This is not least because in India there is a significant overlap between rules and (informal) deals-based decision-making. (As a further parallel, which goes far beyond this chapter, there are structural similarities over interpretations of the *contemporary* United States of America, with explicit or implicit support for economic rent creation, underpinned by political finance and the lobby system, in sectors ranging from finance, oil and gas, to agriculture. An important contrast is that these relationships have been largely institutionalized in formally rules-based processes; this is the legalization of rent-sharing.)

REACTION: THE PROGRESSIVE ERA RESPONSE AND THE INDIAN PARADOX

For India, even more interesting than the comparison with the Gilded Age is that with the Progressive Era and its sequel in the New Deal. This was a multi-decade period of reform, which can be seen as an important manifestation of the second part of Polanyi's 'double movement'. While Polanyi characterized this as a response to 'unregulated capitalism', we have seen that the preceding period was more complicated, especially with respect to the tight links between the state and business. The outcome was the formation of a combination of regulated capitalism and the core trappings of a twentieth-century social state. Crabtree (2018) concludes his book on the 'billionaire Raj' with an optimistic speculation that India could follow such a US transition from Gilded Age to Progressive reform.

This is especially interesting for India since these developments are occurring in the context of a vigorous democracy, which had in turn emerged from a 'clientelistic' polity, based on reciprocal favours between political elites and both social groups or business. F. Fukuyama (2014) has recently argued that the shift from clientelistic polity to rules-based democracy is a particularly difficult political transition—compared with transitions from authoritarian polities—with the United States of America a rare exception. Here we outline an interpretation of the US transition, followed by an exploration of what looks like an apparent Indian paradox.

The US Transition

How could change occur? A simple contemporary view is captured in Figure 11.11: that electoral processes would be more powerful against the 'trusts' (monopolies) than the 'old' method of strikes. The Australian (secret) ballot was introduced soon after the presidential election of 1884. This provided an institutional basis for more equitable influence. However, of equal importance was an effective alliance between a heterogeneous range of popular movements and political parties—Grangers, Populists, Progressives, the reform movement in

FIGURE 11.11 The Vote against the Monopolies: A Contemporary View
Source: Sherman Anti-Trust (Library of Congress).

cities—that provided impetus to action by the executive (from Teddy Roosevelt on), the legislature, and judiciary.[5] This was underpinned by the 'muckraking' journalism that brought out the dark side of the existing system. J. Robinson (2009) argues that the link to political movements was central to the effectiveness of state action. A particular strand of interest was the confluence of moral movements with reformist action (Morone, 2003), which in later decades tended to split, reducing the effectiveness with respect to political-economic reforms. An early split—with a parallel with contemporary India—was the focus on the prohibition of alcohol. In more recent decades, there have been moral movements of a 'progressive' character (civil rights, women's rights), as well as 'conservative/reactionary' (Moral Majority, Tea Party, the alt-right). The role of 'morality' in social movements is highly relevant to contemporary India, in Gandhian groups, the anti-corruption movement, and, of currently greatest salience, the role of Hindu nationalism in social and political action.

In the US case, the result in state action was a series of measures that preserved capitalism whilst managing its excesses—often conceptually correcting market failures. Some major examples are:

- Sherman Antitrust Act (1890)
- Clayton Antitrust Act (1914)
- Pure Food and Drug Act (1906)
- State-level minimum wages (from 1912)

The sources of public action were typically heterogeneous. For example, in a fascinating analysis of the Pure Food and Drug Act, M.T. Law and G.D. Libecap (2006) argue that action flowed from three sources: reformist motives to correct market failures; rent-seeking and regulatory influence from business groups who would relatively gain; and rent-seeking (for work, not bribes) from bureaucrats interested in extending their regulatory reach. The role of the bureaucracy is of particular interest, in light of parallels with India. The key legal change was in the federal Pendleton Act Civil Service Reform Act of 1883,

---

[5] See Kazin (1995) on the evolution of populism in the United States of America in this period.

which overturned the 'spoils system' in which winning political parties awarded government jobs to its supporters, instead requiring that government jobs be awarded on merit. While a necessary condition, D.P. Carpenter (2001) argues that genuine bureaucratic autonomy evolved in some, but not all, agencies as a product of agency leadership, internal organizational change, and, crucially, the development of support from external interest groups that gave a degree of countervailing power to politicians.

The second reform phase occurred in the New Deal in response to the Great Depression and its underlying distributive fights. This can again be seen as capitalism-preserving resolution, in a form of social democracy, paralleling developments in Scandinavia and Britain, as an alternative political resolution to European fascism (see Walton, 2013). Key actions included:

- The Glass–Steagall Act (1933)
- National Labor Relations Act (1935)
- Unemployment insurance (1935)
- Social Security (1935)

It is interesting that the United States of America was ahead of Scandinavia in important respects—and also that some of the more established capitalists were an important part of the *support* for social democratic transition in both the United States of America and Sweden, as this provided protection from entry of competing firms who could undercut them through weaker provisioning for labour (Swenson, 2004).

The Indian Paradox

As we turn to India, there is a striking contrast. Since Independence, there has been an apparent leapfrogging compared with the history of the United States of America and other now-rich countries. India's experience, indeed, looks like a simultaneous, as opposed to sequential, Polanyian double movement. Capitalist change has occurred in parallel with a range of regulatory and social provisioning measures that were institutional 'victories' of the Progressive movement. This includes:

- A bureaucracy that is formally meritocratic, vividly so in the elite Indian Administrative Service (IAS) and other national services, but also, in principle, in state-level services.
- A wide range of business regulation, including anti-monopoly/ competition commissions, and, especially since 1991, the institution of a range of capitalism-supporting regulatory structures, notably the Securities and Exchange Board (SEBI).
- Substantially greater social provisioning than in the late nineteenth- or early twentieth-century United States of America (with the important exception of basic education noted earlier), with a wide range of poverty programmes, union rights, and, more recently, for- mal rights to work, food and education.
- Last, but not least, electorates more than willing to vote out incum- bents, at state and national levels, ever since the dominance of the Congress Party disappeared after the early post-Independence decades.

Yet, we have argued that despite the more extensive range of state action and associated rights, India still has many of the characteristics of the Gilded Age business–state links, weak protections for many groups, and an often ineffective and problematic state. This may seem familiar to students of contemporary developing countries—the Indian para- dox surely has parallels elsewhere. But the point of this chapter is to step back. Here are four India-specific reasons explaining this apparent paradox.

First, the extensive state has become a fertile domain of both cap- ture and effective rent-creation and rent-sharing. This has *risen* as the stakes from access to the state have increased in the post-liberalization and high-growth period. This is evident in the rising price of elections at all levels, the associated importance of political finance, the centrality of land deals in the currency of business–politician exchanges, and the increasing movement of businessmen into politics, and politicians into business—with criminals in politics an extreme manifestation of this (Vaishnav, 2017).

Second, while formally Weberian, the bureaucracy has largely failed to become an autonomous social-welfare-maximizing instrument of the state. Bureaucrats are often subservient to or complicit with the deals of politicians, with the power of politicians to move obstructive bureaucrats around a key part of the equation (see also Chapter 8). More broadly, few parts of the bureaucracy have experienced the US transition to bureaucratic autonomy documented by Carpenter (2001). L. Pritchett (2009) characterized India as a 'flailing' state—with extensive state presence, but ineffective capacity to respond to the intentions of its top echelons. Exceptions, such as the Election Commission, the Comptroller and Auditor General (CAG), and the Reserve Bank of India, only provide a vivid contrast to the more common practice and culture of the Indian state—and even the Reserve Bank has lost its independent allure in the wake of the 2016 demonetization and the December 2018 resignation of its governor. More profoundly, the development of a bureaucratic culture of solving societal or citizen problems is rare, with most services being rule-bound, with an admixture of daily administrative corruption.[6] Finally, there is a sheer lack of capacity—India actually has an extensive state in terms of citizen contact, but a relatively small civil service.

Third, social and political mobilization in India has been dominated by particularist interests, in contrast to the admittedly complex set of alliances in the United States of America. This is evident in farmer movements seeking the sustaining of multiple subsidies or loan forgiveness, and the resistance to evictions or specific areas of exploitation, whether in forests or slums. It is particularly manifest in the deeply institutionalized demand for various forms of group-based reservations—originally conceived by Ambedkar as a temporary measure for Dalits and Scheduled Tribes—but extended to increasing identity-based groups in the wake of the Mandal Commission. R. Somanathan (2010) termed this the 'demand for disadvantage'. Add to this the fact that the most effective 'moral' movement has been that of Hindutva, or Hindu nationalism. Meanwhile, the media is largely owned by business. The result is the absence of a coordinated alliance to reconstruct the state. The 2011 and 2012 anti-corruption movement looks like an exception, but this was a product of a highly contingent middle-class

---

[6] See Akshay Mangla's fascinating account of the contrast between 'deliberative' problem solving in Himachal Pradesh, with the much more typical cases of Uttarakhand and Uttar Pradesh, which he characterizes as 'legalistic' (Mangla, 2014).

alliance, in which 'neo-Gandhians conferred legitimacy; India Shining provided energy and finances; and Legal Activists helped navigate the legislative path' (Sitapati, 2011: 39). This is not easy to replicate.

Fourth, and very much a reflection of these other factors, electoral strategies that emphasize populist or clientelistic approaches are both dominant and largely successful within a competitive political environment. While the campaign and election of Modi's BJP in 2014 was often characterized as being about better governance and development, we would argue that it very much fits within a populist frame, as discussed later.

These factors interact and tend to support a self-enforcing political equilibrium. The next section sketches this.

UPDATING THE POLITICAL ECONOMY EQUILIBRIUM

In 1984, *PEDI* argued that India was stuck in a political economy equilibrium that resisted the systemic change necessary for dynamic growth. There has since been dramatically more dynamism than then anticipated, albeit a dynamism that created Gilded Age-style private wealth accumulation and high-level corruption. Yet, we have argued that the reaction has not coalesced into Progressive Era-style systemic reform for a set of structural reasons. Here we suggest an update of *PEDI* in the form of a sketch of a self-enforcing political economy equilibrium that is consistent both with episodes of dynamism and resilience to systemic change.

First, we need a re-interpretation of *PEDI* in light of the private investment acceleration from the 1980s through the 2000s. As noted in the introduction, this is inconsistent with a central part of *PEDI's* thesis. We would argue that there was indeed a restructuring of state–business relations, initially as a new overall deal: with business gaining from domestic deregulation, and (to varying degrees) having to face increased foreign competition. How did the shift from the old equilibrium occur? At a systemic level, there was an important shift in dominant narratives around economic growth, favouring greater reliance on markets—both globally and in some domestic arenas. This coincided with the emergence of new business elites at a subnational level, allied with local political elites. Then an unfolding macroeconomic crisis (centred on 1991) provided a moment of state autonomy to a group that embraced or at least tolerated the market-oriented narrative. Arguably, the collective action problems that had prevented a systemic shift earlier now impeded coordinated resistance.[7]

While there was a real shift in this core relationship, the 'new' set of state–business relations remained a hybrid of rules and deals, with rent-sharing between political elites and business a central feature. Business has indeed consolidated its position as a 'DPC', while the state's relationship with other groups remained one of complex particularist measures, deploying a range of clientelistic and populist strategies. However, in terms of the broader society the major rise in living conditions has led to the rising political salience of additional groups, from lower-caste mobilization to an emergent, urban middle class (see Chapters 9 and 10 of this volume).

To extend the analysis, it is useful to focus on the subnational state. The system can be conceptualized as an interlocking set of rent-creating and rent-sharing mechanisms. A sketch is presented diagrammatically in Figure 11.12. This was developed with a particular state in mind—Andhra Pradesh prior to the 2014 division into Andhra Pradesh and Telangana.[8] This is of particular interest both because India's subnational states are the core locus of political economy and because Andhra Pradesh has been one of the more dynamic Indian states. It is suggested that similar structures prevail in other states and at the national level.

Two sets of relationship are central: between political and economic elites and between politicians and the electorate. Bureaucrats intermediate both.

The first set of relations are familiar from the discussion earlier. The past 25 years have been a period of major rent creation in India—of both extractive and productivity-based rents. These rents were shared systematically between politicians and business families—with an important subplot of political support for emerging new regional business elites (Damodaran, 2008). In the case of Andhra Pradesh, a big story

---

[7] See also discussion in McCartney (2009).

[8] This was originally developed for presentations on the political economy of Andhra Pradesh at King's College, London, and the Centre for Policy Research, on the basis of discussion with informed observers of the state.

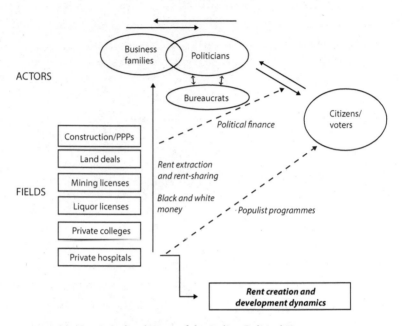

FIGURE 11.12 A Stylized View of the Indian Political Economy Equilibrium
Source: Author's design.

was the development of the local construction industry, initially on the basis of state-level infrastructure, for example, in irrigation and then in major national programmes, often through public–private partnerships. This nurtured genuine capabilities in major firms such as GVK and GMR that have since become international players (this formed the basis of the wealth of their owners, who became billionaires for a while, as noted earlier). There is also a range of smaller construction firms that are linked into the more local political hierarchy.

This relationship is supported by a wide network of relations between politicians and businessmen, with the growing phenomenon of overlapping activities. For example, in the case of Andhra Pradesh, prior to the state's 2014 bifurcation and election, 14 of the state's 61 Members of Parliament (MPs) in the national Parliament were rich individuals whose wealth was based on infrastructure and construction contracts. For local construction contracts, the overlap was typically with state-level Members of the Legislative Assembly (MLAs).

Bureaucrats are an important part of the implementation of any government-related action. India remains highly rule- and procedure-bound, so without the implicit or explicit complicity of bureaucrats the exercise of influence would not work. Some bureaucrats are honest and some dishonest. The fact that powerful politicians can transfer them means this part of the system can be made to work in the interests of rent-sharing deals, for most of the time.

Politicians then have to be re-elected in India's vigorous democracy, and there are often changes in the party in power. Two mechanisms are particularly important for obtaining support: populist programmes and political finance. Both are used competitively by all parties. India is rife with populist programmes—some good, some bad, in terms of their development impact. Particularly inventive from a political economy perspective were two programmes developed in pre-bifurcation Andhra Pradesh for tertiary health care (Aarogyasri) and college education. These have a common overall structure. The state provides bursaries for individuals with Below Poverty Line (BPL) certificates to make use of (mainly private) hospitals and colleges, for example, in engineering and medicine. So far so good. This is highly effective politically because many of these organizations have links to politicians, and, even better, some 80 per cent of the state's households have been granted a BPL certificate (this is substantially higher than the poverty rate as measured by the National Sample Survey). So this nicely closes the loop, creating a highly popular programme that generates rents for connected individuals and is financed by the state budget.

The second mechanism concerns political finance. Legal limits to political finance have been very low in India, which means that virtually all the finance is illegal.[9] Indian elections are becoming more expensive at all levels, so finance is critical to electoral success. There are many mechanisms.[10] One that helps solve the legality challenge is said to work through liquor licences: since there is great scope for overcharging for liquor and appropriating the surplus, such licences

---

[9] There may be a shift with the introduction of 'electoral bonds' in January 2019. However, as these will be anonymous, this creates a new form of opaqueness in electoral finance.

[10] For example, D. Kapur and M. Vaishnav (2018) suggest a link with the construction industry, with evidence of a political cement cycle.

can become an excellent source of black (illegal) money. Unlike the usual challenge of converting black to white money, the electoral challenge in India is to have stashes of black money (this was alleged to be one of the reasons behind Prime Minister Modi's 2016 demonetization; see Mody and Walton, 2017).

There is of course much greater complexity to such a system. The point of this sketch is to take the spirit of *PEDI*'s seminal abstraction and update it. It is also to outline a system that is good at extracting and sharing rents, is self-enforcing, and, at least for certain periods, can also generate particular types of economic and development dynamism—specifically when rent-sharing mechanisms are aligned with productivity increases in the business sector. This increasingly involves a political blend of cronyism and populism, discussed later.

RECENT PRO–GOVERNANCE SOCIAL AND POLITICAL ACTION: NOT (YET) A CRITICAL JUNCTURE?

The account so far has explored why the Indian political economy is likely to be resistant to the kind of systemic changes that typified the Progressive Era. And yet movements to improve governance have a long-standing history in India. The 'anti-corruption' theme has been periodically used by politicians for decades, just as the 'anti-monopoly' theme was so present in the Progressive Era United States of America. In recent years, there have been a variety of social movements, state action, and electoral successes that have seemed, at least from some angles, to herald a more profound shift. We interpret three categories here: the response to scams and the anti-corruption movement; the right to public service; and the election and performance of Modi's BJP, including the 2016 demonetization.

From Scams to Auctions

Consider first the fallout from the anti-corruption mobilization of 2011 and 2012. As discussed earlier, this was an unusual coalition of disparate social groupings, as opposed to a qualitative shift from India's largely particularist and group-based social action. However, it did have consequences. Major scams were one of the spurs to social action. What is interesting is that in some domains of government resource

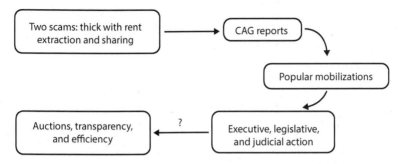

FIGURE 11.13 From Scams to Auctions of Telecoms Spectrum and Coal Mining Blocks: A Progressive Era–Type Response
Source: Author's design.

allocation there was then focused institutional reform, specifically in shifting from administrative to auction-based allocations of telecoms spectrum and coal mining blocks. The sequence is schematically illustrated in Figure 11.13. The public documentation of scams by the CAG helped fuel the anti-corruption movement (along with many other factors). This made the scams and associated questions of institutional design salient within the executive, legislature, and judiciary. Individuals were convicted, and in due course auctions became designated as the required method for selling publicly controlled resources and opportunities to the private sector, including the spectrum and coal mining blocks. The details are not the issue here, as what we are interested in is the overall shape of this change: there were interactions between autonomous checks-and-balance institutions, social movements, and action by different parts of the state. This echoes the mix of changes in the Progressive Era.

In principle, this was a good change in institutional design. But it is not clear that it heralds a broader systemic shift. Rent extraction and sharing remain central in many other domains, even assuming the auctions are genuinely run as fully competitive and efficient affairs.

Right to Public Service

From within the executive, and especially at the level of states, has come a sequence of so-called Right to Public Services (RTS) laws. Madhya

Pradesh was the first to introduce such a law in 2010, followed by Bihar in 2011; some 18 other states have since enacted or notified such legislation. The pattern is to guarantee delivery of particular services within a specific time, with failure leading to punishment of—usually frontline—civil servants. At one level, it is an achievement of the broader accountability movement that such RTS acts are becoming an increasingly common, and politically supportable, part of state-level bureaucracies. However, they only make sense for a very specific class of measurable deliverables of an administration, and arguably divert attention from the administrative failures that caused problems of failures in service delivery in the first place (Aiyar and Walton, 2015). Robinson (2012) finds from field studies that fears of penalties cause bureaucrats to prioritize the affected activities over others that may be of equal importance, while Hasan and Narayana (2013) suggest that officials in Karnataka adjust the rules such that there is 'legal' but not substantive delivery. This approach is the opposite of true accountability, with a shift to a more problem-solving bureaucracy that will respond to the real problems that citizens face.

Governance under Modi

Governance has been an important theme in recent electoral politics, both in a series of state elections and dramatically in the 2014 national election won by the Modi-led BJP. The dominant narrative of Modi's campaign was of governance and development. And indeed, there has been activism in policy in Delhi aligned with this good governance and development discourse. There appear to be boundaries on high-level corruption at the national level (which was revealed to be politically toxic), and there is a popular discourse amongst technical elites on reforming poverty and social programmes, with shifts to a cash-plus-universal ID-based approach. There have been a range of measures ostensibly around improving the business environment, including a new bankruptcy law.

But the overall strategy appears to be politically constrained, with limited major reforms, for example, with only selective shifts on subsidy regimes and the continued centrality of state banks in the lending domain. Indeed, a symptom of the history of favoured relations between the state and business is the substantial levels of non-performing assets in the state banks (not least for major businesses). At the time of writing early in 2019, evidence on the process of state–business interactions remains anecdotal for the Modi era. However, what is clear is that the truly wealthy businessmen, including those alleged to have close connections to the governing regime, have continued to prosper. Mukesh Ambani enjoyed a rise in his net worth of 115 per cent and Gautam Adani of almost 250 per cent between early 2014 and early 2018.

The government also bears the shadow of its close links to Hindu nationalist organizations that mobilize around a national Hindu identity. While Modi campaigned on a development platform, the BJP periodically mobilizes on sectarian lines, and 'patriotism' around Hindu (and implicitly anti-Muslim) themes has been a frequent dimension of government action. This reinforces particularist formations, and, unlike US moral movements in the Progressive Era, is not aligned with cleaning up the system.

One area of emphasis has been 'cooperative federalism' with greater fiscal decentralization to states, implementing a recommendation of the Fourteenth Finance Commission. However, this only shifts more of the action to the domain of state–business rent-sharing,

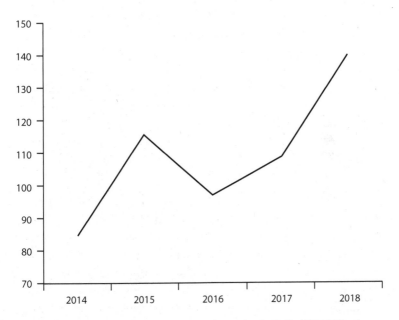

FIGURE 11.14   Net Worth of the Ten Richest Men in India (US$ Billion)

Source: Forbes.

Note: The ten richest men refers to the ten richest individuals among those who appeared every year on the Forbes India rich list.

patronage, and populist measures that lie in the states—as schematized in the section 'Updating the Political Economy Equilibrium'. And unlike the United States of America, Indian cities are not domains for effective political and social movements and contestation, as they are largely subservient to the states.[11] While city governments and local urban politicians are often dispensers of patronage, they have not even gone through the phase of machine politics that preceded the city reform movements in the United States of America.

A final example concerns the Modi administration's remarkable decision to 'demonetize' the economy in November 2016, removing 500 and 1,000 rupee notes—accounting for 86 per cent of the total money supply. This was portrayed (by Modi) variously as an attack on black money, a spur to cashless transactions, and as part of a strategy to take from the undeserving rich and give to deserving groups. This was an absurd move in economic terms, and caused major economic and social damage—at least in the short run. We interpret it as essentially political, and as part of a populist strategy that, if successful, will undermine rather than deepen democracy (see Mody and Walton, 2017). If it strengthens a narrative of direct political connection between a strongman leader and middle and poorer groups, it could lead to a further restructuring in the political processes with respect to 'dominant classes'. The overall political economy continues to have features best described as 'crony populist', as opposed to essentially reformist (Walton, 2018).

★★★

This chapter sought to bring a comparison with the US Gilded Age and Progressive Era to bear on contemporary India. We have argued that Gilded Age dynamics are indeed at work in state–business relations in twenty-first-century India. This occurs in the more extensive domains of state regulatory action compared with the historical United States of America, but with structural similarities around rent creation, rent-sharing, political finance, and networks of relations between businessmen and politicians. This has also been consistent with much greater

---

[11] For discussion of India's urban regime as a rent-sharing 'cabal', see Heller, Mukhopadhyay, and Walton (2019).

dynamism—and specifically investment—than anticipated in *PEDI*'s 1984 account. However, the overall political equilibrium, including the state's relations with other social groups, can be conceptualized in ways that parallel *PEDI*'s assessment.

We also reviewed the potential for change, and in particular for the kind of alliance of political and social movements and parts of the state that generated the multi-decade reforms that built a system of regulated capitalism and the beginnings of a social state in the United States of America. Here, there was an apparent paradox: India already has many of the legislative victories that characterized the Progressive Era and New Deal. But the political economy remains stuck, owing to the predominance of particularist social demands and associated political and bureaucratic strategies. The electorate often appears to be seeking an alternative equilibrium, and there are a number of 'pro-governance' initiatives. But neither social movements nor political elites have the broad coalition and cognitive maps to effect systemic change. There may well be short-run growth surges and expanded service delivery, when rent-sharing is aligned with private investment or public action, but longer-term development remains problematic. At the time of writing, there is concern that India under Modi is sharing in what seems to be widespread global move to authoritarian populism. In a democracy as competitive and vigorous as India's, there is always hope that there will be an eventual coalescence around a Progressive Era-style political coalition. But the paths to such a transition remain unclear.

Bibliography

Agarwal, B. 2015. 'Budget Silences'. *Indian Express*, 9 March. Available at: https://indianexpress.com/article/opinion/columns/budget-silences/ (accessed on 14 August 2019).

Ahluwalia, I.J. 1985. *Industrial Growth in India: Stagnation since the Mid-Sixties*. New Delhi: Oxford University Press.

Ahluwalia, M.S. 1995. 'First Raj Krishna Memorial Lecture: Economic Reform for the Nineties'. University of Rajasthan. Available at: http://planningcommission.nic.in/aboutus/speech/spemsa/msa033.pdf (accessed on 3 January 2017).

Aiyar, Y., and M. Walton. 2015. 'Rights, Accountability and Citizenship: India's Emerging Welfare State'. In *Governance in Developing Asia: Public Service Delivery and Empowerment*, edited by A.B. Deolalikar, J. Shikha, and F.Q. Pilipinas, 260–95. Cheltenham: Edward Elgar Publishing.

Alavi, H. 1972. 'The State in Post-Colonial Societies: Pakistan and Bangladesh'. *New Left Review* I/74: 59–80.

Alfaro, L., and A. Chari. 2012. 'Deregulation, Misallocation, and Size: Evidence from India'. NBER Working Paper 18650, National Bureau of Economic Research, Cambridge, MA.

Altvater, E. 1993. *The Future of the Market: An Essay on the Regulation of Money and Nature after the Collapse of 'Actually Existing Socialism'*. London: Verso.

Anand, M., and S. Chaudhury. 2007. 'Government Employment and Employees' Compensation'. *Economic and Political Weekly* 42(31): 3225–32.

Aslany, M. 2019. 'The Indian Middle Class, Its Size, and Urban–Rural Variations'. *Contemporary South Asia* 27(2): 196–213.

Baddeley, M., K. McNay, and R. Cassen. 2006. 'Divergence in India: Income Differentials at the State Level, 1970–97'. *Journal of Development Studies* 42(6): 1000–22.

Bakshi, A., A. Das, and M. Swaminathan. 2014. 'Household Incomes in Rural India: Results from PARI Village Studies'. Paper presented at the

Foundation for Agrarian Studies, Tenth Anniversary Conference, Kochi, 9–12 January 2014.

Balakrishnan, P. 2014. 'The Great Reversal: A Macro Story'. *Economic and Political Weekly* 49(21): 29–34.

———. 2015. 'A Budget to Transform'. *The Hindu*, 14 February.

Balakrishnan, P., and M. Parameswaran. 2007. 'Understanding Economic Growth in India: A Prerequisite'. *Economic and Political Weekly* 42(27/28): 2915–22.

Banik, D. 2001. 'The Transfer Raj: Indian Civil Servants on the Move'. *European Journal of Development Research* 13(1): 106–34.

Bardhan, P. 1984. *The Political Economy of Development in India*. New Delhi: Oxford University Press.

———. 1986. 'Marxist Ideas in Development Economics: An Evaluation'. In *Analytical Marxism*, edited by J. Roemer, 64–77. Cambridge: Cambridge University Press.

———. 1988a. 'Alternative Approaches to Development Economics: An Evaluation'. In *Handbook of Development Economics*, Vol. 1, edited by H. Chenery and T.N. Srinivasan, 40–71. Amsterdam; Oxford: Elsevier.

———. 1988b. 'Dominant Proprietary Classes and India's Democracy'. In *India's Democracy: An Analysis of Changing State–Society Relations*, edited by A. Kohli, 214–24. Princeton: Princeton University Press.

———. 1989a. 'The Third Dominant Class'. *Economic and Political Weekly* 24(3): 155–6.

———. 1989b. *Conversations Between Economists and Anthropologists: Methodological Issues in Measuring Economic Change in Rural India*. New Delhi: Oxford University Press.

———. 1990. 'Symposium on the State and Economic Development'. *Journal of Economic Perspectives* 4(3): 3–7.

———. 1993. 'The "Intermediate Regime": Any Sign of Graduation?' In *Development and Change: Essays in Honour of K.N. Raj*, edited by P. Bardhan, T.N. Krishnan, and M. Datta-Chaudhuri, 341–52. Bombay: Oxford University Press.

———. 1998. *The Political Economy of Development in India*. Expanded edition. Delhi: Oxford University Press.

———. 2005a. 'An Economist's Approach to the Problem of Corruption'. *World Development* 34(2): 341–8.

———. 2005b. *Scarcity, Conflicts, and Cooperation: Essays in the Political and Institutional Economics of Development*. Cambridge, MA; London: MIT Press.

———. 2006. 'Awakening Giants, Feet of Clay: A Comparative Assessment of the Rise of China and India'. *Journal of South Asian Development* 1(1): 1–17.

————. 2009. 'Notes on the Political Economy of India's Tortuous Transition'. *Economic and Political Weekly* 44(49): 31–6.

————. 2010. *Awakening Giants, Feet of Clay: Assessing the Economic Rise of China and India*. Princeton, NJ; Oxford: Princeton University Press.

————. (n.d.). *An Autobiography of Professional Life*. University of Berkeley website. Available at: http://eml.berkeley.edu/~webfac/bardhan/papers/autobioessay.pdf (accessed on 11 January 2017).

Bardhan, P., M. Luca, D. Mookherji, and F. Pino. 2014. 'Evolution of Land Distribution in West Bengal, 1967–2004: Role of Land Reform and Demographic Changes'. *Journal of Development Economics* 110: 171–90.

Baru, S. 2000. 'Economic Policy and Development of Capitalism in India: The Role of Regional Capitalists and Political Parties'. In *Transforming India: Social and Political Dynamics of Democracy*, edited by F. Frankel, Z. Hasan, R. Bhargava, and B. Arora, 207–30. New Delhi: Oxford University Press.

————. 2009. 'The Growing Influence of Business and Media on Indian Foreign Policy'. ISAS Insights No. 49, Institute of South Asian Studies, National University of Singapore, Singapore, 5 February. Available at: https://www.files.ethz.ch/isn/96448/50.pdf (accessed on 25 July 2019).

Basile, E. 2013. *Capitalist Development in India's Informal Economy*. London, New York: Routledge.

Basile, E., and B. Harriss-White. 2000. 'Corporative Capitalism: Civil Society and the Politics of Accumulation in Small Town India'. QEH Working Paper Series 38, Queen Elizabeth House, University of Oxford, Oxford, UK.

————. 2010. 'Introduction'. *International Review of Sociology*, Special Issue on *India's Informal Capitalism and its Regulation* 20(3): 457–71.

Basu, Deepankar, and Debarshi Das. 2015. 'A Flawed Approach to Food Security'. *The Hindu*, 17 February.

Bavadam, L. 2018. 'The Long Road Ahead'. *Frontline*, 13 April.

Benbabaali, D. 2008. 'Questioning the Role of the Indian Administrative Service in National Integration'. *South Asia Multidisciplinary Academic Journal* [online]. Available at: http://samaj.revues.org/633 (accessed on 25 July 2019).

Berg, A., J.D. Ostry, and J. Zettelmeyer. 2011. 'What Makes Growth Sustained?' EBRD Working Paper No. 133, European Bank for Reconstruction and Development, London.

Berman, E., R. Somanathan, and H.W. Tan. 2005. 'Is Skill-Biased Technological Change Here Yet? Evidence from Indian Manufacturing in the 1990s'. *Annales d'Économie et de Statistique* 79/80: 299–321.

Bernstein, H. 2010. *Class Dynamics of Agrarian Change*. Sterling, VA: Kumarian Press; Black Point, Nova Scotia: Fernwood.

Bertrand, M., P. Mehta, and S. Mullainathan. 2000. 'Ferreting Out Tunneling: An Application to Indian Business Groups'. NBER Working Paper 7952, National Bureau of Economic Research, Cambridge, MA.

Béteille, A. 1989. 'Are the Intelligentsia a Ruling Class?' *Economic and Political Weekly* 24(3): 151–5.

Bhagwati, J.N. 1982. 'Directly Unproductive, Profit-Seeking (DUP) Activities'. *Journal of Political Economy* 90(5): 988–1002.

———. 1993. *India in Transition: Freeing the Economy*. Oxford: Clarendon Press.

Bhagwati, J.N., and A. Panagariya. 2013. 'Introduction'. In *Reforms and Economic Transformation in India*, edited by J.N. Bhagwati and A. Panagariya, 1–12. New Delhi: Oxford University Press.

———. 2014. *Why Growth Matters: How Economic Growth in India Reduced Poverty and the Lessons for Other Developing Countries*. New York: Public Affairs.

Bhagwati, J.N., and P. Desai. 1970. *India: Planning for Industrialization*. New Delhi: Oxford University Press.

Bhagwati, J.N., and T.N. Srinivasan. 1975. *India: Foreign Trade Regimes and Economic Development*. New York: Columbia University Press.

Bhalla, G.S., and G. Singh. 2009. 'Economic Liberalisation and Indian Agriculture: A Statewise Analysis'. *Economic and Political Weekly* 44(52): 34–44.

Bhalla, S. 2014. 'Scarce Land: Issues, Evidence and Impact'. IHD Working Paper WP 02/2014, Institute for Human Development, New Delhi. Available at: https://pdfs.semanticscholar.org/072b/1c98f23283aa6592bebfcd8227608 2a3b2f5.pdf (accessed on 25 July 2019).

Bhattacharya, A.K. 2015. 'Structured Procrastination?' *Business Standard*, 23 August. Available at: https://www.business-standard.com/article/ opinion/a-k-bhattacharya-structured-procrastination-115082300752_1. html (accessed on 14 August 2019).

Bhattacharya, B.B., and A. Mitra. 1990. 'Excess Growth of Tertiary Sector in Indian Economy: Issues and Implications'. *Economic and Political Weekly* 25(44): 2445–50.

———. 1991. 'Excess Growth of Tertiary Sector'. *Economic and Political Weekly*, 26(22–3): 1423–4.

Bhattacharya, S. 2014. 'Is Labour Still a Relevant Category for Praxis? Critical Reflections on Some Contemporary Discourses on Work and Labour in Capitalism'. *Development and Change* 45(5): 941–62.

Bhowmick, S.K. 2002. 'Hawkers and the Urban Informal Sector: A Study of Street Vending in Seven Cities'. Report Prepared for the National Alliance of Street Vendors.

BJP. 2014. Bharatiya Janata Party Election Manifesto 2014. Available at: http://ipv6.bjp.org/images/pdf_2014/full_manifesto_english_07.04.2014.pdf (accessed on 25 November 2015).

Block, F. 1977. 'The Ruling Class Does Not Rule'. *Socialist Revolution* 33(May/June): 6–28.

Bolt, J., R. Inklaar, H. de Jong, and J.L. van Zanden. 2018. 'Rebasing "Maddison": New Income Comparisons and the Shape of Long-Run Economic Development'. Maddison Project Working Paper 10.

Bourdieu, P. 1984. *Distinction: A Social Critique of the Judgment of Taste.* Cambridge, MA: Harvard University Press.

Braudel, F. 1982. *Civilization and Capitalism, 15th–18th Century,* Vol. II: *The Wheels of Commerce.* London: Fontana.

Brenner, J., and M. Ramas. 1984. 'Rethinking Women's Oppression'. *New Left Review* I/144: 33–71.

Business Standard. 2016. 'Avoiding Reform'. 29 May. Available at: https://www.business-standard.com/article/opinion/avoiding-reform-11605 2900714_1.html (accessed on 14 August 2019).

Byres, T.J. 1979. 'Of Neo-Populist Pipe-Dreams: Daedalus in the Third World and the Myth of Urban Bias'. *Journal of Peasant Studies* 6(2): 210–44.

———. 1981. *The New Technology, Class Formation and Class Activism in the Indian Countryside.* London: Frank Cass.

Calì, M., and K. Sen. 2011. 'Do Effective State-Business Relations Matter for Economic Growth? Evidence from Indian States'. *World Development* 33(9): 1542–57.

Carpenter, D.P. 2001. *The Forging of Bureaucratic Autonomy: Reputations, Networks, and Policy Innovation in Executive Agencies, 1862–1928.* Princeton, NJ: Princeton University Press.

Chakrabarty, D. 1989. *Rethinking Working-Class History: Bengal, 1890–1940.* Princeton, NJ: Princeton University Press.

Chakraborty, S. 2013. *The Price of Land.* New Delhi: Oxford University Press.

Chakravarty, S. 1979. 'On the Question of Home Market and Prospects for Indian Growth'. *Economic and Political Weekly* 14(30/32 [Special Number]): 1229–42.

———. 1987. *Development Planning: The Indian Experience.* Oxford: Oxford University Press.

Chand, R., S.S. Raju, and L.M. Pandey. 2007. 'Growth Crisis in Agriculture: Severity and Options at National and State Levels'. *Economic and Political Weekly* 42(26): 2528–33.

Chandra, B., M. Mukherjee, and A. Mukherjee. 2008. *India since Independence.* New Delhi: Penguin.

Chandra, K. 2015. 'The New Indian State: The Relocation of Patronage in the Post-Liberalisation Economy'. *Economic and Political Weekly* 50(41): 46–58.

Chandrasekhar, C.P. 1988. 'Aspects of Growth and Structural Change in Indian Industry'. *Economic and Political Weekly* 23(45/47 [Special Number]): 2359–70.

Chari, S. 2004. *Fraternal Capital: Peasant-Workers, Self-Made Men and Globalization in Provincial India*. New Delhi: Permanent Black.

Chatterjee, E. 2014. 'Power-Hungry: The State and the Troubled Transition in Indian Electricity'. In *Indian Capitalism in Development*, edited by B. Harriss-White and J. Heyer, 208–25. New York: Routledge.

———. 2017a. 'Reinventing State Capitalism in India: A View from the Energy Sector'. *Contemporary South Asia* 25(1): 85–100.

———. 2017b. 'The Limits of Liberalization: The Power Sector'. In *The Political Economy of Contemporary India*, edited by R. Nagaraj and S. Motram, 52–74. New Delhi: Cambridge University Press.

Chatterjee, P. 2004. *The Politics of the Governed: Reflections on Popular Politics in Most of the World*. New York: Columbia University Press.

———. 2008. 'Democracy and Economic Transformation in India'. *Economic and Political Weekly* 43(16): 53–62.

Chen, M.A. 2007. 'Rethinking the Informal Economy: Linkages with the Formal Economy and the Formal Regulatory Environment'. DESA Working Paper ST/ESA/2007/DWP/46, United Nations Department of Economic and Social Affairs, New York, NY.

Chibber, V. 2003. *Locked in Place: State-Building and Late Industrialization in India*. Princeton, NJ: Princeton University Press.

———. 2006. 'On the Decline of Class Analysis in South Asian Studies'. *Critical Asian Studies* 38(4): 357–87.

CNBC: Money Control. 2015. 'Modi Govt Hasn't Delivered on Promised Reforms'. 31 July. Available at: http://www.moneycontrol.com/news/economy/modi-govt-hasnt-deliveredpromised-reforms-moodys_2241381.html (accessed on 25 July 2019).

Cohen, G.A. 1978. *Karl Marx's Theory of History: A Defence*. Oxford: Clarendon Press.

———. 2002. 'Deeper into Bullshit'. In *Contours of Agency: Essays on Themes from Harry Frankfurt*, edited by S. Buss and L. Overton, 321–40. Cambridge, MA; London: MIT Press.

Collier, P., P. Honohan, and K.O. Moene. 2001. 'Implications of Ethnic Diversity'. *Economic Policy* 16(32): 129–66.

Corbridge, S., and J. Harriss. 2000. *Reinventing India: Liberalization, Hindu Nationalism and Popular Democracy*. Cambridge: Polity.

Crabtree, J. 2018. *The Billionaire Raj: A Journey through India's New Gilded Age*. London: Oneworld.

Crossette, Barbara. 1988. 'Angry Farmers Camp in New Delhi's Stately Core'. *New York Times*, 28 October.

Cuberes, D., and M. Jerzmanowski. 2009. 'Democracy, Diversification and Growth Reversals'. *Economic Journal* 119(540): 1270–302.

Damodaran, H. 2008. *India's New Capitalists: Caste, Business and Industry in a Modern Nation*. New York: Palgrave Macmillan.

Das, G. 2006. 'The India Model'. *Foreign Affairs* 85(4): 2–16.

Das, S.K. 2005. 'Reforms and the Indian Administrative Service'. In *The Politics of Economic Reforms in India*, edited by J.E. Mooij, 171–96. New Delhi; London: Sage.

———. 2013. *The Civil Services in India*. New Delhi; Oxford: Oxford University Press.

Dasgupta, C. 2016. *State and Capital in Independent India: Institutions and Accumulation*. Cambridge: Cambridge University Press.

Datt, G., and M. Ravallion. 2010. 'Shining for the Poor Too?' *Economic and Political Weekly* 45(7): 55–60.

Deaton, A., and J. Drèze. 2009. 'Food and Nutrition in India: Facts and Interpretations'. *Economic and Political Weekly* 44(7): 42–65.

Deaton, A., and V. Kozel. 2005. 'Data and Dogma: The Great Indian Poverty Debate'. *World Bank Research Observer* 20(2): 177–99.

Deccan Herald. 2012. 'Gujarat BJP Manifesto Targets Neo-Middle Class'. 3 December. Available at: http://www.deccanherald.com/content/296228/gujarat-bjp-manifesto-targets-neo.html (accessed on 25 November 2015).

Deokar, B.K., and S.L. Shetty. 2014. 'Growth in Indian Agriculture: Responding to Policy Initiative since 2004–05'. *Economic and Political Weekly* 49(26/27): 101–4.

Desai, A.V. 1981. 'Factors Underlying the Slow Growth of Indian Industry'. *Economic and Political Weekly* 16(10/12 [Annual Number]): 381–92.

———. 2001. 'A Decade of Reforms'. *Economic and Political Weekly* 36(50): 4627–30.

Deshpande, S. 2003. *Contemporary India: A Sociological View*. New Delhi: Penguin.

Dev, S.M. 2009. 'Challenges for Revival of Indian Agriculture'. *Agricultural Economics Research Review* 22(1): 21–45.

Dhawan, D.B. 1996. 'Relationship between Public and Private Investments in Indian Agriculture with Special Reference to Public Canals'. *Indian Journal of Agricultural Economics* 51(1/2): 209–19.

Dixit, A.K. 2009. 'Agriculture in a High Growth State: Case of Gujarat (1960 to 2006)'. *Economic and Political Weekly* 44(50): 64–71.

Doner, R., and B.R. Schneider. 2000. 'Business Associations and Economic Development: Why Some Associations Contribute More than Others'. *Business and Politics* 2(3): 261–88.

Drèze, J. 2015. Interview. *Outlook*, 14 December.

Drèze, J. 2015. 'Nehruvian Budget in the Corporate Age'. *The Hindu*, 5 March. Available at: https://www.thehindu.com/opinion/lead/nehru-vian-budget-in-the-corporate-age/article6959755.ece (accessed on 14 August 2019).

Drèze, J., and A. Sen. 2013. *An Uncertain Glory: India and Its Contradictions.* Princeton, NJ: Princeton University Press.

Drèze, J., and R. Khera. 2014. 'The PEEP Survey: Water for the Leeward India'. *Outlook*, 24 March.

Dutta, M. 2009. 'Nokia SEZ: Public Price of Success'. *Economic and Political Weekly* 44(40): 23–5.

Easterly, W., and R. Levine. 1997. 'Africa's Growth Tragedy: Policies and Ethnic Divisions'. *Quarterly Journal of Economics* 112(4): 1203–50.

Economic and Political Weekly. 2009. 'Editorial: Populism and Patronage'. 44(37): 5–6.

Economic Survey of India (various years). New Delhi: Government of India (Ministry of Finance).

Economic Times. 2015. 'BJP, Led by PM Narendra Modi, to Clear the Air on Land Bill'. 5 April.

The Economist. 2014. 'Our Crony-Capitalism Index: Planet Plutocrat'. 15 March.

Elster, J. 1985. *Making Sense of Marx.* Cambridge; New York: Cambridge University Press.

EPW Research Foundation. 2008. 'The Loan Waiver Scheme'. *Economic and Political Weekly* 43(11): 28–34.

Evans, P. 1995. *Embedded Autonomy: States and Industrial Transformation.* Princeton, NJ: Princeton University Press.

———, ed. 1997. *State–Society Synergy: Government and Social Capital in Development.* Berkeley, CA: University of California Press.

Evans, P., and P. Heller. 2015. 'Human Development, State Transformation, and the Politics of the Developmental State'. In *The Oxford Handbook of Transformations of the State*, edited by S. Leibfried, E. Huber, M. Lange, J.D. Levy, F. Nullmeier, and J.D. Stephens, 691–713. Oxford: Oxford University Press.

Ferguson, J.P., and S. Hasan. 2013. 'Specialization and Career Dynamics: Evidence from the Indian Administrative Service'. *Administrative Science Quarterly* 58(2): 233–56.

Fernandes, L. 2006. *India's New Middle Class: Democratic Politics in an Era of Economic Reform.* Minneapolis: University of Minnesota Press.

———. 2009. 'The Political Economy of Lifestyle: Consumption, India's New Middle Class and State-Led Development'. In *The New Middle Classes:*

Globalizing Lifestyles, Consumerism, and Environmental Concern, edited by H. Lange and L. Meier, 219–36. New York, NY: Springer.

———. 2015. 'India's Middle Classes in Contemporary India'. In *Routledge Handbook of Contemporary India*, edited by K.A. Jacobsen, 232–42. London: Routledge.

———. 2018 'Conceptualizing the Post-Liberalization State: Intervention, Restructuring, and the Nature of State Power'. In *Feminists Rethink the Neoliberal State: Inequality, Exclusion, and Change*, edited by L. Fernandes, 1–31. New York: New York University Press.

FICCI [Federation of Indian Chambers of Commerce and Industry]. n.d. 'Memorandum: The Land Acquisition, Rehabilitation and Resettlement Bill 2011'. Submission to Lok Sabha Select Committee, New Delhi.

Firstpost. 2016. 'Parliamentary Panel Gets Sixth Extension on Land Bill after Many States Failed to Furnish Vital Details'. 16 March. Available at: http://m.firstpost.com/india/parliamentary-panel-gets-sixth-extension-on-land-bill-after-many-states-failed-to-furnish-vital-details-2678398.html? (accessed on 25 July 2019).

Frankel, F.R. 1978. *India's Political Economy, 1947–1977: The Gradual Revolution*. Princeton, NJ; Guildford: Princeton University Press.

Fukuyama, F. 2014. *Political Order and Political Decay: From the Industrial Revolution to the Globalization of Democracy*. New York: Macmillan.

Fuller, C.J., and J. Harriss. 2001. 'For an Anthropology of the Modern Indian State'. In *The Everyday State and Society in Modern India*, edited by C.J. Fuller and V. Bénéï, 1–30. London: Hurst.

Gadgil, S., and S. Gadgil. 2006. 'The Indian Monsoon, GDP and Agriculture'. *Economic and Political Weekly* 41(47): 4887–95.

Gandhi, A., and M. Walton. 2012. 'Where Do India's Billionaires Get Their Wealth?' *Economic and Political Weekly* 47(40): 10–14.

Ganguly-Scrase, R., and T. Scrase. 2008. *Globalisation and the Middle Classes in India: The Social and Cultural Impact of Neoliberal Reforms*. London: Routledge.

Ghate, C., and S. Wright. 2012. 'The "V-factor": Distribution, Timing and Correlates of the Great Indian Growth Turnaround'. *Journal of Development Economics* 99(1): 58–67.

Ghosal, S., and P. Eugenio. 2009. 'Democracy, Collective Action and Intra-Elite Conflict'. *Journal of Public Economics* 93(9–10): 1078–89.

Ghose, A. 2016. *India Employment Report 2016*. New Delhi: Oxford University Press.

Glaeser, E.L., and C. Goldin, eds. 2009. *Corruption and Reform: Lessons from America's Economic History*. Chicago: University of Chicago Press; National Bureau of Economic Research.

Goetz, A.M., and R. Jenkins. 2005. *Reinventing Accountability: Making Democracy Work for Human Development*. New York: Palgrave Macmillan.

Goldberg, P., A. Khandelwal, and N. Pavcnik. 2013. 'Variety In, Variety Out: Imported Inputs and Product Scope Expansion in India'. In *Reforms and Economic Transformation in India*, edited by J.N. Bhagwati and A. Panagariya, 168–99. New Delhi: Oxford University Press.

Government of India. 2006. *Social, Economic and Educational Status of Muslims in India: A Report*. New Delhi: Government of India.

———. 2007. *Report of the Expert Group on Agricultural Indebtedness*. New Delhi: Department of Economic Affairs, Ministry of Finance, Government of India.

———. 2015. *Report of the Seventh Central Pay Commission*. New Delhi: Government of India.

Gulati, A., and A. Sharma. 1995. 'Subsidy Syndrome in Indian Agriculture'. *Economic and Political Weekly* 30(39): A93–A102.

Gulati, A., and S. Bathla. 2001. 'Capital Formation in Indian Agriculture: Re-visiting the Debate'. *Economic and Political Weekly* 36(20): 1697–708.

Gupta, A. 1995. 'Blurred Boundaries: The Discourse of Corruption, the Culture of Politics, and the Imagined State'. *American Ethnologist* 22(2): 375–402.

Gupta, A., and K. Sivaramakrishnan. 2011. 'Introduction: The State in India after Liberalization'. In *The State in India after Liberalization: Interdisciplinary Perspectives*, edited by A. Gupta and K. Sivaramakrishnan, 1–27. London; New York: Routledge.

Gupta, D. 2005. 'Whither the Indian Village: Culture and Agriculture in "Rural" India'. *Economic and Political Weekly* 40(8): 751–8.

Hansen, T.B. 1999. *The Saffron Wave: Democracy and Hindu Nationalism in Modern India*. Princeton, NJ: Princeton University Press.

Harriss, J. 1982. 'Character of an Urban Economy: "Small-Scale" Production and Labour Markets in Coimbatore'. *Economic and Political Weekly* 17(23): 945–54.

———. 1987. 'The State in Retreat: Why Has India Experienced Such Half-hearted "Liberalisation" in the 1980s?' *IDS Bulletin* 18(4): 31–8.

———. 1993. 'What Is Happening in Rural West Bengal: Agrarian Reform, Growth and Distribution'. *Economic and Political Weekly* 28(24): 1237–47.

———. 1999. 'Comparing Political Regimes across Indian States: A Preliminary Essay'. *Economic and Political Weekly* 34(48): 3367–77.

———. 2013. 'Does "Landlordism" Still Matter? Reflections on Agrarian Change in India'. *Journal of Agrarian Change* 13(3): 351–64.

Harriss-White, B. 1996a. 'Liberalization and Corruption: Resolving the Paradox'. *IDS Bulletin* 27(2): 31–9.

———. 1996b. *A Political Economy of Agricultural Markets in South India: Masters of the Countryside*. New Delhi: Sage.

———. 2003. *India Working: Essays on Society and Economy*. Cambridge: Cambridge University Press.

———. 2006. 'Poverty and Capitalism'. *Economic and Political Weekly* 41(13): 1241–6.

———. 2008. *Rural Commercial Capital: Agricultural Markets in West Bengal*. New Delhi: Oxford University Press.

———. 2010. *Local Capitalism and the Foodgrains Economy in Northern Tamil Nadu, 1973–2010*. New Delhi: Three Essays Press.

———. 2012. 'Capitalism and the Common Man: Peasants and Petty Production in Africa and South Asia'. *Agrarian South: Journal of Political Economy* 1(2): 109–60.

———. 2014. 'Labour and Petty Production'. *Development and Change*, Special Issue: Forum 2014, 45(5): 981–1000.

———. 2015. '"Local Capitalism" and the Development of the Rice Economy, 1973–2010'. In *Middle India and Urban-Rural Development: Four Decades of Change*, edited by B. Harriss-White, 97–130. New Delhi: Springer.

———. 2017. 'Matter in Motion: Work and Livelihoods in India's Economy of Waste'. In *Critical Perspectives on Work and Employment in Globalizing India*, edited by E. Noronha and P. D'Cruz, 95–111. New Delhi: Springer.

Harriss-White, B., and S. Janakarajan, eds. 2004. *Rural India Facing the 21st Century*. London: Anthem Press.

Hasan, N., and A. Narayana. 2013. 'Governance Reforms and Welfare—A Study of Karnataka Guarantee of Services to Citizens Act'. Paper presented at Second Azim Premji University International Conference on Law, Governance and Development: Right to Welfare, Work, Food and Education, Bangalore.

Hasan, Z. 1998. *Quest for Power: Oppositional Movements and Post-Congress Politics in Uttar Pradesh*. New Delhi: Oxford University Press.

Hatekar, N., and A. Dongre. 2005. 'Structural Breaks in India's Growth: Revisiting the Debate with a Longer Perspective'. *Economic and Political Weekly* 40(14): 1432–5.

Hausmann, R., L. Pritchett, and D. Rodrik. 2005. 'Growth Accelerations'. *Journal of Economic Growth* 10(4): 303–29.

Haynes, D. 2012. *Small Town Capitalism in Western India: Artisans, Merchants and the Making of the Informal Economy, 1870–1960*. Cambridge: Cambridge University Press.

Heller, P., P. Mukhopadhyay, and M. Walton. 2019. 'Cabal City: India's Urban Regimes and Accumulation without Development'. In *Business and Politics in India*, edited by C. Jaffrelot, A. Kohli, and K. Murali, 151–82. New York: Oxford University Press.

Herring, R.J. 1986. 'Review: *The Political Economy of Development in India* by Pranab Bardhan'. *Journal of Asian Studies* 45(3): 622–3.

———. 1999. 'Embedded Particularism: India's Failed Developmental State'. In *The Developmental State*, edited by M. Woo-Cumings, 306–34. Ithaca, NY; London: Cornell University Press.

Herring, R.J., and R. Agarwala. 2006. 'Introduction—Restoring Agency to Class: Puzzles from the Subcontinent'. *Critical Asian Studies* 38(4): 323–56.

———, eds. 2008. *Whatever Happened to Class?* New York: Routledge.

Heyer, J. 2014. 'Dalit Women Becoming "Housewives": Lessons from the Tiruppur Region, 1981–2 to 2008–9'. In *Dalits in Neoliberal India: Mobility or Marginalisation?* edited by C. Still, 208–35. New Delhi: Routledge.

The Hindu. 2015. 'Land Ordinance Gets a Burial'. 31 August.

———. 2015. 'Arun Shourie Tears into Modi Govt'. 27 October. Available at: https://www.thehindu.com/news/national/arun-shourie-tears-into-modi-govt/article7807149.ece (accessed on 14 August 2019).

Hindu Business Line. 2011. 'Land Acquisition Bill Will Push up Prices Five Times: CII Chief'. 9 November.

———. 2015. 'India Most Attractive Investment Destination: EY Survey'. 14 October.

IANS. 2015. 'Government to Achieve 3.9 Fiscal Deficit Target: Jaitley'. *The Pioneer,* 27 October. Available at: dailypioneer.com/2015/top-stories/government-to-achieve-39-fiscal-deficit-target-jaitley.html (accessed on 28 August 2019).

India Today. 1987. 'Powerful Farmers' Organisations Rise on Political Horizon'. 30 November.

Indian Express. 2015. 'RSS Affiliates Up in Arms Against Modi Govt on Land Acquisition Bill'. 21 June.

Iyer, L., and A. Mani. 2011. 'Traveling Agents: Political Change and Bureaucratic Turnover in India'. *Review of Economics and Statistics* 94(3): 723–39.

Jaffrelot, C. 2003. *India's Silent Revolution: The Rise of the Lower Castes in North India.* New York: Columbia University Press.

———. 2019. 'Business-Friendly Gujarat in 2000s: The Implications of a New Political Economy'. In *Business and Politics in India*, edited by C. Jaffrelot, A. Kohli, and K. Murali, 211–33. New York: Oxford University Press.

Jaffrelot, C., A. Kohli, and K. Murali, eds. 2019. *Business and Politics in India.* New York: Oxford University Press.

Jairaj, A., and B. Harriss-White. 2006. 'Social Structure, Tax Culture and the State: Tamil Nadu, India'. *Economic and Political Weekly* 41(51): 5247–57.

Jan, M.A. 2012. '"Ideal Types" and the Diversity of Capital: A Review of Sanyal'. CSASP–SIAS Working Paper 12, School of Interdisciplinary Area Studies, University of Oxford, UK. Available at: https://pdfs.semanticscholar.org/3c9d/1b9cd213f94f1d663dbdb0c70b738c96fb20.pdf (accessed on 25 July 2019).

Jan, M.A., and B. Harriss-White. 2019. 'Petty Production and India's Development'. In *Karl Marx's Life, Ideas, and Influences: A Critical Examination on the Bicentenary*, edited by S. Gupta, M. Musto, and B. Amini. New York: Palgrave Macmillan.

Janakarajan, S. 2004. 'A Snake in the Grass! Unequal Power, Unequal Contracts and Unexplained Conflicts: Facilitating Negotiations over Water Conflicts in Peri-Urban Catchments'. IRC website. www.irc.nl/negowat (accessed on 27 December 2016).

———. 2008. 'Unequal Power, Unequal Contracts and Unexplained Resistance: The Case of the Peri-urban Areas in Chennai'. In *Water Conflicts in India: A Million Revolts in the Making*, edited by K.J. Joy, S. Paranjape, B. Gujja, V. Goud, and V.G. Vispute, 54–9. New Delhi: Routledge.

Jebaraj, P. 2018. 'Why Are Farmers All Over India on the Streets?' *The Hindu*, 9 December.

Jeffrey, C. 2010. *Youth, Class and the Politics of Waiting in India*. Stanford: Stanford University Press.

Jeffrey, C., P. Jeffery, and R. Jeffery. 2008. *Degrees Without Freedom? Education, Masculinities and Unemployment in North India*. Stanford, CA: Stanford University Press.

Jenkins, R. 1999. *Democratic Politics and Economic Reform in India*. Cambridge: Cambridge University Press.

———. 2004. 'The Ideologically Embedded Market: Political Legitimation and Economic Reform in India'. In *Markets in Historical Context: Ideas and Politics in the Modern World*, edited by M. Bevir and F. Trentmann, 201–23. Cambridge: Cambridge University Press.

———. 2017. 'Advice and Dissent: The Federal Politics of Reforming India's Land Acquisition Legislation'. In *The Political Economy of Contemporary India*, edited by R. Nagaraj and S. Motiram, 307–30. Cambridge: Cambridge University Press.

Jenkins, R., and J. Manor. 2016. 'Politics of Social Protection: The Mahatma Gandhi National Rural Employment Guarantee Act in Rajasthan and Madhya Pradesh'. In *Politics of Welfare: Comparisons across Indian States*, edited by L. Tillin, R. Deshpande, and K.K. Kailash, 168–99. New Delhi: Oxford University Press.

———. 2017. *Politics and the Right to Work: India's Mahatma Gandhi National Rural Employment Guarantee Act*. New Delhi: Oxford University Press.

Jenkins, R., L. Kennedy, and P. Mukhopadhyay, eds. 2014. *Power, Policy and Protest: The Politics of India's Special Economic Zones.* New Delhi: Oxford University Press.

Jerath, Arati R. 2011. 'Tikait, Farmer Leader Who Laid Seige to Delhi, Dead'. *Times of India,* 16 May.

Jha, P.S. 1980. *India: A Political Economy of Stagnation.* Oxford: Oxford University Press.

———. 2013. 'In India: Where Democracy Has Gone Wrong'. In *India since 1947: Looking Back at a Modern Nation,* edited by A.K. Thakur. New Delhi: Niyogi Books.

Jodhka, S.S. 2006. 'Beyond "Crises": Rethinking Contemporary Punjab Agriculture'. *Economic and Political Weekly* 41(16): 1530–7.

Jodhka, S.S., and A. Prakash, eds. 2015. *The Middle India: The Politics and Economics of Middle Class in India.* Oxford: Oxford University Press

Jones, B.F., and B.A. Olken. 2008. 'The Anatomy of Start-Stop Growth'. *Review of Economics and Statistics* 90(3): 582–7.

Jong-a-Pin, R., and J. De Haan. 2011. 'Political Regime Change, Economic Liberalization and Growth Accelerations'. *Public Choice* 146(1–2): 93–115.

Joseph, R.K. 2011. 'The R&D Scenario in Indian Pharmaceutical Industry'. RIS Discussion Paper No. 176, Research and Information System for Developing Countries, New Delhi.

Joshi, V., and I.M.D. Little. 1994. *India: Macroeconomics and Political Economy, 1964–1991.* New Delhi: Oxford University Press.

Juluri, V. 2003. *Becoming a Global Audience: Longing and Belonging in Indian Music Television.* New York: Lang.

Kale, S. 2014. *Electrifying India: Regional Political Economies of Development.* Palo Alto: Stanford University Press.

Kalecki, M. 1972. *Selected Essays on the Economic Growth of the Socialist and the Mixed Economy.* Cambridge: Cambridge University Press.

Kapur, D., and M. Vaishnav. 2018. 'Builders, Politicians, and Election Finance'. In *Costs of Democracy: Political Finance in India,* edited by D. Kapur and M. Vaishnav, 74–118. New Delhi: Oxford University Press.

Kapur, D.V. 2015. *The Bloom in the Desert: The Making of NTPC.* Noida: HarperCollins.

Kazin, M. 1995. *The Populist Persuasion: An American History.* Ithaca, NY: Cornell University Press.

Keen, S. 2001. *Debunking Economics: The Naked Emperor of the Social Sciences.* Annandale: Pluto Press.

Khan, M.H. 1998. 'Patron-Client Networks and the Economic Effects of Corruption in Asia'. *European Journal of Development Research* 10(1): 15–39.

Khan, M.H., and K.S. Jomo, eds. 2001. *Rents, Rent-seeking and Economic Development: Theory and Evidence in Asia*. Cambridge: Cambridge University Press.

Khanna, S. 2015. 'The Transformation of India's Public Sector: Political Economy of Growth and Change'. *Economic and Political Weekly* 50(5): 47–60.

Kidron, M. 1965. *Foreign Investments in India*. Oxford: Oxford University Press.

Kijima, Y. 2006. 'Why Did Wage Inequality Increase? Evidence from Urban India, 1983–99'. *Journal of Development Economics* 81(1): 97–117.

Klepper, M., and R. Gunther. 1996. *The Wealthy 100: From Benjamin Franklin to Bill Gates—A Ranking of the Richest Americans, Past and Present*. New York: Citadel Press.

Kochanek, S.A. 1974. *Business and Politics in India*. Berkeley, CA: University of California Press.

———. 1996. 'Liberalisation and Business Lobbying in India'. *Journal of Commonwealth and Comparative Politics* 34(3): 155–73.

Kohli, A. 1990. *Democracy and Discontent: India's Growing Crisis of Governability*. Cambridge: Cambridge University Press.

———. 2006a. 'Politics of Economic Growth in India, 1980–2005. Part I: the 1980s'. *Economic and Political Weekly* 41(13): 1251–9.

———. 2006b. 'Politics of Economic Growth in India, 1980–2005. Part II: The 1990s and Beyond'. *Economic and Political Weekly* 41(14): 1361–70.

———. 2012. *Poverty Amid Plenty in the New India*. Cambridge: Cambridge University Press.

Kothari, R. 1964. 'The Congress System in India'. *Asian Survey* 4(12): 1161–73.

Kotwal, A., B. Ramaswami, and W. Wadhwa. 2011. 'Economic Liberalization and Indian Economic Growth: What's the Evidence?' *Journal of Economic Literature* 49(4): 1152–99.

KPMG, CII, FICCI, and World Bank. 2015. *Assessment of State Implementation of Business Reforms*. Delhi.

Krishna, A. 2010. 'Continuity and Change: the Indian Administrative Service 30 Years Ago and Today'. *Commonwealth & Comparative Politics* 48(4): 433–44.

Krishnan, K.P., and T.V. Somanathan. 2017. 'The Civil Service'. In *Rethinking Public Institutions in India*, edited by D. Kapur, P.B. Mehta, and M. Vaishnav, 339–416. Delhi: Oxford University Press.

Krishnaswamy, R., and J.D. Rajakumar. 2015. 'Recent Trends in Inter-sectoral Terms of Trade'. *Economic and Political Weekly* 50(5): 82–4.

Krueger, A.O. 1974. 'The Political Economy of the Rent-seeking Society'. *American Economic Review* 64(3): 291–303.

Kulshreshtha, A.C. 2011. 'Measuring the Unorganized Sector in India'. *Review of Income and Wealth* Series 57, Special Issue: S123–S134.

Kumar, A.G. 1992. 'Falling Agricultural Investment and Its Consequences'. *Economic and Political Weekly* 27(42): 681–94.

Kuznets, S. 1955. 'Economic Growth and Income Inequality'. *American Economic Review*, 45(1): 1–28.

Lal, D. 1984. 'The Political Economy of the Predatory State'. Development Research Department Working Paper 105, Washington, DC: World Bank.

Law, M.T., and G.D. Libecap. 2006. 'The Determinants of Progressive Era Reform: The Pure Food and Drugs Act of 1906'. In *Corruption and Reform: Lessons from America's Economic History*, edited by E.L. Glaeser and C. Goldin, 319–42. Chicago: University of Chicago Press; National Bureau of Economic Research.

Lebergott, S. 1966. 'Labor Force and Employment, 1800–1960'. In *Output, Employment, and Productivity in the United States after 1800*, edited by D.S. Brady, 117–204. Washington: NBER Books.

Leftwich, A. 1995. 'Bringing Politics Back In: Towards a Model of the Developmental State'. *Journal of Development Studies* 31(3): 400–27.

Lengala, C., and R. Ram. 2010. 'Growth Elasticity of Poverty: Estimates from New Data'. *International Journal of Social Economics* 37(12): 923–32.

Lerche, J. 2010. 'From "Rural Labour" to "Classes of Labour": Class Fragmentation, Caste and Class Struggle at the Bottom of the Indian Labour Hierarchy'. In *The Comparative Political Economy of Development: Africa and South Asia*, edited by B. Harriss-White and J. Heyer, 66–87. London: Routledge.

———. 2013. 'The Agrarian Question in Neoliberal India: Agrarian Transition Bypassed?' *Journal of Agrarian Change* 13(3): 382–404.

———. 2014. 'Regional Patterns of Agrarian Accumulation in India'. Paper presented at the Foundation for Agrarian Studies, Tenth Anniversary Conference, Kochi, 9–12 January.

———. 2015. 'Regional Patterns of Agrarian Accumulation in India'. In *Indian Capitalism in Development*, edited by B. Harriss-White and J. Heyer, 46–65. London: Routledge.

Levien, M. 2013. 'The Politics of Dispossession: Theorizing India's Land Wars'. *Politics and Society* 41(3): 351–94.

Leys, C. 1976. 'The "Overdeveloped" Post-Colonial State: A Re-evaluation'. *Review of African Political Economy* 3(5): 39–48.

Lindert, P.H. 2004. *Growing Public: Social Spending and Economic Growth since the Eighteenth Century*, Vol. 1: *The Story*. Cambridge: Cambridge University Press.

Lipton, M. 1977. *Why Poor People Stay Poor: A Study of Urban Bias in World Development*. London: Temple Smith.

Lokanathan, P.S. 1945. 'The Bombay Plan'. *Foreign Affairs* 23(4): 680–6.

Lukose, R.A. 2009. *Liberalization's Children: Gender, Youth, and Consumer Citizenship in Globalizing India*. Durham, NC: Duke University Press.

Maheshwata, J. 2009. 'Gujarat: BJP Scrapes Through'. *Economic and Political Weekly* 44(39): 133–6.

Mangla, A. 2014. 'Bureaucratic Norms and State Capacity: Implementing Primary Education in India's Himalayan Region'. Harvard Business School Working Paper 14-099, Cambridge, MA.

Mani, M., ed. 2014. *Greening India's Growth: Costs, Valuations and Trade-offs*. London: Routledge.

Mankekar, P. 1999. *Screening Culture, Viewing Politics: An Ethnography of Television, Womanhood and Nation in Postcolonial India*. Durham, NC: Duke University Press.

Manor, J. 1995. 'The Political Sustainability of Economic Liberalization in India'. In *India: The Future of Economic Reform*, edited by R. Cassen and V. Joshi, 339–64. New Delhi: Oxford University Press.

———. 2010. 'Prologue: Caste and Politics in Recent Times'. In *Caste in Indian Politics*. New edition, edited by R. Kothari, xi–lxi. Hyderabad: Orient Blackswan.

———. 2011a. 'The Congress Party and the Great Transformation'. In *Understanding India's New Political Economy: A Great Transformation?*, edited by S. Ruparelia, S. Reddy, J. Harriss, and S. Corbridge, 204–20. London; New Delhi: Routledge.

———. 2011b. 'Did the Central Government's Poverty Initiatives Help to Re-Elect It?' In *New Dimensions of Politics in India: The United Progressive Alliance in Power*, edited by L. Sáez and G. Singh, 13–25. London; New Delhi: Routledge.

———. 2015a. 'Modi Stuck between Two Promises'. *Nikkei Asian Review*. 27 July.

———. 2015b. 'A Precarious Enterprise: Multiple Antagonisms during Year One of the Modi Government'. *South Asia*. December.

———. 2016a. 'As Caste Hierarchies Wane: Explaining Inter-caste Accommodation in Rural India'. In *Politics and State-Society Relations in India: The Writings of James Manor*, 284–303. New Delhi; London; New York: Orient BlackSwan; Hurst; Oxford University Press.

———. 2016b. 'India's States: The Struggle to Govern'. *Studies in Indian Politics* 4(1): 8–21.

Martin, L.A., S. Nataraj, and A. Harrison. 2014. 'In With the Big, Out with the Small: Removing Small-Scale Reservations in India'. NBER Working Paper 19942, National Bureau of Economic Research, Cambridge, MA.

Mathur, A.S., S. Das, and S. Sircar. 2006. 'Status of Agriculture in India: Trends and Prospects'. *Economic and Political Weekly* 41(52): 5327–36.

Mazumdar, S. 2011. 'The State, Industrialisation and Competition: A Reassessment of India's Leading Business Enterprises under Dirigisme'. *Economic History of Developing Regions* 26(2): 33–54.

Mazzarella, W. 2003. *Shoveling Smoke: Advertising and Globalization in Contemporary India*. Durham, NC: Duke University Press.

McCartney, M. 2009. *India: The Political Economy of Growth, Stagnation and the State, 1951–2007*. London: Routledge.

———. 2010. *Political Economy, Growth and Liberalisation in India, 1991–2008*. London; New York: Routledge.

———. 2013. 'Going, Going but not yet Quite Gone: The Political Economy of the Indian Intermediate Classes During the Era of Liberalization'. In *Two Decades of Market Reform in India: Some Dissenting Views*, edited by S. Bhattacharyya, 243–59. New York: Anthem Press.

McDonald, H. 2010. *Mahabharata in Polyester: The Making of the World's Richest Brothers and their Feud*. Sydney: University of New South Wales Press.

Mead, W.R., and S. Schwenninger. 2002. *The Bridge to a Global Middle Class: Development, Trade and International Finance*. New York: Springer.

Mehta, P.B. 2015. 'Loud but Silent'. *Indian Express*, 7 August. Available at: https://indianexpress.com/article/opinion/columns/loud-but-silent/ (accessed on 14 August 2019).

———. 2016. 'After Mandal'. *Indian Express*. 23 April. Available at: http://indianexpress.com/article/opinion/columns/after-mandal-jat-patidar-protests-2766166/ (accessed on 25 July 2019).

Mehta, P.B., and M. Walton. 2014. 'Ideas, Interests and the Politics of Development Change in India: Capitalism, Inclusion and the State'. ESID Working Paper No. 36, University of Manchester, Manchester, UK.

Menes, R. 2006. 'Limiting the Reach of the Grabbing Hand: Graft and Growth in American Cities, 1880 to 1930'. In *Corruption and Reform: Lessons from America's Economic History*, edited by E.L. Glaeser and C. Goldin, 63–93. Chicago: University of Chicago Press; National Bureau of Economic Research.

Mezzadri, A. 2010. 'Globalisation, Informalisation and the State in the Indian Garment Industry'. *International Review of Sociology* 20(3): 491–511.

———. 2014. 'Indian Garment Clusters and CSR Norms: Incompatible Agendas at the Bottom of the Garment Commodity Chain'. *Oxford Development Studies* 42(2): 238–58.

Michelutti, L. 2008. *The Vernacularisation of Democracy: Politics, Caste and Religion in India*. New Delhi: Routledge.

Miliband, R. 1983. 'State Power and Class Interests'. *New Left Review* I 138(March/April): 57–68.

Min, B., and M. Golden. 2014. 'Electoral Cycles in Electricity Losses in India'. *Energy Policy* 65: 619–25.

Mishra, D., and B. Harriss-White. 2015. 'Mapping India's Regions of Agrarian Capitalism'. In *Mapping India's Capitalism: Old and New Regions*, edited by E. Basile, B. Harriss-White, and C. Lutringer, 9–41. Houndmills, Basingstoke; New York: Palgrave Macmillan.

Mishra, S.N., and R. Chand. 1995. 'Public and Private Capital Formation in Indian Agriculture: Comments on Complementarity Hypothesis'. *Economic and Political Weekly* 30(25): A64–A79.

Mitra, A. 1977. *Terms of Trade and Class Relations: An Essay in Political Economy*. London: Frank Cass.

Mitra, S.K. 2011. 'From Comparative Politics to Cultural Flow: The Hybrid State, and Resilience of the Political System in India'. In *Conceptualizing Cultural Hybridization: A Transdisciplinary Approach*, edited by P.W. Stockhammer, 107–32. Heidelberg: Springer.

Mody, A., A. Nath, and M. Walton. 2011. 'Sources of Corporate Profits in India: Business Dynamism or Advantages of Entrenchment?' In *India Policy Forum 2010–11*, Vol. 7, edited by S. Bery, B. Bosworth, and A. Panagariya, 43–84. New Delhi: SAGE.

Mody, A., and M. Walton. 2012. 'A Wasted Sweet Spot'. *Indian Express*. 21 September.

———. 2017. 'Note Ban and the Allure of Authoritarian Populism'. *Business Standard*. 10 January.

Mohan, R., and M. Kapur. 2015. 'Pressing the Indian Growth Accelerator: Policy Imperatives'. IMF Working Paper WP/15/53. International Monetary Fund, Washington, DC.

Mohan, T.T.R. 2005. *Privatisation in India: Challenging Economic Orthodoxy*. London: Routledge Curzon.

Mooij, J. 1999. 'Food Policy in India: The Importance of Electoral Politics in Policy Implementation'. *Journal of International Development* 11(4): 625–36.

———. 2005. *The Politics of Economic Reforms in India*. New Delhi; London: SAGE.

Morone, J.A. 2003. *Hellfire Nation: The Politics of Sin in American History*. New Haven: Yale University Press.

Mukherjee, A. 2009. 'Indian Business, State, and Civil Society: Implications for Global Participation'. In *Chinese and Indian Business: Historical Antecedents*, edited by M. Kudaisya and N. Chin-keong, 143–61. Singapore: Brill Asia.

Mukherji, R. 2014. *Political Economy of Reforms in India*. New Delhi: Oxford University Press.

———. 2017. 'Governance Reform in a Weak State: Thirty Years of Indian Experience'. *Governance* 30(1): 53–8.

Mundle, S., and M. Govinda Rao. 1991. 'Volume and Composition of Government Subsidies in India, 1987–88'. *Economic and Political Weekly* 26(18): 1157–72.

Mundle, S., P. Chakraborty, S. Chowdhury, and S. Sikdar. 2012. 'The Quality of Governance: How Have Indian States Performed?' *Economic and Political Weekly* 47(49): 41–52.

Mundle, S., and S. Sikdar. 2017. 'A Note on Budget Subsidies in India and 14 Major States'. National Institute of Public Finance and Policy, note prepared for the *Economic Survey of the Government of India, 2016–17*.

———. 2019. 'Level and Composition of Subsidies in India: 1987–88 to 2015–16'. Report for the National Institute of Public Finance and Policy.

Murthy, K.N., and A. Soumya. 2007. 'Effects of Public Investment on Growth and Poverty'. *Economic and Political Weekly* 42(1): 47–59.

Nadkarni, M.V. 1991. 'The Mode of Production Debate: A Review Article'. *Indian Economic Review* 26(1): 99–104.

Nagaraj, R. 1990. 'Growth Rates of India's GDP, 1950–51 to 1987–88: Examination of Alternative Hypotheses'. *Economic and Political Weekly* 25(26): 1396–403.

———. 1991. 'Discussion: Increase in India's Growth Rate'. *Economic and Political Weekly* 26(15): 1002–4.

———. 2000. 'Indian Economy since 1980: Virtuous Growth or Polaris-ation?' *Economic and Political Weekly* 35(32): 2831–9.

———. 2006. 'Public Sector Performance since 1950: A Fresh Look'. *Economic and Political Weekly* 41(25): 2551–7.

———. 2008. 'India's Recent Economic Growth: A Closer Look'. *Economic and Political Weekly* 43(15): 55–61.

———. 2013. 'India's Dream Run, 2003–08: Understanding the Boom and its Aftermath'. *Economic and Political Weekly* 48(20): 39–51.

———. 2015. 'Can the Public Sector Revive the Economy? Review of the Evidence and a Policy Suggestion'. *Economic and Political Weekly* 50(5): 41–6.

———. 2017. 'Public Sector Employment: What Has Changed?' In *The Political Economy of Contemporary India*, edited by R. Nagaraj and S. Motiram, 157–78. Delhi: Cambridge University Press.

Narayan, A., and R. Murgai. 2016. 'Looking Back on Two Decades of Poverty and Well-Being in India'. World Bank Policy Research Working Paper 7626, World Bank, Washington, DC.

Nayar, B.R. 2006. 'When Did the "Hindu" Rate of Growth End?' *Economic and Political Weekly* 41(19): 1885–90.

———. 2009. *The Myth of the Shrinking State: Globalization and the State in India*. Delhi; New York: Oxford University Press.

Nayyar, D. 1978. 'Industrial Development in India: Some Reflections on Growth and Stagnation'. *Economic and Political Weekly* 13(31/33): 1265–78.

————. 1994. 'Introduction'. In *Industrial Growth and Stagnation: The Debate in India*, edited by D. Nayyar, 1–17. New Delhi: Oxford University Press.

————. 2014. 'India's Law from Hell'. *Bloomberg Opinion*. 7 November. www.bloomberg.com/opinion/2014-11-07/indias-law-from-hell (accessed on 25 July 2019).

Ninan, T.N. 2016. 'Oh, for a Crisis!' *Business Standard*, 27 May. Available at: https://www.business-standard.com/article/opinion/t-n-ninan-oh-for-a-crisis-116052701131_1.html (accessed on 14 August 2019).

Olson, M. 1965. *The Logic of Collective Action: Public Goods and the Theory of Groups*. Cambridge, MA: Harvard University Press.

————. 1982. *The Rise and Decline of Nations: Economic Growth, Stagflation, and Social Rigidities*. New Haven, CT: Yale University Press.

Omvedt, G. 2005. 'Farmers' Movements and the Debate on Poverty and Economic Reforms in India'. In *Social Movements in India: Poverty, Power and Politics*, edited by R. Ray and M. Katzenstein, 179–202. Lanham, MD: Rowman and Littlefield.

Owensby, B. 1999. *Intimate Ironies: Modernity and the Making of the Middle Class Lives in Brazil*. Stanford: Stanford University Press.

Pai, S. 2014. *Dalit Assertion*. New Delhi: Oxford University Press.

Pal, R. 2013. 'Out-of-Pocket Health Expenditure: Impact on the Consumption of Indian Households'. *Oxford Development Studies* 41(2): 258–79.

Panagariya, A. 2004. 'India in the 1980s and 1990s: A Triumph of Reforms'. IMF Working Paper WP/04/43, International Monetary Fund, Washington, DC.

————. 2008. *India: The Emerging Giant*. New York: Oxford University Press.

Patnaik, P. 2011. 'The Perverse Transformation'. T.S. Rajan Memorial Lecture, Institute of Rural Management, Anand (IRMA), Gujarat. Available at: https://www.youtube.com/watch?v=Vy39RVvV_c4 (accessed on 25 July 2019).

Patnaik, P., and S.K. Rao. 1977. 'Towards an Explanation of Crisis in a Mixed Underdeveloped Economy'. *Economic and Political Weekly* 12(6/8): 205–18.

Patnaik, U. 1976. 'Class Differentiation within the Peasantry: An Approach to Analysis of Indian Agriculture'. *Economic and Political Weekly* 11(39): A82–A101.

Pattenden, J. 2005. 'Trickle-Down Solidarity, Globalisation and Dynamics of Social Transformation in a South Indian Village'. *Economic and Political Weekly* 40(19): 1975–85.

————. 2011. 'Gatekeeping as Accumulation and Domination: Decentralization and Class Relations in Rural South India'. *Journal of Agrarian Change* 11(2): 164–94.

Pattnaik, I., and A. Shah. 2010. 'Is There a Glimpse of Dynamism in Orissa's Agriculture?.' *Economic and Political Weekly* 45(26/27): 756–9.

Pedersen, J.D. 1992. 'State, Bureaucracy and Change in India'. *Journal of Development Studies* 28(4): 616–39.

Perlitz, U. 2008. 'India's Pharmaceutical Industry on Course for Globalisation'. Deutsche Bank Research, Asia Current Issues, Frankfurt, Germany, 9 April.

Piketty, T. 2014. *Capital in the Twenty-First Century*. Cambridge, MA: The Belknap Press of Harvard University Press.

Piliavsky, A., ed. 2014. *Patronage as Politics in South Asia*. New York: Cambridge University Press.

Planning Commission of India. 2014. *Report of the Expert Group to Review the Methodology for Measurement of Poverty* (Chaired by C. Rangarajan). New Delhi: Government of India.

Polanyi, K. 2001 [1944]. *The Great Transformation*. Boston, MA: Beacon Press.

Potter, D.C. 1996. *India's Political Administrators: From ICS to IAS*. New Delhi: Oxford University Press.

Poulantzas, N. 1972. 'The Problem of the Capitalist State'. In *Ideology in Social Science: Readings in Critical Social Theory*, edited by R. Blackburn, 238–53. New York: Pantheon Books.

———. 1973. *Political Power and Social Classes*. London: New Left Books.

———. 2014. *Dalit Capital*. New Delhi: Routledge.

Prakash, Akash. 2015. 'Too Early to Give Up'. *Business Standard*, 12 November.

Prakash, Aseem. 2014. *Dalit Capital*. New Delhi: Routledge.

———. 2017. 'The Hybrid State and Regulation of Land and Real Estate: A Case Study of Gurugram, Haryana'. *Review of Development and Change* 2(1): 173–97.

Pritchett, L. 2009. 'Is India a Flailing State? Detours on the Four Lane Highway to Modernisation'. HKS Faculty Research Working Paper Series RWP09-013, Kennedy School of Government, Harvard University.

PTI. 2015. 'Indirect Tax Collection Grows by 34% in Apr–Nov Period'. *The Pioneer*, 10 December. Available at: dailypioneer.com/2015/business/indirect-tax-collection-grows-by-34-in-apr-bov-period.html (accessed on 28 August 2019).

Radjou, N., J. Prabhu, and S. Ahuja. 2012. *Jugaad Innovation*. New York: Random House.

Raj, K.N. 1973. 'The Politics and Economics of Intermediate Regimes'. *Economic and Political Weekly* 8(27): 1189–98.

Rajagopal, A. 2001. 'Thinking About the New Middle Class: Gender, Advertising and Politics in an Age of Globalisation'. In *Signposts: Gender Issues in Post-Independence India*, edited by R.S. Rajan, 57–99. New Brunswick: Rutgers University Press.

Raju, R.S. 1989. *Urban Unorganised Sector in India*. New Delhi: Mittal.

Ramachandran, V.K., V. Rawal, and M. Swaminathan, eds. 2010. *Socio-Economic Surveys of Three Villages in Andhra Pradesh*. New Delhi: Tulika Books.

Ramakumar, R. 2014. 'Economic Reforms and Agricultural Policy in India'. Paper presented at the Foundation for Agrarian Studies, Tenth Anniversary Conference, Kochi, Kerala, 9–12 January 2014.

———. 2016. 'Jats, *Khaps* and Riots: Communal Politics and the Bharatiya Kisan Union in North India'. *Journal of Agrarian Change* 17(1): 22–42.

Ramakumar, R., and A. Bakshi. 2015. 'New Data Show Continuing Agrarian Distress for Small and Marginal Farmers'. *Peoples Democracy* 39(9). Available at: http://peoplesdemocracy.in/2014/1228_pd/new-data-show-continuing (accessed on 4 March 2015).

Rangarajan, C. 1982. 'Industrial Growth: Another Look'. *Economic and Political Weekly* 17(14/16): 589–604.

Rao, M. Govinda, and S. Mundle. 1992. 'An Analysis of Changes in State Government Subsidies: 1977–87'. In *State Finances in India*, edited by A. Bagchi, J.L. Bajaj, and W.A. Byrd, 107–43. National Institute of Public Finance and Policy.

Rawal, V. 2008. 'Ownership Holdings of Land in Rural India: Putting the Record Straight'. *Economic and Political Weekly* 43(10): 43–7.

RBI. 2011. *Handbook of Statistics on the Indian Economy 2010–11*. Mumbai: Reserve Bank of India.

Robinson, J. 2009. 'The Political Economy of Equality and Growth in Mexico: Lessons from the History of the United States'. In *No Growth without Equity? Inequality, Interests and Competition in Mexico*, edited by S. Levy and M. Walton, 87–107. Washington, DC: World Bank; New York: Palgrave Macmillan.

Robinson, N. 2012. 'Right to Public Service Acts in India: The Experience from Bihar and Madhya Pradesh'. Accountability Initiative Policy Brief Series, Centre for Policy Research, New Delhi.

Rodrik, D., ed. 2003. *In Search of Prosperity: Analytic Narratives on Economic Growth*. Princeton: Princeton University Press.

———. 2012. 'Why We Learn Nothing from Regressing Economic Growth on Policies'. *Seoul Journal of Economics* 25(2): 137–51.

Rodrik, D., and A. Subramanian. 2005. 'From "Hindu Growth" to Productivity Surge: The Mystery of the Indian Growth Transition'. *IMF Staff Papers* 52(2): 193–228.

Roemer, J.E., ed. 1986. *Analytical Marxism*. Cambridge: Cambridge University Press.

Roy, R. 1996. 'State Failure: Political-Fiscal Implications of the Black Economy'. *IDS Bulletin* 27(2): 22–31.

Roy, T. 2012. *India in the World Economy: From Antiquity to the Present*. New York: Cambridge University Press.

Rudolph, L.I., and S.H. Rudolph. 1987. *In Pursuit of Lakshmi: The Political Economy of the Indian State*. Chicago: University of Chicago Press.

Rudra, A. 1985. 'Review: Political Economy of Indian Non-Development'. *Economic and Political Weekly* 20(21): 914–16.

———. 1989. 'Emergence of the Intelligentsia as a Ruling Class in India'. *Economic and Political Weekly* 24(3): 142–50.

Rukmani, R. 1994. 'Urbanisation and Socio-Economic Change in Tamil Nadu, 1901–91'. *Economic and Political Weekly* 29(51/52): 3263–72.

Ruparelia, S., S. Reddy, J. Harriss, and S. Corbridge, eds. 2011. *Understanding India's New Political Economy: A Great Transformation?* London: Routledge.

Ruthven, O. 2008. 'Of Metal and Morals in Moradabad: Perspectives on Ethics in the Workplace Across a Global Supply Chain'. Unpublished PhD Thesis, University of Oxford, UK.

Rutten, M. 1995. *Farms and Factories: Social Profile of Large Farmers and Rural Industrialists in West India*. New Delhi: Oxford University Press.

Sáez, L. 2002. *Federalism without a Centre: The Impact of Political and Economic Reform on India's Federal System*. New Delhi; Thousand Oaks: Sage.

Sanyal, K. 2007. *Rethinking Capitalist Development: Primitive Accumulation, Governmentality and Post-colonial Capitalism*. New Delhi: Routledge India.

Saraswati, J. 2013. 'The IT Industry and Interventionist Policy in India'. In *Beyond the Developmental State: Industrial Policy into the Twenty-First Century*, edited by B. Fine, J. Saraswati, and D. Tavasci, 169–86. London: Pluto Press; New York: Palgrave Macmillan.

Sarkar, S., and B.S. Mehta. 2010. 'Income Inequality in India: Pre- and Post-Reform Periods'. *Economic and Political Weekly* 45(37): 45–55.

SCOPE. 2010. *The Emerging Public Sector: New Vision of a National Treasure*. New Delhi: Standing Conference of Public Enterprises.

Sen, A. 2002. 'Agriculture, Employment and Poverty: Recent Trends in Rural India'. In *Agrarian Studies: Essays on Agrarian Relations in Less-Developed Countries*, edited by V.K. Ramachandran and M. Swaminathan, 111–43. Chennai: Tulika Books.

Sen, A., and Himanshu. 2004. 'Poverty and Inequality in India: I'. *Economic and Political Weekly* 39(38): 4247–63.

Sen, A.K. 1999. *Development as Freedom*. Oxford: Oxford University Press.

Sen, K. 2007. 'Why Did the Elephant Start to Trot? India's Growth Acceleration Re-examined'. *Economic and Political Weekly* 42(43): 37–47.

———. 2009. 'What a Long, Strange Trip It's Been: Reflections on the Causes of India's Growth Miracle'. *Contemporary South Asia* 17(4): 363–77.

Sen, K., and S. Kar. 2014. 'Boom and Bust? A Political Economy Reading of India's Growth Experience, 1993–2013'. IEG Working Paper No. 342, Institute of Economic Growth, New Delhi.

Sen, R. 2015. 'House Matters: The BJP, Modi and Parliament'. *South Asia* 38(4): 776–90.

Sengupta, M. 2004. 'Ideas and Interests: The Role of Lateral Entrants in Indian Policymaking'. Paper presented at the Observer Research Foundation Development Seminar Series, New Delhi, 6 September.

Sharma, M.S. 2014. 'An Obituary for Reform'. *Business Standard*, 23 November. Available at: https://www.business-standard.com/article/opinion/mihir-s-sharma-an-obituary-for-reform-115112200758_1.html (accessed on 14 August 2019).

Shastri, V. 1997. 'The Politics of Economic Liberalization in India'. *Contemporary South Asia* 6(1): 27–56.

Shetty, S.L. 1978. 'Structural Retrogression in the Indian Economy since the Mid-Sixties'. *Economic and Political Weekly* 13(6/7): 185–244.

———. 1990. 'Investment in Agriculture: Brief Review of Recent Trends'. *Economic and Political Weekly* 25(7/8): 389–98.

Sidhu, H.S. 2002. 'Crisis in Agrarian Economy in Punjab: Some Urgent Steps'. *Economic and Political Weekly* 37(30): 3132–8.

Singh, S.B. 2005. 'Limits to Power: Naxalism and Caste Relations in a South Bihar Village'. *Economic and Political Weekly* 40(29): 3167–75.

Sinha, A. 2005. *The Regional Roots of Developmental Politics in India: A Divided Leviathan*. Bloomington, IN: Indiana University Press.

———. 2016. *Globalizing India: How Global Rules and Markets Are Shaping India's Rise to Power*. Cambridge: Cambridge University Press.

Sinha, A., and C. Adams. 2007. 'Modelling the Informal Economy in India'. In *Trade Liberalization and India's Informal Economy*, edited by B. Harriss-White and A. Sinha, 307–64. New Delhi; New York: Oxford University Press.

Sinha, J., and A. Varshney. 2011. 'It Is Time for India to Rein in Its Robber Barons'. *Financial Times*, 6 January.

Sitapati, V. 2011. 'What Anna Hazare's Movement and India's New Middle Classes Say about Each Other'. *Economic and Political Weekly* 46(30): 39.

Sivasubramonian, A. 2004. *The Sources of Economic Growth in India, 1950–1 to 1999–2000*. New Delhi; New York: Oxford University Press.

Skocpol, T. 1979. *States and Social Revolutions: A Comparative Analysis of France, Russia and China*. Cambridge, MA: Harvard University Press.

———. 1982. 'Bringing the State Back In: Strategies of Analysis in Current Research'. In *Bringing the State Back In*, edited by P.B. Evans, D. Rueschemeyer, and T. Skocpol, 3–37. Cambridge: Cambridge University Press.

Skocpol, T., and K. Finegold. 1982. 'State Capacity and Economic Intervention in the Early New Deal'. *Political Science Quarterly* 97(2): 255–78.

Society for Promotion of Wasteland Development & Rights and Resources Initiative. 2014. 'Land Acquisition Related Disputes'. Available at: http://www.rightsandresources.org/wp-content/uploads/Land-Conflicts-Map-updated-2013-14.pdf (accessed on 25 July 2019).

Sokoloff, K.L., and S.L. Engerman. 2000. 'History Lessons: Institutions, Factor Endowments, and Paths of Development in the New World'. *Journal of Economic Perspectives* 14(3): 217–32.

Somanathan, R. 2010. 'The Demand for Disadvantage'. In *Culture, Institutions, and Development: New Insights into an Old Debate*, edited by J.P. Platteau and R. Peccoud, 125–40. New York: Routledge.

Sridharan, E. 1993. 'Economic Liberalisation and India's Political Economy: Towards a Paradigm Synthesis'. *Journal of Commonwealth & Comparative Politics* 31(3): 1–31.

Srinivas, G. 2016. *Dalit Middle Class: Mobility, Identity and Politics of Class.* New Delhi: Rawat Publications.

Srinivas, M.N. 1959. 'The Dominant Caste in Rampura'. *American Anthropologist* 61(1): 1–16.

Srinivasa-Raghavan, T.C.A. 2015. 'Lessons from the First Year'. *Business Standard*, 4 July. Available at: https://www.business-standard.com/article/opinion/t-c-a-srinivasa-raghavan-lessons-from-the-first-year-115070400012_1.html (accessed on 14 August 2019).

Srinivasan, M.V. 2015. 'Arni's Workforce: Segmentation Processes, Labour Market Mobility, Self-Employment and Caste'. In *Middle India and Urban-Rural Development: Four Decades of Change*, edited by B. Harriss-White, 65–96. New Delhi: Springer.

Srivastava, D.K., C.B. Rao, P. Chakraborty, and T.S. Rangamannar. 2003. *Budgetary Subsidies in India: Subsidising Social and Economic Services.* Background study for the Planning Commission, National Institute of Public Finance and Policy, New Delhi. Available at: http://planningcommission.nic.in/reports/sereport/ser/stdy_bgdsubs.pdf (accessed on 25 July 2019).

Srivastava, D.K., and H.K. Amar Nath. 2001. 'Central Budgetary Subsidies in India'. National Institute of Public Finance and Policy, New Delhi.

Srivastava, D.K., T.K. Sen, H. Mukhopadhyay, C.B. Rao, and H. K. Amarnath. 1997. *Government Subsidies in India.* Background study for the Ministry of Finance, National Institute of Public Finance and Policy, New Delhi. Available at: https://www.nipfp.org.in/media/pdf/books/BK_45/Government%20Subsidies%20In%20India.pdf (accessed on 25 July 2019).

Srivastava, S. 2015. *Entangled Urbanism: Slum, Gated Community, and Shopping Mall in Delhi and Gurgaon.* New Delhi: Oxford University Press.

Stepan, A.C. 1978. *The State and Society: Peru in Comparative Perspective.* Princeton: Princeton University Press.

Stewart, F. 2010. 'Power and Progress: The Swing of the Pendulum'. *Journal of Human Development and Capabilities* 11(3): 371–95.

Stiglitz, J.E. 2013. *The Price of Inequality.* London: Penguin.

Stivens, M. 1998. 'Sex, Gender and the Making of the New Malay Middle Class'. In *Gender and Power in Affluent Asia*, edited by K. Sen and M. Stivens, 87–127. London; New York: Routledge.

Sundar, N. 2010. 'The Rule of Law and the Rule of Property: Law Struggles and the Neoliberal State in India'. In *The State in India After Liberalization: Interdisciplinary Perspectives*, edited by A. Gupta and K. Sivaramakrishnan, 175–93. Abingdon, UK: Routledge.

Sundaresan, J. 2014. 'Urban Planning in Vernacular Governance'. Unpublished PhD thesis, London School of Economics, London, UK.

Swenson, P. 2002. *Capitalists against Markets: The Making of Labor Markets and Welfare States in the United States and Sweden.* New York: Oxford University Press.

Tewari, M. 1998. 'Intersectoral Linkages and the Role of the State in Shaping the Conditions of Industrial Accumulation: A Study of Ludhiana's Manufacturing Industry'. *World Development* 26(8): 1387–411.

Thamarajakshi, R. 1990. 'Intersectoral Terms of Trade Revisited'. *Economic and Political Weekly* 25(13): A48–A52.

Thorat, S., and K.S. Newman. 2007. 'Caste and Economic Discrimination: Causes, Consequences and Remedies'. *Economic and Political Weekly* 42(41): 4121–4.

Times of India. 2015. 'Budget Cuts Impacting Healthcare Will Be Like "Starving a Sick Child": Activists'. 28 February.

Tiwari, A.C. 1996. 'Volume and Composition of Subsidies in the Government, 1992–93'. Report, Indian Council for Research on International Economic Relations, New Delhi.

Topalova, P. 2004. 'Trade Liberalization and Firm Productivity: The Case of India'. IMF Working Paper WP/04/28, International Monetary Fund, Washington, DC.

Toye, J. 1988. 'Political Economy and the Analysis of Indian Development'. *Modern Asian Studies* 22(1): 97–122.

Trimberger, E.K. 1978. *Revolution From Above: Military Bureaucrats and Development in Japan, Turkey, Egypt, and Peru.* New Brunswick: Transaction Books.

Tyabji, N. 1981. 'Stratification of Indian Business'. In *Change and Choice in Indian Industry*, edited by K. Bagchi and N. Banerjee, 149–71. Calcutta: Centre for Studies in Social Sciences.

Upadhya, C. 1988. 'The Farmer-Capitalists of Coastal Andhra Pradesh'. *Economic and Political Weekly* 23(27): 1376–82.

———. 1997. 'Social and Cultural Strategies of Class Formation in Coastal Andhra Pradesh'. *Contributions to Indian Sociology* 31(2): 169–93.

———. 2007. 'Employment, Exclusion and "Merit" in the Indian IT Industry'. *Economic and Political Weekly* 42(20): 1863–8.

Vaidyanathan, A. 1977. 'Constraints on Growth and Policy Options'. *Economic and Political Weekly* 12(38): 1643–50.

———. 2006. 'Farmers' Suicides and the Agrarian Crisis'. *Economic and Political Weekly* 41(38): 4009–13.

Vaishnav, M. 2017. *When Crime Pays: Money and Muscle in Indian Politics*. New Haven, CT: Yale University Press.

Vakulabharanam, V. 2010. 'Does Class Matter? Class Structure and Worsening Inequality'. *Economic and Political Weekly* 45(29): 67–76.

Vakulabharanam, V., and S. Motiram. 2011. 'Political Economy of Agrarian Distress in India Since the 1990s'. In *Understanding India's New Political Economy: A Great Transformation?*, edited by S. Ruparelia, S. Reddy, J. Harriss, and S. Corbridge, 101–26. Abingdon, Oxon; New York: Routledge.

Vanaik, A. 1990. *The Painful Transition: Bourgeois Democracy in India*. London: Verso.

Varma, P. 1998. *The Great Indian Middle Class*. Delhi: Viking.

Varshney, A. 1984. 'Political Economy of Slow Industrial Growth in India'. *Economic and Political Weekly* 19(35): 1511–17.

———. 1998. 'Mass Politics or Elite Politics? India's Economic Reforms in Comparative Perspective'. *Journal of Policy Reform* 2(4): 301–35.

Verma, S. 2014. 'Constitutional Law: Doctrine of Repugnancy and the Constitution of India (Centre-State Relations)'. *Desi Kanoon*, 26 May. Available at: http://www.desikanoon.co.in/2014/05/doctrine-of-repugnancy-and-constitution-of-india.html (accessed on 25 July 2019).

Virmani, A. 2004. 'India's Economic Growth from Socialist Rate of Growth to Bharatiya Rate of Growth'. ICRIER Working Paper No. 122, Indian Council for Research on International Economic Relations, New Delhi.

Virmani, A., and D.A. Hashim. 2011. 'J-Curve of Productivity and Growth: Indian Manufacturing Post-Liberalization'. IMF Working Paper WP/11/163, International Monetary Fund, Washington, DC.

Wacquant, L. 1991. 'Making Class: The Middle Class(es) in Social Theory and Social Structure'. In *Bringing Class Back in Contemporary and Historical Perspectives*, edited by S. McNall, R. Levine, and R. Fantasia, 39–64. Boulder, CO: Westview Press.

Wade, R. 1982. 'The System of Administrative and Political Corruption: Canal Irrigation in South India'. *Journal of Development Studies* 18(3): 287–328.

———. 1985. 'The Market for Public Office: Why the Indian State Is Not Better at Development'. *World Development* 13(4): 467–97.

Wallack, J.S. 2003. 'Structural Breaks in Indian Macroeconomic Data'. *Economic and Political Weekly* 38(41): 4312–15.

Walton, M. 2013. 'Can a Social Democratic Resolution Resolve Issues of Inequality and Growth for India?' In *An Indian Social Democracy: Integrating Markets, Democracy and Social Justice*, edited by S. Khilnani and M. Malhoutra. New Delhi: Academic Foundation.

———. 2018. 'Can India Escape a Crony Populism Trap?' *Business Standard.* 27 August.

Waterbury, J. 1993. *Exposed to Innumerable Delusions: Public Enterprise and State Power in Egypt, India, Mexico and Turkey.* Cambridge: Cambridge University Press.

Weiner, M. 1987. *The Indian Paradox: Essays in Indian Politics.* New Delhi: SAGE.

White, R. 2011. *Railroaded: The Transcontinentals and the Making of Modern America.* New York: W.W. Norton & Company.

Wielenga, K.D. Forthcoming. 'The Emergence of the Informal Sector: Labour Legislation and Politics in South India, 1940–1960'. *Modern Asian Studies.*

Williamson, J. 1994. 'In Search of a Manual for Technopols'. In *The Political Economy of Policy Reform*, edited by J. Williamson, 11–28. Washington, DC: Institute for International Economics.

Witsoe, J. 2013. *Democracy against Development: Lower-Caste Politics and Political Modernity in Postcolonial India.* Chicago: University of Chicago Press.

World Bank. 2010. *Investing Across Borders: Indicators of Foreign Direct Investment Regulation in 87 Countries.* Washington, DC: World Bank.

———. 2015. *Assessment of State Implementation of Business Reforms.* New Delhi: World Bank.

Yadav, Y. 1996. 'Reconfiguration in Indian Politics: State Assembly Elections, 1993–1995'. *Economic and Political Weekly* 31(2–3): 95–104.

———. 1999. 'Electoral Politics in the Time of Change: India's Third Electoral System, 1989–1999'. *Economic and Political Weekly* 34(34–5): 2393–9.

Editors and Contributors

EDITORS

Elizabeth Chatterjee is a Lecturer at the School of Politics and International Relations at Queen Mary University of London, UK, a Fellow of All Souls College, Oxford, and of the Initiative for Sustainable Energy Policy at Johns Hopkins, United States of America, and an Associate Editor of the journal *Politics*. She was previously a postdoctoral scholar at the University of Chicago. Chatterjee's research examines energy politics and state capacity in the face of climate change, with a particular focus on South Asia. Her publications have explored aspects of contemporary Indian politics from blame games to the relationship between electoral competition and energy reforms. She is currently completing a book, *Rewiring India*, on electricity and the transformations of Indian state capitalism in the economic reform era.

Matthew McCartney is Associate Professor of Political Economy and Human Development of South Asia at the University of Oxford. Previously, he lectured on the economic development of South Asia at SOAS, London, arriving in Oxford in 2011 to take over from Barbara Harriss-White as director of the South Asia programme in the School of Global and Area Studies. Matthew has taught in South Korea, India, Pakistan, Denmark, and Japan, and worked with the UNDP, USAid, World Bank, and the European Union in Zambia, Botswana, Bangladesh, Georgia, Egypt, and Bosnia, including spending two years in the Ministry of Finance in Zambia as an Overseas Development Institute Fellow. His research examines the political economy of macroeconomics in India and Pakistan, in particular economic growth, investment, and the role of the state. He is the author of several books on the political economy of growth and stagnation in South Asia, most recently *Economic Growth and Development: A Comparative Introduction* (2015), *New Perspectives on Pakistan's Political Economy: State, Class and Social Change* (with Akbar Zaidi, 2019), and *The Indian Economy, 1947–2017* (forthcoming).

CONTRIBUTORS

Asha Amirali teaches at the Institute of Development Studies, University of Sussex, UK. She received her PhD from the Department for International Development at the University of Oxford for a thesis on the politics of accumulation in Pakistan's informal economy, and her current research focuses on the politics of tax compliance in Pakistan.

Pranab Bardhan is Professor of Graduate School in the Department of Economics at the University of California, Berkeley. He was educated at Presidency College, Kolkata, and University of Cambridge, UK, and taught at Massachusetts Institute of Technology, USA; the Indian Statistical Institute, Kolkata; and Delhi School of Economics before joining Berkeley in 1977. He has also been a visiting professor or fellow at Trinity College, Cambridge, St. Catherine's College, Oxford, and the London School of Economics and Political Science (LSE), UK. He held the Fulbright Siena Chair at the University of Siena, Italy, in 2008–9 and was the BP Centennial Professor at LSE for 2010 and 2011.

Bardhan is the author of 14 books and editor of 12 other volumes, and has authored more than 150 journal articles, many in leading economics journals such as *American Economic Review*, *Quarterly Journal of Economics*, *Econometrica*, *Review of Economic Studies*, and the *Journal of Political Economy*. He served as chief editor of the *Journal of Development Economics* from 1985 to 2003. A prolific commentator in Bengali, he has also contributed essays to *The New York Times*, *Scientific American*, *Financial Times*, *Boston Review*, *Project Syndicate*, *Business Standard*, and *The Indian Express*. He now writes a regular column for the blog *3 Quarks Daily*. His books on India include *Awakening Giants, Feet of Clay: Assessing the Economic Rise of China and India* (expanded edition, 2013) and *The Political Economy of Development in India* (expanded edition, 1998)—the slender classic which prompted this collection of essays.

Leela Fernandes is Glenda Dickerson Collegiate Professor of Women's Studies and Professor of Political Science at the University of Michigan. Her research examines the relationship between politics and culture through both qualitative empirical research and theoretical scholarship, with a special focus on gender, social inequality, and theorizing class identity. Fernandes is the author or editor of several books on India and on knowledge production about the Global South. These include *India's New Middle Class: Democratic Politics in an Era of Economic Reform* (2006), *Transnational Feminism in the United States: Knowledge, Ethics, Power* (2013), and *Feminists Rethink the Neoliberal State: Inequality, Exclusion, and Change* (2018). Her forthcoming book *Governing Water in India: Urbanization, Inequality and the Liberalizing State* analyses the remaking of the Indian state in the post-liberalization period through an in-depth institutional analysis of India's water bureaucracy.

Maitreesh Ghatak is Professor of Economics at the LSE, a post he has held since 2004, having earlier taught at the Department of Economics at the University of Chicago. He has published extensively on topics related to development economics in the *Journal of Political Economy*, *Journal of Development Economics*, *Quarterly Journal of Economics*, *The Review of Economic Studies*, and the *Economic and Political Weekly*. He is currently working on a project on poverty traps with longitudinal data from Bangladesh. He is an elected fellow of the British Academy, a board member and elected fellow of the Bureau for Research in the Economic Analysis of Development (BREAD), USA, and an elected fellow of the development economics programme of the Centre for Economic Policy Research (CEPR), London.

John Harriss is Professor Emeritus of International Studies at Simon Fraser University, Canada. He was previously Dean of the School of Development Studies at the University of East Anglia, UK, founder-director of the Development Studies Institute and Centre for the Study of Global Governance at LSE, and South and Central Asia regional head for Save the Children, UK. He is the (co-)author of twelve books on aspects of Indian politics and international development, and is currently working both on a book on Indian rural society and on a new edition of *India Today: Economy, Politics and Society* (with Stuart Corbridge and Craig Jeffrey). John's research interests include the political economy of development, Indian politics, political participation and civil society in India, social policy in India and other 'emerging economies', institutional theories, and agrarian change (especially in south India). He was recently named a fellow of the Royal Society of Canada.

Barbara Harriss-White is Emeritus Professor of Development Studies at the University of Oxford and a senior research fellow at the Oxford School of Global and Area Studies. Before retiring in 2011, she directed the Oxford Department of International Development and also founded Oxford's Contemporary South Asian Studies Programme. She is the (co-)author of 17 books; (co-)editor of a further 21; (co-)author of 13 consultancy reports to UN agencies; and has (co)published 139 chapters in edited books, 121 journal papers, and 96 working papers and web-based presentations. Her research interests are grounded in Indian fieldwork and span political economy, agriculture, energy and food, informal capitalism, rural and local development, and low-carbon transition. Harriss-White has also been an adviser to the UK's Department for International Development and to seven UN organizations, and a trustee of ActionAid and the International Food Policy Research Institute. She sits on the advisory boards of SOAS, London; the Institute for the Study of Economic and Social Development (IEDES), Paris; and the South Asia Institute (SAI), Heidelberg. She is a contributing editor of the *Socialist Register* and currently serves on the French government's Conseil national du développement et de la solidarité internationale.

Muhammad Ali Jan is Junior Research Fellow at Wolfson College, University of Oxford, and an affiliate of the Contemporary South Asian Studies Programme at Oxford. He was previously at the Department of International Development, University of Oxford, where he completed his DPhil. He works on agrarian change in Pakistan, and his research interests include the politics of development in South Asia and the institutions regulating the informal economy in Pakistan. His forthcoming publications in the *Journal of Agrarian Change* and *Journal of Peasant Studies* explore the making of commercial capital in colonial Punjab, and land and rural labour relations in colonial and post-colonial Punjab. He is currently preparing a manuscript on the agrarian sociology of Pakistani Punjab through the class and status struggles between merchants, landlords, and peasants in two districts of the province.

Rob Jenkins is Professor of Political Science at Hunter College and The Graduate Center, City University of New York. Previously he was professor of political science at Birkbeck College, University of London, and has undertaken advisory work and commissioned research for the United Nations Development Programme, Britain's Department for International Development, the World Bank, and other agencies. Jenkins's research in the area of Indian politics and political economy has covered a range of topics, from local-level anti-corruption movements to India's engagement with the World Trade Organization. Most recently, he has authored (with James Manor) *Politics and the Right to Work: India's National Rural Employment Guarantee Act* (2017) and co-edited (with Loraine Kennedy and Partha Mukhopadhyay) *Power, Policy, and Protest: The Politics of India's Special Economic Zones* (2014).

James Manor is Emeritus Professor at the Institute of Commonwealth Studies, University of London. He has taught at SOAS University of London, the Australian National University, Yale University, University of Leicester, MIT, Harvard University, and the University of Sussex, and was previously director of the Institute of Commonwealth Studies and founding head of research at the School of Advanced Studies, University of London. Manor has worked as a consultant for the Ford Foundation, the World Bank, the World Economic Forum, the United Nations Development Programme, and many other international development agencies, and has advised the governments of Bangladesh, Colombia, India, Zambia, and the United Kingdom. His research interests include democratic decentralization, state–society relations, elections, political leadership, political institutions, and poverty. Among numerous volumes on South Asian politics, he is the author (with Rob Jenkins) of *Politics and the Right to Work: India's National Rural Employment Guarantee Act* (2017). Recently, a collection of his classic essays from the last six decades of his research has been published as *Politics and State–Society Relations in India* (2017).

Ritwika Sen is a PhD candidate in managerial economics and strategy at the Kellogg School of Management, Northwestern University, USA. She has previously worked as a Country Economist for the International Growth Centre in Uganda (2016–18) and as an Overseas Development Institute Fellow at the Ministry of Agriculture and Animal Resources in Rwanda (2014–16). Ritwika holds a B.A. (Hons) in Economics from St. Stephen's College, University of Delhi, and an MSc in Economics from LSE. Her research interests are at the intersection of development, trade, and agriculture.

Michael Walton is Senior Lecturer in Public Policy at the Harvard Kennedy School, USA, and a Senior Visiting Fellow at the Centre for Policy Research, Delhi. He worked across four continents during a twenty-five-year career with the World Bank, where he co-authored and directed several editions of the *World Development Report*. He was previously the V.K.R.V. Rao Chair Professor, Institute of Social and Economic Change, Bangalore. A development economist, Michael has published widely on the political economy of India, including articles and reports on inequality, civil society, urban development, education, political leadership, rent-seeking, and institutional change.

Index